TELE
SE

*Terry Nation*

Published in our
centenary year
~ **2004** ~
MANCHESTER
UNIVERSITY
PRESS

# THE TELEVISION SERIES

*series editors*

SARAH CARDWELL
JONATHAN BIGNELL

*already published*

*Jimmy Perry and David Croft* SIMON MORGAN-RUSSELL

JONATHAN BIGNELL
AND ANDREW O'DAY

---

# *Terry Nation*

**Manchester University Press**
MANCHESTER AND NEW YORK

distributed exclusively in the USA by Palgrave

Copyright © Jonathan Bignell and Andrew O'Day 2004

The right of Jonathan Bignell and Andrew O'Day to be identified as the authors of this work has been asserted by them in accordance with the Copyright, Designs and Patents   Act 1988.

*Published by* Manchester University Press
Oxford Road, Manchester M13 9NR, UK
*and* Room 400, 175 Fifth Avenue, New York, NY 10010, USA
www.manchesteruniversitypress.co.uk

*Distributed exclusively in the USA by*
Palgrave, 175 Fifth Avenue, New York, NY 10010, USA

*Distributed exclusively in Canada by*
UBC Press, University of British Columbia, 2029 West Mall,
Vancouver, BC, Canada V6T 1Z2

*British Library Cataloguing-in-Publication Data*
A catalogue record for this book is available from the British Library

*Library of Congress Cataloging-in-Publication Data applied for*

ISBN 0 7190 6546 1 *hardback*
EAN   978 0 7190 6546 0
ISBN 0 7190 6547 X *paperback*
EAN   978 0 7190 6547 7

First published 2004

13  12  11  10  09  08  07  06  05  04        10  9  8  7  6  5  4  3  2  1

Typeset in Scala with Meta display
by Koinonia, Manchester
Printed in Great Britain
by Bell & Bain Limited, Glasgow

# Contents

LIST OF ILLUSTRATIONS                                *page* vi
GENERAL EDITORS' PREFACE                                  vii
ACKNOWLEDGEMENTS                                           ix

**Introduction**                                            1

1  **Biographical sketch**                                  9

2  **Collaboration at the BBC**                            25

3  **Science fiction genre and form**                      67

4  **Nation, space and politics**                         113

   **Conclusion**                                         179

APPENDIX: LIST OF TELEVISION PROGRAMMES                   189
BIBLIOGRAPHY                                              207
INDEX                                                     219

# List of illustrations

1 The scientist and the deadly virus, from the *Survivors* title sequence

2 A space battle in *Blake's 7* 'Duel'

3 Barbara (Jacqueline Hill) menaced by a Dalek, *Doctor Who* 'The Daleks'                                    *page* 110

4 Pixillated image of Blake, from *Blake's 7*'s title sequence

5 Tom Price (Talfryn Thomas) by a Rolls-Royce, from *Survivors* 'Genesis'

6 The map, from *Doctor Who* 'Genesis Of The Daleks'

7 Community, from *Survivors* 'A Beginning'

8 Looking up at the Thal Alydon, from *Doctor Who* 'The Daleks'

9 Looking down on Wormley's mob, from *Survivors* 'Genesis'          111

10 Drugged citizens, from *Blake's 7* 'The Way Back'

11 Blake (Gareth Thomas) in frame, from *Blake's 7* 'The Way Back'

12 The graveyard, from *Blake's 7* 'Duel'

13 Sinofar (Isla Blair) against the statue, from *Blake's 7* 'Duel'

14 Sinofar (Isla Blair) and Giroc (Patsy Smart), from *Blake's 7* 'Duel'

15 Portrait of Servalan (Jacqueline Pearce), from *Blake's 7* 'Traitor'          112

# General editors' preface

Television is part of our everyday experience, and is one of the most significant features of our cultural lives today. Yet its practitioners and its artistic and cultural achievements remain relatively unacknowledged. The books in this series aim to remedy this by addressing the work of major television writers and creators. Each volume provides an authoritative and accessible guide to a particular practitioner's body of work, and assesses his or her contribution to television over the years. Many of the volumes draw on original sources, such as specially conducted interviews and archive material, and all of them list relevant bibliographic sources and provide full details of the programmes discussed. The author of each book makes a case for the importance of the work considered therein, and the series includes books on neglected or overlooked practitioners alongside well-known ones.

In comparison with some related disciplines, Television Studies scholarship is still relatively young, and the series aims to contribute to establishing the subject as a vigorous and evolving field. This series provides resources for critical thinking about television. While maintaining a clear focus on the writers, on the creators and on the programmes themselves, the books in this series also take account of key critical concepts and theories in Television Studies. Each book is written from a particular critical or theoretical perspective, with reference to pertinent issues, and the approaches included in the series are varied and sometimes dissenting. Each author explicitly outlines the reasons for his or her particular focus, methodology or perspective. Readers are invited to think critically about the subject matter and approach covered in each book.

Although the series is addressed primarily to students and scholars of television, the books will also appeal to the many people who are interested in how television programmes have been commissioned, made and enjoyed. Since television has been so much a part of personal and public life in the twentieth and twenty-first centuries, we hope that the series will engage with, and sometimes challenge, a broad and diverse readership.

Sarah Cardwell
Jonathan Bignell

# Acknowledgements

We thank the following people and organisations for their assistance: BBC Written Archives Centre, David Bickerstaff, Isla Blair, Chris Boucher, Susanna Capon, Nicholas Courtney, Paul Darrow, Terrance Dicks, Paul Dunn, Andrew Evans, Tim Farr, Gavin French, Julian Glover, as well as Derek Hambly, Paul Huzzey and Paul Taylor of the 10th Planet store, Tim Harris (who deserves special recognition for his generosity with time and resources and for contributing greatly to the overall appearance of the book), David Hipple, Les Hollis, Catherine Johnson, Paul R. Jones, Verity Lambert, Barry Letts, Fiona Moore, John Nathan-Turner, Jacqueline Pearce, Mark J. Pilkington, Andrew Pixley, Dave Price, Ruth and Richard Rhodes, David Rolinson, Tom Spilsbury, Alan Stevens, Gareth Thomas, Paul Vazquez, Helen Wheatley and Paul Winter. We are grateful to BBC Worldwide for permission to reproduce images from television programmes in this book. Every attempt has been made to contact actors who can be seen in the illustrations, to gain consent for reproduction of their images. We will be happy to rectify in future editions any errors or omissions made in this regard.

On a personal level, Jonathan Bignell would like to thank Sarah Cardwell and Matthew Frost for their support for The Television Series of which this book is a part, and the academics, research students and undergraduates whose interests and enthusiasms have contributed to the blossoming of Television Studies as a vigorous discipline. In particular, he thanks colleagues in the Centre for Television Drama Studies and the Department of Film, Theatre and Television at the University of Reading. The Arts and Humanities Research Board funded the research project 'Cultures of British Television Drama, 1960–82', and this book is just one of many initiatives connected with it that have been made possible by the AHRB's generous support. Jonathan thanks Lib Taylor once again for her encouragement, support and love. Andrew O'Day wishes to extend his gratitude for friendship and support over the years to, as well as many of the people previously mentioned: Colin Hill, Anthony Granato, Amy Reiswig, Jim MacLean, Shelley Charlesworth, Richard Robeson, Adam Emanuel, Grace Knight, Kristian Griffiths, Dave Workman, Andrew Atkins, Ian Beard, Colin Jones, Steve Few, all at Café Coco, Oxford, Andi Whiting, the LGB at Royal

Holloway University of London, and all the teaching staff who have offered encouragement in his academic pursuits, not least to Professor Leonée Ormond, Dr Miles Bradbury and to 'The Lady', who truly knows the value of being last, and whose teachings have been nothing but an inspiration.

Jonathan Bignell dedicates this book to his brother Richard, with whom he watched many of programmes discussed herein. Andrew O'Day dedicates this book to his parents and family with devotion, offers special thanks and love to Colonel Helen E. O'Day for technical support needed for the completion of this book, and remembers the days when he could *actually* persuade *his* younger brothers Daniel and Matthew Englander to sit and watch such exciting escapades.

# Introduction

## Authorship and authority

This book raises, and repeatedly returns to, the issue of where and with whom the authorship and authority over a television production lies. The books published in The Television Series construct boundaries around the contribution that individual writers or producers have made to British television. To an extent, these boundaries are necessary to group a series of works together. This particular book, *Terry Nation*, is named after a man who is credited with creating and/or writing some of the most significant television science fiction of the 1960s and 1970s, and also occupied writing and production roles in British adventure series in the period. Among Nation's notable contributions were stories for the BBC science fiction drama series *Doctor Who*, where he created the ever-popular Daleks, and he was also the brains behind the BBC programmes *Survivors* and *Blake's 7*. The title of this book would therefore suggest that what we are looking at is a unified authority figure, Terry Nation, and that the works credited to Nation actually 'belong' to him. The word 'belonging' connotes an enormous amount of power on the part of the owner, and indeed Terry Nation part-owned the Daleks having negotiated a 50 per cent share of the copyright of the creatures and he was continually associated with them.

However, within the boundaries of our author-based study, and within the boundaries of the series of books to which this one is an early contribution, we are concerned to challenge the authority vested in the creator or the writer. Unlike in literary works, for example, authority does not entirely revolve around the role of the creator or writer because, in the case of television, boundaries are set by generically coded formats and the script must be transferred to the screen by a production team and performers. To label a programme as created by and/or written by someone like Terry Nation, and indeed to title a book such as this one after a creator/writer is to grant that person an enormous amount of power. Authorship has been associated with power since the beginning of history in the Judeo-Christian worldview, since God was seen as the author of the world and of humankind. Up until the nineteenth century the literary writer was seen as an artist inspired and authorised by the divine. Indeed, the words 'author' and 'authority' are etymologically connected, both in the original Latin terms *auctor* and *auctoritas*, in the French *auteur* and *autorité*, and in our English derivatives from these. In the case of television production, that power and authority is in fact spread out over a number of people, and because of the long-standing connection between author and authority the screenwriter of popular television, and even to a degree the creator of programmes and formats, has instead been labelled a 'craftsperson' who does a paid job within the constraints of the industry, often following guidelines provided by people higher up in the institutional hierarchy (see Murdoch 1980).

We shall therefore argue throughout this book that the author(ity) behind television programmes is far from being a unified creator or writer figure. We note some of the evidence for a Terry Nation 'signature' in the programme ideas, genres, plot structures and political subtexts of his different works, which often stand out as examples of repetition, but we stress the combination of forces of writer, producer, script editor, director and so forth that were involved in bringing these works to the screen. This was particularly the case with Nation whose work was subject to extensive revision by script editors, as well as different realisation by varying directors. Indeed, the fact that Nation's work is often characterised by repetition enables the way in which his works were realised by different directors, for instance, to stand out markedly. Authorship and authority are therefore multiple, with flexible boundaries where the different roles of those who 'crafted' the works flow into one another to create the finished product that audiences see on the screen. Different genres and forms also introduce constraints on authorship and allow for creative possibilities within and between them. Furthermore, television audiences possess author(ity) status over programmes by interpreting them in ways not necessarily intended by either writer or production team. We therefore believe that while this book concentrates on the role that Terry Nation played in British television science fiction it is also of wider interest to an academic readership and indeed to 'fans' of popular television because of its detailed discussion of television authorship, authority and the 'crafts' of television production more generally. The interactions between authorship, authority, and crafting constitute a thread that runs through the structure of the book as we challenge the idea that Nation's programme ideas, storylines and scripts can be understood as free-standing works. Each of these is conditioned by the collaborative contexts in which they were created, realised as television programmes and viewed by audiences. As the focus of the book moves towards the interpretation of programmes that Nation worked on, we are also aware of the collaborative context in which viewers, critics and we ourselves have made meanings from those programmes, further removing them from the complex of intentions that might lie behind Nation's authorship and authority. For as theoretical work on television and other media has argued, meanings are made by negotiations between authors, institutions, programme texts and audiences, rather than following the contours set by their creators.

## Popular television and 'quality'

The academic study of television has had little interest in valuing one programme or kind of television over another. Yet in the ways people talk about television, these evaluative issues are high on the agenda. 'Quality television' is an informal category that often separates one-off television plays and films, literary adaptations and authored serials from the rest, from 'popular' television (see Brunsdon 1990). Attaching the label 'quality' involves assigning cultural importance to programmes or kinds of television that have acquired a valued position in culture, rather like theatre's distinctions between 'serious' theatre and musicals or pantomime. There is a social and cultural framework that enables the study of some television to carry value, and the programmes or kinds of television labelled as 'quality' to carry value, in a way that popular television does not. The academic subject of Television Studies has taken popular television seriously, because it is the television many people watch the most. This is despite the common criticism in the press, and sometimes in the television industry itself, that popular television is unimportant, 'just' commercial, and lacking in artistic value.

Our focus on the science fiction series that Nation is credited with creating and/or writing is partly intended as a contribution to this debate about quality. Nation's work is important in terms of a history and practice of writing television texts within dominant institutions and programme types including the drama series, and it is also important because of Nation's consistent concern to connect with a popular audience. We believe that the work credited to Nation as creator and/or writer fails to fit some of the traditional criteria of 'quality'. It is largely in familiar generic forms, was made on comparatively low budgets, and is addressed to a mass audience. As Bernadette Casey *et al.* (2002: 209) have noted, 'Cultural critics have long regarded science fiction as a low-status, somewhat disreputable form, frequently regarded as "pulp" fiction', and much of Nation's television work falls into the science fiction genre. But we believe that Nation's works are significant in the ways they engage audiences, even though many viewers would not articulate this, and are therefore important for study. Furthermore, work credited to Nation as a writer exhibits some of the more traditional signs of 'quality' that viewers and critics recognise such as an authorial 'signature' that unites aspects of his work, and engages with significant social and political ideas, even though these features were probably not intended by the writer or members of the production team. Casey *et al.* (2002: 209) argue that science fiction 'allows a framework for difficult philosophical and political debate', and despite popular television's limitations in realising complex ideas in dramatic form, we argue that Nation has contributed to this.

Our focus on the popular television that Nation created and/or wrote is also in dialogue therefore with academic criticism's formation of canons of work that have been considered worthy of study. Canon, a term deriving from the ancient Greek word *kanon* for a measuring rod and later acquiring the sense of 'rule' or 'law', operates according to a principle of inclusion and exclusion, setting up boundaries around what may be worthy of study. The word 'canon' is often used by fans of television programmes, in publications, and in Internet newsgroups, for example. Its function is to authorise value judgements about whether only television programmes can form part of a canon, or whether subsequent novelisations, audiotapes, or fan-produced texts should be considered part of a corpus or body of texts. Value judgements are also made by academics determining what is canonical, and evidently we consider work credited to Nation as creator and/or writer to be worthy of study, and implicitly therefore as part of an enlarged canon in the discipline of Television Studies. Our focus is primarily on the science fiction television that Nation worked on, and adds to earlier academic work (Tulloch and Alvarado 1983; Tulloch and Jenkins 1995) that has brought this genre to academic attention and implicitly drawn it into the canon. Recent publications have also focused on action and adventure television (Osgerby and Gough-Yates 2001; Chapman 2002), including many of the programmes to which Nation contributed, to similar effect.

## The aims and structure of the book

Despite considerable non-academic publication on his work, and a small amount of published academic work, no book has yet focused solely on the contribution to British television of the work credited to Nation as creator and/or writer. No existing study has explored the networks of multiple authorship that affected Nation's writing career, or addressed it from the theoretical and methodological concerns of Television Studies. This book sets out to accomplish these aims, and we hope that it will interest academics, researchers and students, and also the large international readership of books on science fiction television and popular and 'cult' television in general. We are interested in how the concerns of television theory shape the understandings of Nation and his work that are in circulation in the discourses of Television Studies, as our brief comments on questions of authorship and quality demonstrate. Conversely, we aim to explore how the study of Nation's work might shape or reshape the terms in which Television Studies theorists understand popular television drama. These issues feature at intervals throughout the book.

Like any academic subject, Television Studies is diverse and evolving, and there are articulate points of view within it that differ greatly in aims, assumptions, emphases and conclusions. For example, the study of television drama might adopt a focus on the authorship and authority of the writer and the multiple figures involved in the realisation of scripts and storylines. It is illuminating to explore the television industry as an institution and its production practices and organisation. Because of television's pervasiveness and contribution to society, it would be significant to study the role of television in culture and the activity of audiences in interpreting programmes. So Television Studies' discourses of analysis do not translate neatly one into another, and this book draws on a range of theoretical issues in current approaches to television. We aim to recognise that our approach to Nation's work is part of a struggle around the proper concerns and methods of Television Studies, and since many of our readers will not be television scholars, we aim to show why these approaches have a significant role in the field.

For example, in exploring issues of authorship, authority and 'craft', the first chapter will adopt one strand of Television Studies' focus on the primacy of the writer, providing a biographical sketch of Nation's life and work. The chapter briefly outlines his career as a professional writer earning his living from contributing scripts, storylines and programme ideas, which were realised and often controlled by others. This individual focus contrasts with later parts of this book in which we address selected programmes scripted or devised by Nation, which were added to by other production team members, focusing on the meanings that critical analysis, and actual or possible viewers, may derive from them. Our biographical sketch aims to demonstrate the range of his work in television and the genres with which he was familiar, providing greatest detail on the BBC science fiction work for which he is best known.

The second chapter, 'Collaboration at the BBC', fully restores the work credited to Nation to the conditions in which it was created. For the chapter traces the institutional contexts in which Nation's work was developed, in order to emphasise the notion of television authorship as a collaborative enterprise between different production personnel, rather than located solely in the agency of the creator and/or writer. Working in popular series television for most of his career, Nation was constrained by the demands of television institutions for long-running series that could attract and retain significantly large and diverse audiences, and we explore these institutional contexts to discuss the practices of authorship that were, and were not, available to him. Although we aim to provide some background knowledge about how Nation's work connects with developments in television across the period of the 1960s and 1970s, we are concerned less with the detail of that history than with how Nation's work and its historical contexts can be approached critically, revealing much about the roles of different author(ity) figures who we shall see at work in our analysis of television programmes in chapters 3 and 4. But this part of the book is therefore, at the same time, necessarily about particular aspects of British television history. Our approach to telling this story is to draw on a range of types of evidence such as detailed production files contained in the archives of broadcasting institutions, especially the BBC, which contextualise Nation's work in these institutions. We cite these archival sources by indicating their presence in the BBC Written Archives Centre (BBC WAC) followed by the file number concerned.

The chapter will also stress the fact that the science fiction television programmes credited to Nation were widely watched, and we use further types of historiography in this examination. For example, the pages of the BBC's listings magazine *Radio Times* can be instructive in understanding how programmes and programme schedules were offered and advertised to their audiences. There are also some records of viewer responses to programmes. The BBC's Audience Research department gathered information by questionnaire and interview in order to gauge audience sizes, and viewers' approval or disapproval of programmes written by Nation. These sources provide a glimpse of how people responded to his work. Their responses were partly based on the promotional and publicity discourses about programmes. We examine these to give a partial snapshot of the ways in which viewers were invited and authorised to establish a relationship with broadcasters and programmes, although an unequal relationship, in a particular period.

The second half of the book will continue to probe the idea of authorship, authority and craft, and adopts a different methodology by shifting from a focus on the writer and the production contexts surrounding Nation's work to a concentration on television programmes as audiovisual texts. The third chapter, 'Science fiction genre and form', addresses multiple authorship by exploring the generic and formal elements of works credited to Nation as creator and/or writer, as popular narrative television designed to engage the audience. We will again look at the multiple production personnel responsible for realising these aspects and also show that by accommodating themselves to existing television genres and forms, the programmes Nation worked on necessarily draw on, borrow from and seek to connect with other television programmes and generic traditions in literature or film, for example. The role of the television writer is seen in relation to works authored by others, taking account of the audience's understanding of these pre-existing genres and forms. So authorship is not only shared between the writer and his or her collaborators realising a programme in television form, but also shared with inherited genre components and the ways that these components circulate as shared knowledge in history and culture. Genre and form opened up possibilities for the author figures, and we argue that the aesthetics of television programmes are worthy of study because of the impact that they had on audiences.

The fourth chapter, 'Nation, space and politics', combines aspects of our approach in chapters 2 and 3 with a specific focus on the ideologies and cultural meanings that can be read in the programmes Nation worked on. We continue to explore the interrelationships between script, direction and design that form part of our interest in multiple authorship and authority over the programme text, and also develop further the detailed interpretative work that was begun in chapter 3. Returning to the question of 'quality', and specifically the criterion that quality involves engagement with political themes, we argue that Nation had a consistently dystopian vision, which crossed the boundaries of the individual programmes he worked on, and which can be contextualised in relation to science fiction in general and British science fiction in particular. Works credited to Nation can critique the simple moralism to be found in other popular television science fiction, and raise questions of politics and gender in television fiction and in television science fiction. These programmes provide a location to think through the tradition of critical work on television drama that interprets programme texts in political terms as either progressive or reactionary.

This chapter therefore begins from the assumption that, as the British theorist Raymond Williams (1981) so powerfully argued, culture is not only the expression of social forces but also an agent of social change. We hope that this book will engage fruitfully in an exchange between the concerns of a working writer who always denied lofty intellectual or political ambitions, and those of us who make our living by bringing the popular medium of television into conversation with intellectual, social and political debates. Part of the context of this book is our wish that Nation's authorship and the discourses of Television Studies might come together, since part of the agenda of television criticism has been the unevenly successful dialogue between academics and television professionals (see, for example, Tulloch and Alvarado 1983; Millington and Nelson 1986; Tulloch 1990; and Bignell *et al.* 2000). Our approach to Nation's work is part of a dialogue about the proper concerns and methods of Television Studies. Rather than assuming that the approaches to television we adopt in this book are like a set of neutral tools, we hope that our eclectic use of different methodologies, addressing authorship, institutions, genre, audience, theme and ideologies, will remind readers that the approaches we use tend to shape the television being studied.

Finally, our conclusion returns to the key emphases on authorship authority and craft, and draws out the importance of television theory in what it can reveal about these issues. We show how Nation's influence on science fiction and popular culture overflowed the boundaries of the decades of the 1960s and 1970s in which his most well-remembered work was launched. At the end of the book, we have included an appendix listing the television programmes that Nation scripted, and a bibliography of the archival, academic and non-academic written sources we have used.

# Biographical sketch

## Introduction

Terry Nation was a prolific writer for British radio and television, and also devised programme formats, adapted stories, edited scripts by other writers, and wrote film screenplays. He is best known for the science fiction television programmes that he scripted and devised for the BBC, and his creation of the Daleks for *Doctor Who* made him nationally famous and significantly wealthy. We give an overview of the span of his career in this chapter, to draw attention both to the wide range of genres for which he wrote and from which he earned a living, and to the primary television forms in which he most consistently worked. Our overview aims to chart Nation's career and provide a sense of the kinds of writing he undertook, while more specific details about the programmes he scripted or devised are given in the appendix. Nation largely wrote for programmes with established series formats, where writers were expected to craft scripts for programmes controlled by production teams who employed writers as freelance contributors. As we explained in the introduction, we employ terminology of authorship in this book because of its etymological links with notions of authority, though we regard Nation not as a sole authority figure but rather as what Graham Murdoch (1980) calls a 'craftsman'. Nation ended up writing a considerable amount at an increasingly rapid rate and was not confined to a particular genre. He wrote in numerous popular genres, rejecting the ideology of 'literary' television authorship in favour of commercial success and recognition in the British television industry of the 1960s and 1970s. Our description and discussion of his work in this chapter does not claim that Nation was an exceptional innovator, therefore, but instead shows how numerous and significant his contributions were to programmes that were central to the television landscape of their time and have, in several cases, acquired cult status and reputation in subsequent years. This biographical sketch is a launching point since Nation's contribution to television was part of a large institutional system, and we consider institutional networks of collaboration in the following chapter. Our later work in chapters 3 and 4, on genre and form, and politics and ideology respectively, therefore brings academic attention to programmes that were not conceived as objects of study. In this biographical sketch we draw attention to the way that phases of Nation's career were marked by consistent involvement in genres such as comedy, science fiction and action drama.

## The birth of a Nation: the 'craftsman' radio writer

While Nation became one of the most successful scriptwriters of his generation, working freelance on various projects for both the BBC and independent broadcasters in Britain, the early years of his career were not auspicious as he attempted to gain a foothold in broadcasting. Instead he can be seen as a craftsperson who aimed to earn a living by working for other people. He was an only child, born in Llandaff on 8 August 1930. He grew up in South Wales, going to school in Cardiff, then briefly joined his father in the family furniture business as a travelling salesman. The business closed and he began to work as a stand-up comedian, but after several unsuccessful auditions his agent told him that he had good material, but very poor delivery. Nation himself said: 'Somebody told me, "The jokes are very good; it's you who's not funny" – that was hurtful, but then I figured I had to make a living' (quoted in Nazzaro 1989: 17).

Instead of trying to make his career in performance, Nation looked for opportunities as a writer. This move was to an extent imposed on him, and required Nation to go to London in 1955 where opportunities for commissions were more easily found. He hung around BBC studios where he met the radio comedian Spike Milligan who took pity on the poverty-stricken Nation and paid him to write a *Goon Show* script (Nazzaro 1989: 17). Milligan was impressed by the script though it was never broadcast, and Nation was often to be found at Milligan's office above a greengrocer's shop in London's Shepherd's Bush, making a start in writing radio comedy for stars of the time including Frankie Howerd, Harry Worth and Peter Sellers (Pixley 1997b). He was hired to write a BBC radio comedy series *All My Eye And Kitty Bluett*, although the show was a disaster. Through his association with Milligan and his comedy writing, he was able to join the agency Associated London Scripts

(ALS), which led to further chances to earn money by writing for radio. ALS privileged the role of the radio writer and so Nation was able to support himself financially by churning out comedy material for other people. ALS was the powerhouse of radio comedy writing at this time, and was formed by the writer-performers Spike Milligan and Eric Sykes, who wanted to create a writers' collective. This privileging of the writer was reflected in the management of the company, whose directors in 1959 included not only Milligan and Sykes but also Alan Galton and Ray Simpson (the writers for Britain's top comedian Tony Hancock), Tony Hancock himself, and Frankie Howerd. Tony Hancock's brother Roger ran the agency, and Nation wrote about 200 comedy scripts at ALS, showing early evidence of the prolific output that would later characterise his career in television.

Nation's comedy writing for radio was largely written with other people for the stars of the time. As early as 1955 Nation was collaborating with fellow writers John Junkin and Dave Freeman on outlines for a new radio comedy series to be called *The Fixers*, but the BBC thought this programme's format and style would be too similar to the hugely successful series *The Goons*. Unable to launch a new programme, in 1955 Nation co-wrote scripts for BBC radio's *Frankie Howerd Show* (Pixley 1997b), and in 1957 he wrote with John Junkin for the BBC radio series *Variety Playhouse*, and supplied sketches and jokes for the established radio comedians Elsie and Doris Waters and Ted Ray. The variety format of songs, sketches, monologues and jokes was a staple of the BBC's Light Programme radio schedules, and Nation also contributed to *Calling The Stars*, which featured Benny Hill, Dickie Valentine, Peter Sellers and Ted Ray. He and Junkin also scripted *Fine Goings On*, a BBC radio comedy drama again starring Frankie Howerd, in 1957–58 (Pixley 1997b). Indeed, when Nation got married on Saturday 29 March 1958 in London, he was well known enough at the BBC for a memo to be circulated informing staff of the date and place of his wedding in case people wanted to send good wishes. Until 1959 the writing team of Nation, Junkin and Freeman was providing material for Elsie and Doris Waters in *Floggits*, a radio vehicle for the Waters sisters in their personae as Gert and Daisy. Nation and Junkin were regarded as versatile writers producing material for various radio stars (BBC WAC SCR1 RCONT1) on *Variety Playhouse*, writing monologues, continuity links and the regular sketch items 'The Case Book Of Eddie Nimbus', a spoof detective playlet, and 'Nidge Of The News' about a Fleet Street journalist and his assistants. The writing team's last work in radio comedy was *It's A Fair Cop*, a Light Programme situation comedy starring Eric Sykes (Pixley 1997b), in 1961.

## The growth of a Nation: breaking into television

During this span of time, Nation was actively trying to break into television writing to further his career and generate income as a 'craftsman' writer. Nation's earliest television writing ran parallel to his radio scripting and began with the comedy genre in which he was experienced. He contributed to the Associated Rediffusion company's television version of the hugely popular BBC radio programme *The Goon Show*, titled *The Idiot Weekly, Price 2d*, in 1956, as did many of the ALS agency's comedy writers. The programme's premise was that 'The Idiot Weekly, Price 2d' was a tatty Victorian tabloid run by Peter Sellers and in each instalment its headlines were used as a link for a number of different sketches featuring Sellers and Spike Milligan. The programme, however, was only broadcast in the London area to a limited public.

In the mid-1950s, with the arrival of Independent Television, variety acts drawn from radio comedy helped to draw large audiences to the new channel. The production company ITC, for instance, was run by Lew Grade who had been booking theatrical acts for many years, as well as by Prince Littler and Val Parnell, one of the most powerful men in the world of variety. Nation contributed to the variety show *Val Parnell's Startime* (Pixley 1997b) for the regional television company ATV, broadcast on the ITV network. The programme was transmitted from the Prince of Wales Theatre, and followed on from the relatively short-lived *Val Parnell's Saturday Spectacular*, giving early television exposure to names such as Anthony Newley, Eric Sykes, Hattie Jacques, Jo Stafford, Tommy Steele, Cliff Richard and Morecambe and Wise, each of whom would be prominent stars in the decades to come.

In 1958–59 Nation also wrote with John Junkin for the variety programme *The Ted Ray Show*, broadcast on the national BBC television network, in the final two seasons of its six season run of 28 hour-long episodes (1955–59). In July 1960 Nation devised the idea for *Comedy Playhouse*, a series of television plays to be performed by actors rather than comedians (BBC WAC T48/445). Johnny Speight, John Junkin and Nation wrote one half-hour play each as samples for BBC consideration, and this anthology (a run of different episodes under the same series title) became a proving-ground for situation comedy-dramas that later developed into series, such as *Steptoe And Son*.

Nation's comedy writing for television continued, although he had contributed a script to the ITV company Associated Rediffusion's police series *No Hiding Place* in 1959. Nation had aimed to gain commissions for sole-authored dramas, and drew on his experience of comedy writing in his play *Uncle Selwyn*, submitted to the BBC in 1960 (BBC

WAC T48/445). The play was referred to readers by the BBC in case there might be offence to Welsh viewers, since the plot centred around a group of Welsh 1920s anarchists bombing an electrical power station to the benefit of the eponymous Uncle Selwyn's oil lamp shop. Nation hoped that its characters and situations could become the basis for six one-hour episodes in a series. But Hywel Davies, Head of Programmes for Wales, thought the play was too crudely farcical and derivative, and it was rejected by BBC television Light Entertainment. It was sent to the BBC Script Department where it was also rejected in 1961.

Nation tried his hand at writing for cinema by scripting the 1961 British film *What A Whoppa!*, a vehicle for the pop star Adam Faith who played a young writer hoping to make his name by selling faked photographs of the Loch Ness monster. At the same time Nation began his involvement with science fiction by contributing screenplays, mostly adaptations of published stories, for the independent broadcaster ABC's science fiction anthology *Out Of This World* (BBC WAC T48/445). Also continuing his work in comedy writing, Nation was a contributing writer and chaperone to Tony Hancock on his new 13-episode ATV television comedy series simply titled *Hancock* (1963) after Hancock had fallen out with his regular writers, Galton and Simpson, who had written the BBC series *Hancock's Half Hour*. Hancock liked Nation's script 'The Assistant' for the new ATV series so much that he put it first in the transmission order, and Nation wrote three more episodes transmitted towards the end of the series. The programme drew on the reputation of its star by casting him in a range of occupations that gave Hancock opportunities to be snobbish, bungling and annoying, as he had been in the BBC series. But Hancock was much less successful by this time than in his earlier BBC work with Galton and Simpson, and his show dropped out of the top 20 in the ratings (Wilmut 1978). Nation was also being paid to chaperone Hancock on a short theatrical tour begun at the Theatre Royal in Nottingham, and as Hancock's anxiety worsened amid bouts of drinking he kept getting nervous and deleting Nation's new material from his stage act. The stage shows were not well received and Nation was doing very little writing, and although he and his wife Kate holidayed with Hancock and his wife on Hancock's converted fishing boat in France, Nation abruptly stopped working for him after an argument (Hancock and Nathan 1975) and while the pair patched up their differences the next morning neither would back down (Pixley 2003: 30). As a result, Nation was left with no income to cover the installation of a new central heating system at his flat in Hampstead.

Therefore Nation accepted the offer to write a story for the new BBC series *Doctor Who*, having been recommended by his friend, the writer

Dennis Spooner, later to become script editor of the programme. The initial 26-page outline entitled 'The Survivors' (Pixley 2003: 30), was retitled 'Doctor Who And The Mutants', extended at producer Verity Lambert's request from six to seven episodes (Pixley 2003: 32), then known as 'Beyond The Sun' (Pixley 2003: 33) and later named 'The Daleks'. It was the need to earn a living from his ability to craft scripts for existing programmes and performers that started Nation's long involvement with *Doctor Who*, since he had initially rejected the commission, spurning writing for a children's series. While he was working on this script, he contributed material for Eric Sykes' BBC/ Swedish Television Service variety special *Wish You Were Here!*, which was broadcast on 7 September 1963 (Pixley 2003: 32). Like his earlier comedy *Uncle Selwyn*, Nation's outline for a one-off drama 'The Thousand And Several Doors' for the BBC's *Suspense* anthology series was rejected as too derivative (BBC WAC T48/445), but *Uncle Selwyn* was finally sold to the independent Associated Rediffusion television company and transmitted in 1964 several years after its conception. However, the play was regarded by reviewers as insufficiently funny. Nation was commissioned in December 1963 (BBC WAC T48/445) to write an offering for the BBC2 anthology *Story Parade*, which each week presented a dramatised version of a novel written in the past 30 years, running as a rule for about 75 minutes. This was quickly followed by a second commission, and the producer Irene Shubik noted in a memo (BBC WAC T48/445) that Nation 'is quick and reliable, so a valuable writer on this type of programme'. *The Times* reviewer John Russell Taylor argued that Nation's first contribution was the best of the series (1964a). Nation also contributed an adaptation to the science fiction anthology series *Out Of The Unknown* (see appendix for details of these plays, following the listing for Nation's work on *Doctor Who*).

## Adventure Nation

Nation's BBC 1960s work ran alongside increasing involvement in ITV action drama as the decade continued, and his skill in rapidly crafting scripts for popular generic television quickly led to financial security and recognition both within the television industry and beyond. The independent broadcaster ABC screened six seasons of the adventure series *The Saint* between 1962 and 1969, made by the ITC production company. Leslie Charteris had authored the novels on which the character of the Saint was based, a gentleman adventurer played in the television series by Roger Moore. The fact that Moore played the lead character is highly significant since the programme saw him in a role prefiguring that of James Bond, which he later assumed in the cinema in the 1970s and 1980s. Nation wrote 13 episodes in all, contributing to the third, fourth and sixth seasons, highlighting his prolific output. *The Saint* was not only a staple part of ITV's British schedule, but was also exported internationally, notably to the United States from 1967 to 1969 once episodes were filmed in colour and were thus more marketable.

After the summer of 1965 Nation took a break from freelance writing and went to Associated British Elstree Studios to work as a writer and script supervisor on *The Baron*, a 30-episode series screened as one season in 1966–67 and produced by Monty Berman. Its premise derived from the character created by the writer John Creasey (under the pseudonym Anthony Morton) in the 1930s, but was developed for television as a contribution to the significant genre of the time that featured gentleman amateur spies. The Baron, John Mannering (Steve Forrest), was an American millionaire antique dealer whose fortune, made as a cattle rancher, enabled him to open antique shops in Washington, London and Paris. The format was designed for American consumption, and was sold to the ABC network in the United States before its British screening. Nation wrote 16 episodes in all (one with Dennis Spooner), comprising over half the series, again illustrating Nation's large volume of work at this time.

With established skills in crafting scripts for adventure series, Nation then wrote episodes of *The Champions* (1968–69) for his friend Dennis Spooner who was producing the series for ITC. This programme, which lasted for one season of 30 episodes, was an action drama centred on a team of two men (Craig Stirling and Richard Barrett) and a woman (Sharron Macready) working for the international agency Nemesis to combat crime and unravel mysterious happenings. The distinguishing feature of the 'hero team' that set them apart from the main characters of the other action dramas that Nation wrote for was their telepathic powers. Following their rescue from a plane crash in Tibet in the first episode, the Champions were endowed with these powers by mysterious beings and gradually discovered their abilities in the course of the series. Nation, however, only wrote two episodes for this programme but they added to his immense contribution to the action drama genre.

The action drama from this period that has acquired greatest subsequent attention is *The Avengers* (see Miller 1997), and Nation contributed six episodes to the series and also acted as script editor for a time. *The Avengers* comprised 161 episodes and ran between 1961 and 1969. The programme began in black and white (seasons one to four) as an espionage thriller and moved in its later colour episodes (seasons five to seven) towards increasingly science-fictional and fantasy storylines during Nation's involvement with the programme. The central characters were a hero team of a man (played by Patrick Macnee) and a woman (most notably Honor Blackman, followed by Diana Rigg then Linda Thorson during Nation's work on the programme) called upon to solve mysteries, undertake espionage missions and combat master criminals. The pairing of the male lead with a female assistant again paralleled the staple format of spy drama and action adventure. This series too was exported to the United States and other international markets, and contributed to Britain's growing reputation for popular television drama that showcased pop culture and 'cool' British fashion.

Nation collaborated again with Spooner on the early episodes of *The Avengers'* successor, *Department S*, which had been created by Spooner along with Monty Berman. *Department S* lasted for one season (1969–70) of 28 episodes, of which Nation was responsible for two. The premise of *Department S* was of international crime fighters Stewart Sullivan, Annabelle Hurst and famous author Jason King taking on cases too bizarre for the ordinary police. The series therefore mixed genres such as the detective story, fantasy and action adventure, genres that were all evident in Nation's contributions to the programme.

Nation was appointed associate producer and story consultant for ITC's next adventure series, *The Persuaders!* Screened between 1971 and 1972, *The Persuaders!* consisted of one season of 24 episodes. This series teamed Roger Moore with the American film star Tony Curtis, as a duo of wealthy playboys coerced into undertaking missions against threatening foreign agents and master criminals, enlivened by witty repartee between the two central characters Brett Sinclair (Moore) and Danny Wilde (Curtis). Nation scripted seven of the episodes, almost a third of the series. As in the case of *The Saint*, the casting of Roger Moore prefigured his role as James Bond in the cinema. But *The Persuaders!*, like much of ITC's output of this kind, was regarded by critics and reviewers as sub-James Bond, and very derivative, and the programme's audience ratings were not helped by its scheduling against the innovative BBC sketch show *Monty Python's Flying Circus*. Nevertheless, *The Persuaders!* was the most expensive television series made in Britain at the time, with a budget of £2.5 million, and made extensive use of location filming and lavish settings and props. It was screened simultaneously in Britain and the United States and was exported to over 50 countries.

Nation then wrote for another ITC series, *The Protectors* (1972–74) starring Robert Vaughan (who would also appear in the spy series *The*

*Man From U.N.C.L.E.*), Nyree Dawn Porter and Tony Anholt, which was another action adventure drama shot on film. *The Protectors* was the producer Gerry Anderson's only contemporary thriller series and consisted of two seasons of 52 episodes in total. The Protectors were three intrepid international private detectives whose services came at the highest price, and as in other programmes we have mentioned such as *Department S*, genres including the detective story and action drama were mixed. Nation contributed four episodes to the second season.

Following this, Nation co-wrote an episode of the series *Thriller* with its creator Brian Clemens who had also worked on *The Avengers*. ATV produced the programme with assistance from Lew Grade's ITC television company. *Thriller*, however, differs from the other programmes considered in this section since it was an anthology series of self-contained plays featuring different performers in each episode. Originally Clemens was given the go-ahead by Lew Grade to author one season of ten plays but the first season was so popular with UK viewers that Clemens was brought back to work on a further five seasons consisting of six or seven episodes each. When Clemens shared the writing responsibility with friends, he always wrote the basic outlines for stories himself. While the programme emphasised mystery and often provided unexpected plot twists, as its title makes clear, the episode co-written by Nation with Clemens returns to the familiar pattern outlined above in relation to other series featuring a pair of detectives, a man and a woman, and action such as rescuing a character from an assassination attempt. Comments within the television industry on Nation's work reveal that his forte was in writing this kind of generic action adventure rather than character-driven drama, as we discuss in chapter 2. There was an informal circle of people writing and producing these action drama programmes and Nation was a significant participant in this group.

### Science fiction Nation

By the mid-1960s Nation had become a recognised name associated with science fiction adventure because of his work on the BBC's *Doctor Who*, running alongside his action drama writing for independent television. Nation's contribution to the Doctor's adventures in space and time would have assured him a place in television history even if his television career had been limited to this. He had achieved professional success and was continually invited to contribute further *Doctor Who* stories, many featuring the Doctor's extraordinarily popular opponents, the Daleks, created for Nation's first screenplay for the series in 1963.

As his commitments to ITC increased he ceased working on BBC programmes in 1966, after writing 'The Keys Of Marinus' (a non-Dalek story), 'The Dalek Invasion Of Earth', 'The Chase', 'Mission To The Unknown' and 'The Daleks' Master Plan' for *Doctor Who*. But writing a *Doctor Who* script normally took him only about eight hours, so after allowing David Whitaker to script the two later 1960s Dalek stories during Patrick Troughton's time as the Doctor ('The Power Of The Daleks' and 'The Evil Of The Daleks'), he accepted invitations from producer Barry Letts and script editor Terrance Dicks to write for *Doctor Who* in the 1970s ('Planet Of The Daleks', 'Death To The Daleks', 'Genesis Of The Daleks'), after being unhappy with the treatment of the Daleks in Louis Marks's script for 'Day Of The Daleks' (1972). He had in the 1960s shaped the direction that *Doctor Who* would take with the emphasis on science fiction as opposed to historical adventures (see chapter 2). So the *Doctor Who* story that David Whitaker had commissioned Nation to write after delivery of 'The Daleks', the seven-episode story 'The Red Fort', which would have had the Indian Mutiny of 1857 against British colonial officers as its setting (Pixley 2001a: 28), was dropped in favour of Nation's science fiction offerings 'The Keys Of Marinus', and later 'The Chase'. Nation had also achieved public success in the 1960s with the Daleks, and became a focus of media attention. Indeed he playfully misled journalists by inventing the myth that he had thought up the Daleks' name from reading the letters 'DAL–LEK' on the spine of an encyclopedia. The Daleks frequently appeared on programmes other than *Doctor Who*, and merchandising quickly revolved around them (BBC WAC T48/445), including several books co-authored by Nation (see chapter 2). The word 'Dalek' was included in the *Oxford English Dictionary*, which pleased Nation enormously. Furthermore, for a person who had initially struggled to make a living he had achieved financial success. Nation received a royalty fee on both Dalek screen appearances and merchandising. All this made Nation wealthy and although he had planned to work flat out for a year so that he could buy a big house in the country, within six months he was able to buy (mostly in cash) an Elizabethan mansion in Teynham, Kent, with 15 rooms, a swimming pool and 35 acres of parkland. Also, although Nation's attempt to obtain BBC backing for a film series deriving from *Doctor Who* and featuring the Daleks did not succeed, he gained further attention and income from the cinema films *Dr Who And The Daleks* (1965) and *Dr Who – Daleks Invasion Earth 2150AD* (1966), adapted by Whitaker from Nation's early *Doctor Who* television serials 'The Daleks' and 'The Dalek Invasion Of Earth'. Nation gained an enduring reputation as 'the Dalek man' (Peel 1997b), and continued to contribute to

*Doctor Who* by devising the character of the Daleks' creator Davros as a mouthpiece for the machines, and writing 'The Android Invasion' (a non-Dalek adventure) and 'Destiny Of The Daleks'. But by the 1970s Nation was keen to develop his own series and turned again to the genres of science fiction and action adventure with which he was familiar.

Nation scripted the 1970 film *And Soon The Darkness*, in which two young nurses on a cycling holiday in France are stalked by a mysterious figure, and stalking was a common motif in Nation's earlier science fiction work, which we discuss in chapter 3. In 1973 he wrote and produced the film *The House In Nightmare Park* (US title *The House Of The Laughing Dead*) with Clive Exton, a comedy thriller starring Frankie Howerd and Ray Milland (who went to the same Cardiff school as Nation), which was very reminiscent of the 1939 Bob Hope film *The Cat And The Canary*. But in 1971 Nation made pitches for two of his own drama series at the BBC. The aim was that these would be commissioned initially as single plays, but if audience response and approval among BBC staff were sufficiently strong they would be turned into television series. Therefore the producer that Nation met was Andrew Osborn, Head of Drama Series, rather than Osborn's colleague in Plays. Nation based the first idea on Victorian Gothic, mixing mystery, suspense and costume drama with science fiction adventure. The programme was titled *The Incredible Robert Baldick* after its aristocratic central character, who, as a late Victorian scientist sleuth, resembled the scientist-investigator the Doctor in *Doctor Who*. The format and genres of *The Incredible Robert Baldick*, then, illustrated Nation's tendency to repeat familiar successful tendencies. Nation's second idea for a series pilot was described in BBC documentation of the pitch meeting as a 'Drama Science Documentary' with the title *Beyond Omega* (BBC WAC T48/445). It is impossible to tell from existing records what this programme may have been, but the connotations of surviving the end that the title *Beyond Omega* possesses hint that the programme may have been an initial attempt at science fiction post-apocalyptic drama. Nation tried unsuccessfully to sell an idea for such a series to ITV with the help of his colleague the writer-producer Brian Clemens, and later devised the programme for BBC under the title *Survivors*. Nation ran late with the two pilot scripts, and since Osborn needed one immediately, he proposed that *The Incredible Robert Baldick* should be the one to deliver. Nation aimed for a contracted post as script adviser if the pilot became a series, as well as commissions for several episode scripts, and in January 1972 Nation's remuneration for a run of 26 episodes was agreed if the pilot succeeded in becoming a series (BBC WAC T48/445).

*The Incredible Robert Baldick*: 'Never Come Night' mixed Gothic mystery with science fiction. It was transmitted in October 1972 in the *Drama Playhouse* slot, an anthology of possible pilots for new series (BBC WAC RCONT20), and was repeated on BBC2 in February 1974. Robert Hardy starred as Baldick, and the play was mainly shot in BBC studios, using sets to represent Baldick's ancestral home, Baldick Park, and the church and crypt in which the Gothic mystery story took place, as well as the main salon of The Tsar, an elaborate private train carriage that acted as Baldick's mobile headquarters. The text of the publicity billing for the play in the *Radio Times* (2 October 1972) was: 'A fear so real, it can kill. A fear so old, it defies reason. A fear which Baldick must overcome – or be smothered by his own terror.' The mysterious deaths of villagers that Baldick was called on to investigate were eventually revealed to be caused by a strange device, buried under an abbey's crypt, which amplified the fears of anyone in close proximity to it. Baldick himself was terrified in this way, but realised that his own reactions were being amplified and fed back to him. At the close of the play, the mysterious device is briefly glimpsed, and is a fragment of a printed circuit board. Baldick wisely concludes that it is not an artefact of the nineteenth century, thus linking what appeared to be a Gothic costume drama with Nation's work in the science fiction genre, also apparent through the fact that Dr Baldick was a scientist. While the pilot was never developed into a series, Nation's contribution progressed further than that for another series which was never made called *No Place Like Home*, about two couples, one American and one British, who retired early to Ireland (BBC WAC T48/445). Nation was commissioned in October 1973 by producer Andrew Osborn to write two episodes, 'Everything In The Garden Is Lovely' and 'The Accident', and delivered scripts that were never used.

Nation wrote a UK bestselling children's book *Rebecca's World* (1975), a fantasy adventure story named after his daughter, as was the character Rebec in the *Doctor Who* story 'Planet Of The Daleks' (Pixley 1993a: 26). The book was published in several countries including the United States, and was read by Bernard Cribbins in five 15-minute episodes on BBC's children's story programme *Jackanory* in April 1976. It was this work with which Nation was ultimately most pleased. But he had again been trying to originate a new television series idea, originally *The Survivors* (Pixley 1999c), later simply titled *Survivors* (1975–77). Nation's bleak premise for *Survivors* concerned a disparate group attempting to cope in the aftermath of a global pandemic, and is explained in greater detail in the following chapter. The series was reminiscent of the similarly bleak BBC series *Doomwatch* (1970–72), which dealt with the inherent dangers to humankind in scientific progress, and indeed many of the people working on *Survivors* had been involved in the earlier series. *Survivors* was shot on location in Wales and Herefordshire as well as in studio sets, and ran for three seasons, totalling 38 episodes. Nation left the series after the first season, having acted as script consultant and written the three-part opening ('The Fourth Horseman', 'Genesis' and 'Gone Away'), and four later episodes including the last episode of the first season ('A Beginning', after he had already contributed 'Garland's War', 'The Future Hour' and 'Something Of Value'). In Nation's view, the perils and challenges established in his series format were not developed with sufficient rigour (taken further in his novel based on the series storylines, published in 1976), which led to bitter disagreements with the producer. In a mid-1970s High Court case, Brian Clemens argued unsuccessfully that he had told Nation the series idea in the late 1960s and registered the concept with the Writer's Guild in 1965 (see Brown 1993).

It was in autumn 1975 that Nation signed a contract for what would become the third of the most well-known television productions credited to him, *Blake's 7*, which would ultimately last for four 13-episode seasons transmitted between 1978 and 1981. We discuss the premise, genre and politics of this programme in detail in subsequent chapters, but it is worth noting here that the premise of *Blake's 7* resembles that of *Survivors* in its similar struggle by a small group to combat seemingly overwhelming circumstances. The format featured the main character of Roj (originally Rog) Blake and on the memo that recorded Nation's commission the BBC producer Ronald Marsh described the new series as an, 'Adventure story set in the future' (BBC WAC RCONT21), and wrote, 'A space western-adventure. A modern swashbuckler'. Initially there were to be a 'group of villains being escorted onto a rocket ship ... which goes astray & lands on an alien planet where inhabitants are planning to invade & destroy earth', though the Earth invasion motif was later abandoned. Nation wrote all 13 episodes of the first season (see appendix), spreading himself rather thin. He then contributed three episodes each to the following two seasons, including the first episodes of both seasons and the last instalment of the third. At this point Nation was attempting unsuccessfully to launch a TV movie called *Bedouin* (Stevens and Moore 2003: 63), and as he completed *Blake's 7*'s planned last episode, 'Terminal', he was about to move to Hollywood (BBC WAC T65/72/1). Indeed Alan Stevens and Fiona Moore (2003: 146) suggest that the name of the planet Califeron in 'Terminal', a planet that would shelter the *Blake's 7* spaceship crew, probably derived from California. Nation was in America when a fourth and final season of *Blake's 7* was made, and was not overjoyed that the last episode, 'Blake', would see all of the regular hero team killed except Avon (Paul Darrow). *Blake's 7's* producer, Vere Lorrimer, has commented that 'although Terry might have been upset at the time, I'm quite sure he can't have been ultimately upset ... it certainly gave people an amazing living memory' (quoted in Airey 1991: 70).

## Cross-Nation

Nation moved to Los Angeles with his family in 1980, and had dreamt of working in Hollywood for many years. But he disapproved of the domination of the US film industry by accountants and was unable to sell a new television format in the United States. However, he did work on development and script doctoring projects for Columbia, 20th Century Fox and MGM, and people including Steven Spielberg who were fans of *Doctor Who* made him welcome in Los Angeles. While in the United States, Nation wrote an episode for the short-lived filmed adventure series *Ticket To Ride* (titled *A Fine Romance* in the United States), a comedy thriller format based around the presenters of a television travel programme fronted by former husband and wife Michael Trent (Christopher Cazenove) and Louisa Phillips (Margaret Whitton).

Nation also worked on the ABC network's action drama *MacGyver*, producing six episodes for its 1985 season, though his writing contribution was limited to the 'opening gambits', short scenes before the main title sequence in which ingenious solutions are found by the eponymous hero to deal with threatening situations, and which showcase MacGyver's talent for quick thinking as well as physical action. The programme made use of inexpensive stock footage in much the same way as the ITC series that Nation had worked on in the mid-1960s. For instance, one *MacGyver* episode featured an international crime caper using drivers of Mini cars, depicted by inserting footage from the film *The Italian Job* (1969), which was based around the same premise.

Along with Andrew J. Fenady, Nation was also involved in writing the made-for-television film *A Masterpiece Of Murder* (1986). The film featured Bob Hope in his first television movie, and mixed the genres of comedy and mystery. *A Masterpiece Of Murder* centres on an over-the-hill detective, Dan Dolan (played by Hope), reluctantly teaming up with a worldly retired master thief to solve a series of art thefts and murders with much mayhem ensuing along the way.

Nation appeared in the New Jersey Network television documentary *Doctor Who Then And Now* in 1987, the BSB documentary *31 Who* in

1990, and collaborated in 1988 with John Peel on *The Official Doctor Who and the Daleks Book*. He remained inextricably associated in the minds of media pundits with the Daleks that he had brought to the screen over 25 years before. He died on 9 March 1997 in Pacific Pallisades, California after several years of poor health, having suffered in his last years from emphysema. He was survived by his wife Kate (née Gaunt), his son Joel and daughter Rebecca.


## Conclusion

The purpose of this chapter has been to provide factual information on the many writing projects with which Terry Nation was involved. Its biographical focus has necessitated our use of two interrelated discourses whose assumptions we will go on to question in the later parts of this book. Moving from Nation's birth to his death, our writing assumes the unity of his life and implicitly suggests a process of progression and development, organised around turning points where significant shifts in his writing career took place. This discourse might seem appropriate to a study of the work of a single individual, and to a series of books on television screenwriters, producers and other creators of television. However, the setting of boundaries around Nation's life tends to exclude the ways in which limits were set to what he was able to accomplish as someone acting in a complex context of collaboration, in dialogue and negotiation with other people and with institutions, in the changing environment of television production and changing social and political times. Nation's activity, or 'agency' as a more academic term would have it, was neither under his sole control nor unaffected by these collaborations, negotiations and external factors. It is this first assumption of unified agency and authority that we seek to deconstruct in the following chapter, where we focus on the collaborative enterprise of television production in which Nation was involved, and in which his role was primarily that of a craftsman writing quickly and prolifically for others.

The second discourse that we have adopted in this chapter is one in which the radio and television programmes and films that are credited to Nation have been discussed one-by-one. Our third chapter, on genre and form, however, extensively explores the ways that programmes are both differentiated from one another, primarily by means of their format, and also connected with each other because of their relationships with existing genres. Again, the assumptions of unity, coherence and the security of boundaries are questioned in chapter 3 as we develop our argument that the programmes Nation worked on need to be understood as part of a wider network of interconnections, repetitions, borrowings and reworkings. Furthermore, the above discussion has shown that while Nation wrote several films, he did not break into that medium in the way he did with television, which is important because it shows how Nation's career in television revolved around particular television forms, whereas cinema conventionally allows the writer rather more freedom in this respect. Nation commonly slotted his work into already defined parameters where there is a relationship between writer and form. In chapter 4, on the cultural and political interpretations that may be made of the programmes associated with Nation, we stress the relationships between programmes and ideas and ideologies that were and are in circulation within and beyond television programme texts. By closely analysing selected examples from Nation's writing career, we show that television programmes can be understood (apart from the intentions of their creators) as participating in the dialogues and negotiations that frame ways of thinking about culture and society. For although our biographical sketch tends, because of its form and remit, to imply that Nation's work was in a sense his 'property', we are keen to demonstrate the ways in which academic analysis can explore the meanings of television that can be shared and exchanged beyond the boundaries set by the authority of authorship.

# Collaboration at the BBC

## Introduction

In this chapter we discuss specific aspects of Terry Nation's collaboration with the BBC, in order to develop our account of what is at stake in the authorship of series and serial television. While we maintain a focus on Nation's particular contribution to BBC programmes, we regard these detailed contexts as broadly representative of the boundaries and constraints on television authorship in general. Our work on Nation's role as a creator of programme formats and writer of television scripts is therefore not only relevant to a study of Nation's body of work but also to Television Studies scholarship on the production of television fiction. In discussing the limitations placed on creators and writers by television's institutional and industrial organisation, the chapter distinguishes between the terms 'form', 'genre', and 'format'. In serial and series television, where single stories and episodes fit within the boundaries of continuing runs of programmes, these concepts are essential to understanding the scope that the creators of programmes and the writers of episodes possess. We therefore extend existing academic discussions of these terms, which often do not connect them with the role of the screenwriter. We shall see how the writer and other production staff are collaborative and interdependent parts of a team in which there are permeable boundaries around the notion of authorship, and where ultimately the author function is dependent on all of its constituent parts. We discuss the role of the writer in British television in the 1960s and 1970s in relation to commissioning and production processes, and explain how institutional support (or the lack of it) for science fiction television, technical and budgetary constraints, scheduling decisions and the responses of audiences circumscribed the contributions Nation could make but also offered opportunities for him to write and devise programmes. The generically coded format and themes in work credited to Nation as creator and writer were sometimes erected and always built upon by other members of the different programmes' production teams. Audiences also have some claim to authorial authority because viewers make programmes their own by interpreting them and responding to them. These interpretive activities are of interest to television production staff and feed back into the planning and realisation of future programmes, so that television authorship needs to be understood as a collaborative and recursive enterprise.

## Creators and writers

Terry Nation was a contributing writer for *Doctor Who* and not its creator, but he was the creator of *Survivors* and *Blake's 7* and wrote the screenplays for some of the episodes of each series. Both creators and writers have author(ity) functions in the British science fiction television work with which Nation was involved, but there is a tension between these two roles. The production of television programmes is a linear process from the initial idea to the pre-production, planning and development of the programme in an audiovisual form. But prior to this, a programme is conceived with regard to a certain television audience, genre, slot and size of budget. The treatment, budgets and storylines are devised with this in mind, through post-production to the final broadcast. So making programmes demands anticipation of later stages at every point in the process. An initial idea will need to be shaped so that it will appeal to the audience imagined by its creators, and this affects the genre, aesthetic form, subject, style and pace of the programme. The creator therefore comes first and is responsible for anticipating the end of the process in which specific audiences will be attracted and retained for a programme scheduled and advertised in particular ways. Creation is an individual originating process with an important author(ity) function, but it demands the imagining of what a programme will have become when it is finished and shown.

While the creator is the originator of a programme, for series and serial television the writers of individual episodes are often not employees of the television institution that makes the programme. They are freelance workers contracted to produce a specified script that is required to conform to the idea that has been approved by the permanent staff within an institution such as the BBC. There are institutional differences between the idea, which is the property of the television institution, and the script, which is effectively a product sold by the writer to that institution.

**Form and generically coded format: definitions**

The notions of form, genre and format are interconnected and reveal much about the limitations and the opportunities for creators and writers of television productions. Form refers to the structure of the programme (i.e. whether it is composed of self-contained episodes or a series of stories comprising linked episodes). Genre involves a process of taxonomy, in other words the identification of common features shared by one programme and a group of others into which it fits. The genre of a programme (such as science fiction) is determined first, followed by format. Format (also a term employed to label types of video recorder or DVD) denotes the aspects of a programme that are largely original and stable, such as the characters and character-types (a hero, a hero and an assistant, or a hero team, for example), and recurring settings that the series or continuing serial forms will involve. The term format is sometimes used pejoratively to indicate that a programme contains nothing new or interesting because it follows guidelines that are already established. But we use this term in a neutral and descriptive way in this chapter to refer to the template that specifies how the episodes of a series or a series of serials will share characters and settings that provide continuity and consistency, and how the screenwriter's role is negotiated in relation to these notions.

**Differing television forms and their relationships to genre and format**

There are a number of forms in television drama. The anthology series written by a multitude of writers consists of self-contained stories and one-off characters, where any individual story may belong to a different genre from the last (as in *The Wednesday Play* and *Play For Today* anthologies in the 1960s and 1970s) or may fall into a specific generic category (as was the case for Nation's science fiction contributions to *Out Of This World* and *Out Of The Unknown*). The boundary between this form and others is relatively rigid, and although the separate stories of the anthology series may be linked by the presence of an on-screen host, the linked episodes in the series and serial forms are most relevant to our study. The form of the episodic series consists of largely self-contained stories, usually all belonging to the same dominant genre, with regular characters and settings linking one episode to the next. As John Tulloch and Manuel Alvarado (1983: x) note, the episodic series involves 'the main protagonists ... and locations ... providing continuity between episodes'. According to Graeme Burton (2000: 109), 'Continuity describes those narrative features which link one programme to another. In the series structure ... those features have to do with character and environment. Sitcoms are a good example of this – same people, same place. But the storylines change: narratives are set up and resolved week by week'. In contrast to the series form, the 'episodic serial' has an ongoing story for a number of episodes, with generically coded characters, settings or modes of transport that recur. As John Ellis (1982: 123) writes, the serial aims 'towards a conclusion which is a number of weeks distant'. In fact, series and serial forms sometimes blur together. One series can contain multiple serials linked together by the main series' dominant genre and format, as in the case of *Doctor Who*'s serial stories within the framework of a series. Some series may also have serial traits, where free-standing episode stories introduce changes to the consistent group of characters, for example, that affect subsequent episodes. The choice of series or serial form is a component in the original creation of a programme's generically coded format.

### Form, generically coded format, and creators and writers

This examination of form and generically coded format reveals much about the structure of television authorship. The distinctions between forms, for example, are useful in understanding the planning and writing of television drama. Within a created series different writers can be employed to contribute parts of the whole, such as individual episodes of anthology series, episodic series or multi-episode episodic serials. While the anthology series gave greater freedom to individual screenwriters in the 1960s and 1970s, this was often not the case with episodic series or a series such as *Doctor Who*, which contained numerous episodic serials. Episodic series and serial forms make a consistent generically coded format possible, and restrict contributing writers within their boundaries.

The boundaries around authorship are explicitly at issue in relation to programme formats, which are created with generic characteristics in mind. Formats consist of what Nick Lacey (2000) calls a 'repertoire of elements' such as constant generically coded settings or modes of transport and characters or types of character. They can, as Graeme Turner (2001: 7) notes, 'be original and thus copyright, franchised under licence, and traded as a commercial property'. According to Turner, 'Format is a production category with relatively rigid boundaries that are difficult to transgress without coming up with a new format'. This contrasts with the genre the programme format participates in, which is necessarily unoriginal since the concept of genre highlights properties that are shared with existing programmes. The creator establishes the dominant genre of the format, exercising authority over the writer. In the case of *Doctor Who*, for example, Nation slotted his multi-episode stories into the boundaries of a stable generically coded format already set up by the production team. Nation could copyright his scripts and storylines for *Doctor Who*, whereas the format of the programme belonged to the BBC (in keeping with Turner's argument), so there were different levels of authority in play. By contrast with *Doctor Who*, Nation's role in shaping *Survivors* and *Blake's 7* and creating the boundaries of their generically coded formats gave him a different and greater authority, although he was still answerable to other production personnel.

The generically coded format of programmes would often be described to prospective writers in a written document composed by an author(ity) figure with responsibility for overseeing them within the television institution. This document is often (though not always) known as the series 'Bible', connoting its authority over a programme and the status of its 'commandments' about genre, characters, settings and types of permissible storyline. It is to these documents that individual writers of programmes must refer so that their story offerings fit in with the overriding generically coded format. Authorship is therefore further complicated by the requirement that an individual writer's storyline or script must contribute to the overall whole of a programme. The role of the written documentation outlining a format that contains specified generic characteristics, thus setting boundaries to prospective writers' individual authorship, can be seen in relation to *Doctor Who* and specifically to Nation's contributions to the series, as well as to *Blake's 7*. But while we explain below how form and generically coded format placed boundaries around Nation's contributions to BBC science fiction television, we shall complicate the distinctions made here, especially in relation to the genre of the programmes he worked on, in the following chapter, and we will also see that genre is intertextual.

### Devising generic programmes

The initial conception of *Doctor Who, Survivors* and *Blake's 7* took place along generic lines. In the former case the BBC Head of Drama, Sydney Newman, and the programme's generically coded format exercised author(ity) functions over the writers who scripted stories for *Doctor Who*. Newman was initially brought from Canada by the independent broadcaster ABC to run the drama anthology series *Armchair Theatre*, which succeeded in gaining top ten ratings for 32 out of 37 weeks between autumn 1959 and summer 1960, with audiences often in excess of 12 million. When Newman moved to the BBC he had extensive authority, and divided the Drama Department into three parts: Plays (for single dramas and operas), Series (for popular drama such as the police drama *Z Cars* and the medical drama *Doctor Finlay's Casebook*), and Serials (for long running weekly drama productions using cliff-hangers to encourage viewer loyalty, such as *Compact* and *Town Hall*, and adaptations of literary works). His authority extended to a form of authorship, in that he suggested a science fiction series composed of different extended stories to be made by Serials for a family audience on early Saturday evenings, and it was this idea that became *Doctor Who*. The programme was therefore conceived along generic lines, although Newman and Donald Wilson, Head of Serials, refused the term 'science fiction' as a satisfactory generic label. A memo written by Wilson, outlining the idea for *Doctor Who* in July 1963 (BBC WAC T5/657/1) stated: 'The serial cannot accurately be described as either space travel or science fiction'. For generically, *Doctor Who* was designed to contain not only futuristic adventures but also historical stories that could be regarded as educational and improving for its youth audience, concerning significant events in the times and places visited by the main characters, such as the Roman invasion of Britain, or the Thirty Years' War. Using the science fiction genre's notion of time travel meant that the main characters' values would be different from those of the people they encountered, thus enabling reflection and debate about historical events. In its futuristic stories, the new programme was to avoid the low-quality, non-educational bug-eyed monster stories of cinematic science fiction, though monster adventure soon became important once Nation introduced the Daleks in *Doctor Who*'s second story. Genre itself exercised a degree of authority over writers for *Doctor Who*, which was at first advertised not by highlighting the contributions of its writers but by emphasising its dominant genre of science fiction. For instance, in the *Radio Times* feature 'DR. WHO' to announce the new series (21 November 1963, p. 7) the Doctor was described as being 'from another world and a distant future', but as we shall see, Nation's stories challenged the direction of the programme within that dominant genre to some extent.

Nation created *Survivors* and *Blake's 7* as science fiction, and generic references in the promotion of the programmes established boundaries for audience interpretation. A pessimistic construction of the future was expressed in *Survivors*, arising from its premise of a decimating plague. The *Radio Times* feature promoting the first episode of *Survivors* suggested its connection with science fiction (Dunkley, 1975: 6–7). Quoting a line of dialogue from Nation's script, it referred to the present-day characters as belonging to the 'generation which landed a man on the moon', thus referencing the Apollo space programme, and the series explored the consequences of an accident in a science lab from which a plague virus escaped and rapidly swept across the world. Similarly, in *Blake's 7* a dark vision of the future as a result of genetic engineering and computers was envisaged for this series, as mentioned in a *Radio Times* feature (Evans, 1977: 114–17).

## Science fiction television formats

Boundaries placed around individual writers by the creators of the series formats led to struggles for authorship and authority on programmes Nation wrote for. The format of *Doctor Who* was largely devised by Cecil Edwin Webber (see Gillatt 1998) following the discussions initiated by Newman's plan for a science fiction serial. The format is manifested in documents that simultaneously exercise authority over potential writers and also authorise the creation of original screenplays that explore its possibilities. Donald Wilson's document (BBC WAC T5/ 647/1) of July 1963 was designed primarily for use in publicity, outlining the regular cast, writers and directors, the recording schedule and promotional photo-call and trailer dates, and reflects the key features of the agreed format. It specifies that the main character of the alien Doctor is an extraordinarily old man, senile but brilliant, of whom the audience would possess little knowledge, hence the title of the programme, *Doctor Who*. He travels through time and space in his TARDIS (Time And Relative Dimensions In Space) machine, meant to blend in with its surroundings but stuck from the very first episode in the shape of a British police box. The format of the series largely drew on H. G. Wells's *The Time Machine* novel, but characters were added, one of whom would be a child, and the others two contemporary school teachers travelling with them. As the programme progressed and actors playing the Doctor's companions left, similar character types replaced them. In our conversation with the first producer Verity Lambert, she was keen to stress the distinction between the parameters set by the format of the programme and the role of individual writers fitting their own stories within those boundaries.

Nation created *Survivors'* premise of a global pandemic and the regular characters of Abby Grant, Jenny Richards, Greg Preston and Tom Price; in the case of *Blake's 7*, he conceived the outer space setting, the spaceship and the main characters. Writing about his role as creator of *Blake's 7* Nation noted that he often found it hard to pin down where his ideas originated from and remembered that for *Blake's 7* he outlined the format at a meeting with the BBC after running out of other suggestions for new programmes (Attwood 1983: 7). After the alien invasion idea (see chapter 1), the pitch highlighted a wrongly convicted patriot being transported to a prison planet who escapes to take over an alien spacecraft and use it to wage war against the evil forces of the Federation. In our discussion with script editor Chris Boucher, he confirmed that the format was wholly Nation's creation, but the fact that Nation referred to *Blake's 7* as 'The Dirty Dozen' in space' shows that the notion of a disparate group of convicts embarking on a dangerous mission may have been suggested by this 1967 film. When the actor playing Blake, Gareth Thomas, left at the end of the second series (to make a couple of brief return appearances), the format, overseen by Nation, remained largely the same. Avon (Paul Darrow) assumed control of the spaceship Liberator, although he was more interested in survival than in saving worlds. When the Jenna Stannis character was written out, the new Dayna Mellanby and Del Tarrant characters replaced her in the Liberator crew.

### Form and generically coded format: Nation as creator and writer

Since *Doctor Who* employed the form of multiple episodic serials, rather like the later *Ace Of Wands* (1970–72) and *The Tomorrow People* (1973–79), it required Newman's and his colleagues' originating authority to devise these and oversee the whole. But many contributing writers were needed to supply episodes since the programme was designed for broadcast 48 weeks per year, with stories of four to six episodes each. Within each story, episodes would end like those of a thriller serial, with a cliffhanger to be picked up by the same writer in the following instalment. Published short stories were initially considered as the basis for the series that became *Doctor Who*, and while this idea was abandoned, after the series began a multitude of writers of science fiction were again considered, this time as possible scriptwriters of original stories. The agents of several science fiction authors were contacted by script editor David Whitaker in September 1964 (BBC WAC T5/647/1) to see whether these authors would write for *Doctor Who*, and these included John Wyndam, Charles Eric Maine and John Brunner. Writers for *Doctor Who* were required to contribute original storylines and scripts, and the recourse to established authors demonstrates a concern for the creative authority associated with the literary work. But the opposing pressure was for writers to stay within the boundaries of the generically coded format and to conform to the disciplines of writing for television (such as meeting tight deadlines and keeping production costs down). The authorship of individual episodes could therefore conflict with the authorship of the format, and attempts to involve literary science fiction writers gave way to commissioning writers with experience of conforming to the disciplines of format and the BBC institution's boundaries around authorial creativity. It was in this context that Nation, as an experienced writer, was contracted to produce his first *Doctor Who* story, 'The Daleks'.

The form of *Survivors* and *Blake's 7*, which were mixtures of the episodic series and the serial (see chapter 3), entailed continuity of setting and regular characters, meaning that Nation's role as the creator of the generically coded format often predominated as author(ity) figure over the scope available to individual screenwriters. A variety of different writers contributed episodes since each episode had a largely freestanding storyline. The identity of both the episodic series with serial elements and the series composed of episodic serials relies on the maintenance of format and the dominant genre across episodes authored by the same person or by different writers, with similar tensions arising between the unity of the programme as prescribed in its format, and the diversity of episodes that were required to be in themselves original. The idea of *Blake's 7* was outlined in a document for other prospective writers from the second season, a 'Bible' written by Boucher and titled 'General Notes and Baffle Gab Glossary' (Stevens and Moore 2003: 63).

## Limitations of format and freedoms of authorship

The generically coded formats of these series are themselves very revealing about the degree of authority that creators and writers had. In *Doctor Who*, for which Nation contributed individual stories, the generically coded science fiction format both placed limitations on writers yet also widened the opportunities for them to transgress its limits. Format therefore paradoxically involved both a closing off yet simultaneously an opening up. Authorship involves steering a narrative and predetermining its co-ordinates. The production team's authorship of the programme is personified in their creation of the Doctor, also an authorial figure who endeavours to steer the narrative through an attempt to control his ship, the TARDIS. But the production team's authorship is therefore characterised by a desire to see where the series would lead rather than limiting it from the outset. An aura of mystery is central, since the Doctor cannot always control the TARDIS and its destination is often random. So individual writers had significant freedom since their stories could be set in any place and at any time. The TARDIS is a boundary object randomly crossing the thresholds of time and space, so individual writers' contributions were not wholly bounded but were also permitted some freedom. The viewer would learn about a new environment with the main characters, thus providing a flexibility not offered to writers in other series and serial genres such as the sitcom or the police drama. Interestingly, however, the success of Nation's first story did impose limits on the type of adventure to which the TARDIS would lead in his subsequent scripts.

Nation created the formats of *Survivors* and *Blake's 7*, and restricted himself and other writers to a greater degree than the creators of *Doctor Who* did, since contributors of episodes were left with less choice of subject matter. The format of *Survivors* involved characters located in a particular time, place and environment, and did not emphasise mystery to the same extent. Furthermore, the requirement that a group of characters living in an England devastated by plague should gradually come to terms with their situation, rather than being able quickly to alter their surroundings, was itself part of the format's premise and therefore extremely difficult to change. This imposed limits on the writers of individual episodes, though different writers had different generic emphases (see chapter 3). The format of *Blake's 7* featured a group of characters on board a spaceship in a fixed time, whose overall mission would be to battle the regular enemy, the Earth Federation. Although, as Stevens and Moore (2003: 24, 26, 29, 31) note, Nation's four opening episodes allowed some mystery as to who the main characters would be, they were established by the time other writers contributed, as were the new characters introduced in the third season. The randomness at the centre of *Doctor Who*'s format and the opportunities for investigation of new environments did not characterise either *Survivors* or *Blake's 7* to the same degree. Yet some *Blake's 7* episodes did not feature the Federation, the third season episode 'Sarcophagus' by Tanith Lee pushed at these boundaries (see Stevens and Moore 2003: 135), and writers could introduce other sub-genres; but in general format limited the authorship and authority of contributing writers.

## Policing formats, selecting writers and revising scripts: producers and script editors

These formats were overseen by producers and script editors. At the BBC, Newman devolved authorial power through the institutional network of producers, script editors and other personnel who thereby gained authority themselves, and this structure remained not only for *Doctor Who* but also for *Survivors* and *Blake's 7*. Television can be regarded as a producer's medium, meaning that the television producer has the predominant authority over, and responsibility for, programmes, though there are several other roles that could claim such creative and managerial authority, particularly that of script editor (known as the story editor until 1968). The producer controls the process of making a programme, and fulfils a responsibility to the television institution that has commissioned it by overseeing the format, budgets, personnel, the production schedule and the delivery of the finished product. For example, for *Doctor Who*, Newman, in consultation with the Head of Serials Donald Wilson, asked his former production secretary at ABC Television, Verity Lambert, who had joined him at the BBC, and who had worked in light entertainment, quiz programmes, music and arts but never on children's programmes, to take on the producer's author(ity) function. Later *Doctor Who* producers for periods in which Nation was contributing included John Wiles, Barry Letts, Philip Hinchcliffe and Graham Williams, with Terence Dudley serving as producer on *Survivors*, while on the first three seasons of *Blake's 7*, David Maloney assumed that role, to be replaced by Vere Lorrimer for the fourth and final season. Newman provided producers with a group of further author(ity) figures such as script editors to deal with the details of script production, whereas previous BBC practice had been to combine in the producer the roles of producer and script editor. Whereas the authority had previously rested with the producer, author(ity) was devolved and became less concentrated and more differentiated. However, there was still a layering of author(ity) with the producer occupying the top of the chain, and the script editor positioned below. There was a hierarchy but with all the parts interconnected, and the top was supported by the contributions made lower down.

The role of the script editor was all-important in determining which screenwriters should be included and excluded as contributors to programmes, and in altering scripts. During the pre-production process, script editors often spend considerable amounts of time in discussions with writers, seeking ideas and negotiating terms for scripts. Script editors may need to commission several more scripts than actually get used, to allow for late delivery, refusal of a script due to cost implications and, all importantly, unsuitability for the agreed format. Production planning typically, but not always, begins more than a year before any shooting takes place, and at this stage storylines and scripts need to be commissioned and approved. Maintaining connections with writers, and finding new writers to contribute to a series, are thus important aspects of the script editor's job.

Nation's connection with the first script editor for *Doctor Who* differed from that with the script editors of *Survivors* and *Blake's 7*. For in the case of *Doctor Who*, script editor David Whitaker supplied potential writers with a six-page briefing document (BBC WAC T5/647/1) explaining the background and approach of the programme, and Whitaker acted as a conduit for the institutional author(ity) of Lambert and the programme format for which she was responsible. The document explained: 'Since this is primarily a series of stories concerning people rather than studio effects, and the original characters and backgrounds have been prepared already, the writer will be asked to submit a story line from which he will be commissioned. This need not go into fractional detail – three or four pages of quarto ought to be sufficient to express the idea.' Since Verity Lambert had no writing experience it was the script editor who initially had more influence on the beginning of *Doctor Who* and who Nation worked with closely. Nation's agent in the early 1960s was Associated London Scripts, and Whitaker went to ALS to find writers for *Doctor Who*, among them Dennis Spooner, John Lucarotti and Bill Strutton who had worked on Newman's ATV series *The Avengers*. Whitaker was very keen on Nation's first storyline for the programme 'The Daleks', about a race of totalitarian creatures, and much less keen on a script by Anthony Coburn called 'The Robots', which he regarded as much more cerebral than Nation's. Whitaker described 'The Daleks' outline as 'a detailed and highly fancied storyline' (BBC WAC T48/445).

In the case of *Survivors* and *Blake's 7*, however, Nation had devised the formats and therefore was not selected by a script editor policing them. However, changes were made to reduce the number of regular characters in *Blake's 7*. The characters Tone Selman, Brell Kline and Arco Trent, who had few lines but made up seven roles in addition to Blake's crew of Avon, Gan, Vila and Jenna, were removed and Cally added. 'Seven' then referred to non-human personae such as the computers (Stevens and Moore 2003: 18), as well as to humanoid characters. Nation wrote the whole first season, although one of his scripts, 'The Invaders', was rejected (Stevens and Moore 2003: 18). Another script, 'Locate And Destroy', was also rejected although storylines involving the villainous character Travis (originally introduced in the first episode but replaced by the spy Dev Tarrant), and Jenna being kidnapped by primitives on a planet, appeared later in Nation's 'Duel' and 'Deliverance' (Stevens and Moore 2003: 18). Nation used a variant of his title for the sixth transmitted episode 'Seek-Locate-Destroy'. His format imposed an approach on other writers for later seasons, which the script editor Chris Boucher was responsible for overseeing, while Nation was writing according to limits he had largely set himself.

Script editors not only select screenwriters to contribute stories to fit within a format, but screenwriters collaborate with them during the process of writing. Script editors are often writers themselves and therefore, in a process of doubling, the two roles are both differentiated and merged, and boundaries between the roles are both erected and collapsed. The script editor advises scriptwriters to edit and sometimes rewrite their work, and to understand the visual and sound technologies that will be used to realise a script. Even when a script has been delivered, the script editor continues to work on it. Revisions may be required in order to make the script shootable within the budget. Extensive rewriting or polishing of the script can be necessary in order to maintain continuing characters, adapt the script to the strengths or weaknesses of performers, or add or remove special effects. It is conventionally agreed in the television industry that writers retain credit for the scripts they produce, although in practice the script used during shooting may well have been extensively revised by a script editor. Because of the numerous other demands on producers, script editors often do much of the work in revising scripts and consulting with writers.

For example, in Nation's involvement with *Doctor Who*, *Survivors* and *Blake's 7* his scripts were subject to a continual process of revision, demonstrating the authority that could be wielded over writers by production teams. In all three series, the script editors were often writers themselves, collapsing the boundaries around authorship noted above: *Doctor Who*'s script editors David Whitaker, Dennis Spooner, Terrance Dicks, Robert Holmes and Douglas Adams all contributed their own stories to the programme. Whitaker aided the success of the Daleks by scripting the Dalek comic strip in the *TV Century 21* comic in 1965–66, by writing the first *Doctor Who* annual, co-writing the first Dalek film and the dialogue for the second, as well as the 1964 theatre play *Curse Of The Daleks*. Spooner had worked on ITC series. Adams would write the hugely successful *The Hitch-Hiker's Guide to the Galaxy*. *Survivors*' script editor Terence Dudley had written for *Doomwatch* and in the early 1980s wrote stories for *Doctor Who*, namely 'Four To Doomsday', 'Black

Orchid' (1982) and 'The Kings' Demons' (1983). The *Blake's 7* script editor Chris Boucher had previously contributed 'The Face Of Evil', 'The Robots Of Death' and 'Image Of The Fendahl' (1977) to *Doctor Who*, and wrote no fewer than nine *Blake's 7* episodes himself – 'Shadow', 'Weapon', 'Trial', 'Star One' (1979), 'City At The Edge Of The World', 'Rumours Of Death', 'Death-Watch' (1980), 'Rescue', and the climactic 'Blake' (1981) – before creating and writing for the BBC2 series *Star Cops*. The requirement for script editors to revise Nation's scripts sometimes came about as a result of input from other forces as the programme was being made, such as Sydney Newman's comments on *Doctor Who* and notes from episode directors. It was made clear in the briefing document for *Doctor Who* (BBC WAC T5/647/1) that the story would be checked and that the writing of the finished script would be partly collaborative: 'Writers may consult the story editor who will work out their plots and situations with them and arrange meetings with the Associate Producer' (Mervyn Pinfield, who gave technical advice).

Nation's weaknesses in character development and plot often required the script editor's assistance. A script report on Nation's first two episodes of the *Doctor Who* story 'The Daleks' (BBC WAC T5/647/1) contains 13 points asking for clarification of plot, suggesting dramatic turning points and offering explanations for events in the story, such as how the Daleks are powered by static electricity. Christopher Barry, the director, asked for the characters' motivations and emotions to be brought out more, and concluded: 'It seems that Terry Nation feels that once he has told the audience something the characters need no longer react to the situation. He is continually having them accept a situation in a most undramatic manner, and therefore losing a lot of potential value' (BBC WAC T5/648/1). He made similar detailed comments on the other episodes. Therefore the script editor, Whitaker, had more work to do. Sydney Newman himself gave feedback to Verity Lambert after watching Nation's story, and this added to other BBC staff's concern for Nation to give greater logic and character drama to his work. A note from Newman to Verity Lambert (BBC WAC T5/647/1) in June 1964 congratulates the team on the success of 'The Daleks' serial, and adds: 'Despite the blonde faeries this last episode, "The Escape" contained one very marvellous thing which you should attempt to duplicate as often as possible. I am referring to the *demonstration* of intelligence by our four heroes – you know the way they figured out how Daleks operated their machines and how to disable them'. Comments such as this from superior positions in the BBC hierarchy were influential for future script editing. Much of the dialogue for Nation's 'The Dalek Invasion Of Earth' was also reworked before rehearsals (Pixley 1999b:

19, 21). Lambert herself, although not experienced in writing, made detailed notes on the scripts that Nation delivered such as the later story 'The Chase' (1965) for its director Richard Martin (BBC WAC T5/1241/ 1). She was happy with the 'movement and action', it being obviously an 'adventure story' where the Doctor and his companions flee the Daleks, but not with the dialogue, which she felt script editor Dennis Spooner could improve. In the case of 'The Daleks' Master Plan' (1965–66), however, the producer John Wiles and script editor Donald Tosh were scarcely involved, which annoyed Wiles who was hoping to make the show more sophisticated and adult even though the story involved an attempt to foil monsters' evil plans.

When Nation returned to *Doctor Who* in the mid-1970s, he wrote 'Planet Of The Daleks' (1973), set in an alien jungle where the Daleks plan to conquer the galaxy and master invisibility, and in 1973 script editor Terrance Dicks was discussing the next story 'Death To The Daleks' with him: a letter to Nation from Dicks in July 1973 (BBC WAC T65/29/1) reveals that they met for a long lunch, well supplied with champagne, and it was in this setting that story ideas were hammered out between them. In his letter to Nation recording the substance of their meeting, Dicks mentioned his concern that Nation should not repeat material, since the original storyline had been set in an alien jungle, stating, 'The main necessity is to avoid any resemblance to your previous show, i.e., a group of fugitives hunted through the jungle by Daleks. Instead of jungle, think of bleak, rocky, foggy quarry'. Nation altered his script accordingly. Dicks at one point tried to persuade Nation to strengthen the roles of female characters, not only of the lead companion Sarah Jane Smith but also of guest characters. As Andrew Pixley (1999c: 38) notes, 'Recalling the blandness of the female Thal Rebec in "Planet Of The Daleks", Dicks ... asked Nation to make the female member of the Earth party one of the main protagonists, or even an expedition leader'. Similarly, in 'Genesis Of The Daleks' (1975), the female Thal Bettan was originally male (Pixley 1997a: 36). Nation was persuaded to write 'Genesis Of The Daleks', exploring the creatures' origins, by the outgoing producer Letts, and his scripts were subject to revision by the new script editor Robert Holmes. Holmes suggested the amalgamation of the two characters General Greiner and Ravon, a soldier of the race that would become Daleks, solely into Ravon, and Greiner's appearance at the start of the third episode was cut (Pixley 1997a: 36). Nation's scripts for 'The Android Invasion' (1975), involving a plan to invade Earth using android duplicates, and his final contribution for the programme 'Destiny Of The Daleks' (1979), where the Daleks seek their creator Davros in order to gain an advantage over the robotic Movellans, were also completed after the script editors' revisions, and in the latter case Douglas Adams added comic scenes. A continuing process of encouragement, revision, criticism and rewriting therefore affected Nation's work, as in the case of other writers commissioned by the BBC.

Nation created the format for *Survivors* and *Blake's 7*, but as one of the writers of the series episodes he was still subject to the producer/script editor's authority and the relationship was fraught with difficulty. Both Nation and the producer/script editor Terence Dudley attempted to assume prime author(ity) status. Nation began to deliver his scripts late after his intention to make Jimmy Garland, introduced in the 'Garland's War' episode, a continuing character was rejected by Dudley who thought the audience would not identify with the youthful aristocratic man of action. Dudley wanted to shift the location of the series and reshape the community of characters by killing off some of them in a fire, and despite Nation's objections Dudley's authority as producer exceeded Nation's and Nation began to consider other projects. Nation lost the role of script consultant, and did not reply to letters from Dudley. This unhappy experience arose partly because of Dudley's interpretation of, and concern about, audience reactions to *Survivors*, as we explain below. But its effects were to encourage Nation to create the new science fiction drama *Blake's 7*.

By the time Nation wrote the format and storylines for *Blake's 7* in 1977–78 he was aiming to gain greater control over, and credit for, his work, with more author(ity) status. However, he was still subject to collaborative working relationships with the script editor, Chris Boucher, who told us that Nation's scripts for *Blake's 7*, while complete first drafts, were not always usable because they were not character-driven. As Stevens and Moore (2003: 18) observe, 'the scriptwriting procedure generally involved Nation writing the first draft, Boucher and Maloney making suggestions on it in the form of detailed notes and then Nation writing the final version'. For the first season of *Blake's 7* Nation was contracted to write all 13 episodes, 'not only because the series was his "baby", but also to allow for it to be promoted on the basis of his strong public profile' (Stevens and Moore 2003: 18), which put enormous pressure on him. As Stevens and Moore (2003: 18) write 'Towards the end of the first season, as Nation began to find the tight writing schedule difficult, he would simply submit the drafts and Boucher would rewrite them – although Nation had the final say, and even on these later episodes the plot remained essentially unchanged from the first drafts'. The role of the script editor was essential to the effective completion of the episodes because of the unusually severe stress on Nation and the difficult production circumstances that included shortages of both time and money (see Nazzaro 1992a: 29).

The cases of *Survivors* and *Blake's 7* also differ from *Doctor Who* since Nation as creator attempted to gain more authority over the selection of other screenwriters and the power to amend their scripts. Nation negotiated successfully for the role of script consultant on *Survivors*, for example, and his agent wrote to the BBC in October 1974 (BBC WAC RCONT20) pointing out that Nation had consulted with other writers on scripts and was owed £400 for this. Terence Dudley had by this time taken over as producer from Andrew Osborn, the producer for whom Nation devised the series. Osborn had commissioned various scripts from Nation, unknown to Dudley. Dudley read these and wrote off a couple as unusable, and commissioned more scripts. The script consultancy was for Michael J. Bird's 'Enter The Soldier' of which two versions were submitted and both were written off, Clive Exton's 'The Spark' which was written off, Jack Ronder's 'Corn Dolly' and 'Gone To Angels', and Exton's 'Promised Land' and 'Law And Order' which reached the screen. So despite devising the programme and writing extensively for it, Nation did not have complete authority.

By the third season of *Blake's 7* Nation had hoped to get a choice of co-writers for some of his *Blake's 7* episodes, and approval of other writers' scripts, since after the first season he was not responsible for every episode, taking on more of the script editor's role in relation to other screenwriters, but the producer Maloney rejected these requests. In discussing plans for the third series, for example (BBC WAC T65/72/1), Maloney wanted to change Nation's storylines since Nation wanted only Avon from the original crew to appear in episode one, whereas Maloney thought that the new female character should be introduced in episode one and also that the character of Vila should be retained. Nation was angling to have the role of producer in the American sense of writer-producer, a role occupied by Gene Roddenberry during the making of *Star Trek* in the 1960s, and by Steven Bochco in the making of the police series *Hill Street Blues* in the 1980s, for example. In the US television context, producers could exercise considerable authority over episode scriptwriters, and intervene to make detailed changes to scripts. Nation's awareness of the greater power and ownership of series drama in US television on the part of such writer-producers, and his occupation of the role of script consultant on *Survivors*, probably underlay this aim.

## Visual Nation: the director and designer as author(ity) figures

All television programmes are produced as a result of collaborative enterprise, where the creator or writer is not the sole author(ity) figure, and neither are members of the production team such as the producer and script editor. But a further level of collaboration becomes significant when the script is realised in visual form by directors and the designers who assist them. Important contributions are also made by personnel such as a costume designer and lighting designer. In science fiction television in particular, the visual realisation of settings and special effects is the responsibility of directors and designers who, although subservient to the demands of the script, have considerable input into the concrete realisation of script ideas. The BBC employed designers to 'service' programmes, but their relatively lowly position in the institutional hierarchy belied their crucial authorial role in creating the finished programme.

Nation's role was largely separated from that of the director. The function of the director is actively to give a programme shape by orchestrating other members of the team. David J. Howe, Mark Stammers and Stephen James Walker (1993: 35) note that in the early 1960s 'the BBC had a large pool of on-staff directors who would be allocated to particular productions according to their respective aptitudes and availability', and Newman wanted *Doctor Who* to become the inexperienced director's testing ground before placing him or her on major dramas. The producer Verity Lambert selected new directors based on short training films they had made or other short programmes, while keeping a couple of experienced directors on board. For instance, for Nation's first *Doctor Who* story in 1963, 'The Daleks', Lambert used two directors, one experienced (Christopher Barry) and the other not (Richard Martin). The separation between Nation and directors is affirmed by Christopher Barry: 'I only met Nation once. He seemed to have as little time for me – or the programme – as I came to have for him' (quoted in Cook 2002: 9–10; see also Hearn 1991: 11). The first season of *Blake's 7* was handled by four on-staff directors: Michael E. Briant, Pennant Roberts, Vere Lorrimer and Douglas Camfield, although producer David Maloney was responsible for directing 'Deliverance' and not Briant as credited (Stevens and Moore 2003: 53). Vere Lorrimer was responsible for directing the later Nation stories, except for 'Powerplay' (directed by Maloney himself), 'Pressure Point' and 'Terminal'. 'The director's job', write Howe *et al.* (1993: 36–7) in relation to *Doctor Who* but with equal relevance to other programmes, 'entailed liasing not only with the production team but also with the other BBC staff who would have been heavily involved in the making of the programme – principally the designers and the technical crew'.

There was therefore a relationship between director and designer and often a lack of connection between the screenwriter and designer. The relationship between Nation and designers is important to the authorship of *Doctor Who, Survivors* and *Blake's 7*. At the very beginning of *Doctor Who*'s history, although the pilot episode was put in the hands of designer Peter Brachacki, two principal designers worked on the programme for the practical reason of easy planning in blocks of episodes. After the first season, however, further designers were brought in to allow the two principal designers leave time (Howe *et al.* 1993: 37). While at first the historical stories were designed by Barry Newbery, the science-based stories were handled by Raymond P. Cusick, although the designer originally allocated to 'The Daleks' was Ridley Scott (later the director of the films *Alien* and *Gladiator*) (Cook 2002: 10). In the case of the first *Doctor Who* Dalek serial there was an important relationship between Nation and the designer, Cusick, that was crucial to the development of *Doctor Who* as a whole and Nation's continued association with the programme. Fans of the programme are often divided as to whether Nation, as the writer, was the creator of the Daleks, or whether their designer Raymond Cusick was. Once assigned to 'The Daleks', Cusick telephoned Nation who told him about a television performance by the Georgian State Dancers, whose female dancers moved with a gliding motion across the stage, taking tiny steps with their feet concealed under long, wide dresses. While having lunch with Christopher Barry (the director) and Mervyn Pinfield, Cusick moved one of the pepper pots on the table to explain the movement he was looking for, and this shape was the inspiration for his eventual design. Nation very rarely specified in detail the design of places or creatures in his stories. Jeremy Bentham (1986: 133) quotes Cusick: 'Terry Nation often used to describe a set as a plain, white room. So when I met him once I asked him "Why do you do that?"; to which he replied, "I couldn't think of anything else. It's up to you. Do what you like"'. As director Christopher Barry puts it, 'I was very enthusiastic about what Ray made of the Daleks, though Nation's black-and-white on the page hadn't given us a lot to go on' (quoted in Cook 2002: 10). Indeed, Nation's script descriptions for 'The Keys Of Marinus' were also vague and costume designer Daphne Dare realised the design of the alien Voord (Pixley 2001a: 30), but for 'The Dalek Invasion Of Earth' Nation outlined in depth the objects that the Doctor would use to escape from the flying saucer prison cell (Pixley 1999b: 19). Nation often relied on the skills of designers such as Cusick to realise the places and creatures outlined in his scripts, though as a BBC employee Cusick received no additional payment for this work whereas Nation had negotiated a 'Dalek royalty' whenever the creatures appeared on the screen.

Nation gave an unusually detailed description of the Dalek creator Davros's appearance in the script for part two of 'Genesis of the Daleks': 'Davros is contained in a specially constructed self-powered wheel chair. It has similarities to the base of a Dalek. Davros himself is a masterpiece of mechanical engineering. His chair is a complete life-support system for the ancient creature' (quoted in Pixley 1997a, 36). Nation explained the presence of a microphone and amplifier to create Davros's voice, sounding not unlike the voice of a Dalek, a miniature heart and lung machine, and a lens wired to his forehead to replace his eyes. Nation's description concluded: 'The only really humanoid feature we ever see of Davros is an ancient withered hand that plays across the switch packed surface of the control panel that stretches across the front of the chair'. This unusually specific description was realised by Peter Day who constructed the wheelchair, and the visual effects designer and sculptor John Friedlander who made the character's elaborate mask.

## Visual Nation: technical and budgetary constraints

The realisation of Nation's work was also expensive, and this imposed both limits and opportunities on his authorship. The undated briefing document provided to writers for *Doctor Who* (BBC WAC T5/647/1), for instance, notes that this is 'primarily a series of stories concerning people rather than studio effects', but that for creatures, sets, models and effects, 'Technical advice is available insofar as what may or may not be achieved in the studio but every endeavour will be made to meet the requirements of your story. There is a certain film budget, not extensive but sufficient to cover most contingencies'. The film budget that the document refers to was to allow brief sequences shot on location, or sequences involving models and special effects, to be edited into the finished videotape programme.

From *Doctor Who*'s beginnings there was therefore a conflict between the intention to centre the drama on its characters (which, as we have seen, was not Nation's strength), and to make use of special effects and up-to-date methods of production. A strategy that Nation very often employed was to develop strands of the plot that involved separating the four main characters into pairs, for both dramatic and technical reasons. Due to the production system of continuous recording (pre-recording on videotape but in long takes as if performed live), one pair of characters could perform in a bridging scene while the other two moved off to the next studio set, to appear in the subsequent scene. The technology to record television pictures and sound on videotape was introduced in Britain slowly in the late 1950s. It was expensive to buy tape, to store it, and to buy and maintain the recording machines. A long and detailed memo of May 1964 (BBC WAC T5/2239/7) from the BBC's television recording engineers explained the process of assembly editing and dubbing sound on videotape. The tape was very cumbersome, with no facility to pause during a recording, a tape life of only 60 plays, and high internal charges levied by BBC technical departments for editing time and tape storage. This made it preferable to shoot on video in long takes 'as if live', and to avoid any editing of tape sequences after the shoot. When mistakes were made, scenes would be performed again after winding the tape back to a previous start point, rather than editing the mistakes out. This use of the recently available videotape technology made it possible to pre-record *Doctor Who* episodes, and gave a degree of priority to character drama since the actors were working in relatively lengthy takes rather than acting scenes one shot at a time (as actors do in cinema).

On the other hand, the use of videotape enabled some special effects to be produced by the electronic cameras and recording equipment themselves, and other effects and models shot on film to be inserted into the finished programme. This gave a competing priority to the use of creatures, sets and effects rather than actors' performances, and in the *Radio Times'* twentieth anniversary issue on *Doctor Who* in 1983 (unpaginated) Verity Lambert remembered: 'Sydney [Newman] told me it was to be a show that stretched television using all the newest technology'. The associate producer, Mervyn Pinfield, had a key role in establishing what kinds of visual effects and technical requirements would be possible and affordable. The result was that writers such as Nation could write scripts that called for alien creatures, for alien land-scapes fabricated in the studio, models representing alien planets or cities, short sequences in exterior locations that would be shot on film, and camera effects (such as the reversal of light and dark tones, a 'negative' of the camera picture, when Daleks fired their weapons), but with minimum post-production.

Originally, the budget per episode of *Doctor Who* was £2,500, excluding the £3,278 that the TARDIS cost to make; £200 per week was set aside for specially constructed scenery, and £500 per week for studio sets and outside filming. Each episode was allowed seven days design work (BBC WAC T5/647/1). One 25 minute episode of *Doctor Who* could be shot entirely in the studio in a single 13 or 14 hour studio day.

In 1966 a memo from Shaun Sutton (Head of Serials) to producers, directors and production assistants in the Serials Department reminded them not to allow more than five breaks in their studio recording day because of consequent overruns and the costs in overtime this incurred (BBC WAC T5/782/3).

Realising Nation's work was expensive because of the grand scope of its creatures, settings and special effects, and at times this placed limits on his authorship. In the early 1960s the sheer number of sets in Nation's stories caused fire hazards and union health and safety problems in the studios because the space was overfull and stored electrical equipment obstructed fire lanes. For Nation's first story, 'The Daleks', there were estimates for 4,000 hours of labour over the seven episodes and outside contract building of special materials such as the Daleks themselves was estimated at up to £8,000. Sutton acknowledged that the Daleks on *Doctor Who* required more breaks because Dalek operators experienced such discomfort in working them, and technical problems tended to occur. There were five days of filming at the BBC's Ealing studios using set models and special effects (BBC WAC T5/648/1). 'The Daleks' therefore looked a lot more expensive than the budget of £2,500 allotted per episode when Nation's scripts arrived. Donald Baverstock (Chief of Programmes BBC1) wrote on 18 October 1963 to Donald Wilson that *Doctor Who* seemed to be very expensive because of the costs of sets and special props (BBC WAC T5/647/1). He told Newman not to proceed with the production of more than the first four episodes and to prepare plans for a new children's series for New Year 1964. BBC staff sent memos back and forth accusing each other of overspending, not informing each other about the amount of design required and its cost, and the design department requested advance copies of *Doctor Who* scripts one week earlier than usual because of the work involved. So Nation's Dalek stories were expensive, difficult to shoot and broke the pattern of BBC production, but this was ultimately allowed for because of their success.

Nation's story 'The Keys Of Marinus', which involved a quest for keys to bring harmony to a planet, required a very large number of sets and props, including the beach of an alien planet, a pyramid, midget submarines and the construction of the Conscience Machine, as well as a journey through different terrains. Lack of budget led to the use of low key lighting and black drapes substituting for the set in some of the scenes, and inexpensive stock footage being used in the fourth episode, 'The Snows Of Terror', to open out the setting. Nation's story 'The Chase', which involved the protagonists fleeing the Daleks, demanded alien creatures and extensive scenery. Two designers were allocated to it to share the work (Cusick and John Wood). The story also included the

construction of an adversary for the Daleks, the Mechanoids (originally
the Mechons), spherical geodesic robots equipped with flame-throwers,
showing the production team's willingness to use original and expensive creatures and special effects. The flame-throwers actually worked,
so that in episode six, 'The Planet Of Decision', where the Mechanoids
battle the Daleks, production shifted to Ealing film studios where the
potentially dangerous flame-throwers could be more safely filmed. In
the small studios used for recording *Doctor Who*, the Mechanoids were
very difficult to manoeuvre, and to Nation's disappointment they were
never used again. 'The Daleks' Master Plan', produced in 12 episodes
with scripts written by Nation and Dennis Spooner, was the longest and
most elaborate *Doctor Who* story ever made. The protagonists' journey
to defeat the Daleks involved an unequalled number of sets and special
effects, and Nation was asked repeatedly by production staff to cut back
on these. However, 'The Daleks' Master Plan' came in under budget
(BBC WAC T5/1246/1) because costs were spread across 12 episodes.
The actual average cost of a *Doctor Who* episode was £3,140 versus an
average agreed with BBC Programme Planning of £2,750, but Nation's
long stories were both popular with audiences, as we discuss in chapter
3, and also offered opportunities to minimise cost by spreading it out
over more than the usual number of episodes. Indeed, Nation's work
for *Doctor Who*, like that of other writers, was marketed in Britain and
abroad, generating income and making his stories valuable to the BBC.
But sale abroad (for example, to Canada in 1964) was made problematic
by the low quality of the telerecordings (film recordings of master video-
tapes) of the early episodes (BBC WAC T5/647/1) where the low key
lighting meant that some sequences were too dark to see once transferred to film. Nation's attempts to sell a Dalek spin-off series to NBC
television in the United States in late 1966 for which, as decided in
January 1967, the BBC would receive a fee, meant that the Daleks would
be killed off in 'The Evil Of The Daleks' so that they could appear
exclusively in the United States. However, when the BBC Programme
Review Board met in May 1967 and the Head of Drama Serials
announced this, such was the protest that it seems Sydney Newman
ordered that the Dalek Emperor should still be barely alive in the last
episode, allowing for the return of the Doctor's popular adversaries.

These budgetary and technical boundaries around the scripts that
Nation produced continued to be significant throughout his involvement with *Doctor Who*. In 1975, when Philip Hinchcliffe was producing
*Doctor Who*, for example, he wrote to Nation in March (BBC WAC T65/
31/1) about the scripts he had received for 'The Android Invasion',
initially titled 'The Enemy Within':

to be frank we feel the scripts will require a fair amount of rewriting. One of the major problems is the amount of film still required to do justice to the story. Matching studio exteriors with location filming is a difficult and expensive business and I don't think the final result would be very good. Also with 13 interior sets and 6 exterior sets the story is too costly and impractical as it stands.

Hinchcliffe used his authority as producer to place strictures on the scripting work that Nation had done, calling on his institutional position within the BBC to specify budgetary and technical factors that Nation himself had no control over. The collaborative nature of television authorship is apparent here, since in effect Hinchcliffe was asking Nation to rewrite parts of scripts in order to conform to requirements that Hinchcliffe himself could not alter. In *Survivors*, the technical problems were much less than with *Doctor Who*, but involved the combination of essential shooting outside the studio with a large cast who had to be contracted long in advance for planned shooting days. The actors playing regular characters had to be paid retainers to prevent them from undertaking other work that might make them unavailable when needed. *Survivors* had a budget of roughly £21,000 per episode, and this had to include everything from payment of the writer to vehicle hire.

Technical and budgetary factors are also important in relation to Nation's *Blake's 7* episodes, which were grand in scope, sometimes placing a limit on his authorship and authority. Attempts by the BBC to find suitable co-producers who would invest in *Blake's 7* and contribute to its cost were unsuccessful. In 1977 Ronald Marsh (Head of Drama Series) sent London Films storylines for eight episodes and complete scripts for four, indicating that each episode would require £65–70,000 so that the series could compete with the production values of American science fiction. London Films turned the proposal down, as did the American company Time-Life when its request for world rights over *Blake's 7* (which would prevent BBC from exploiting the programme itself) was refused by Alistair Milne, Managing Director, Television (BBC WAC T65/90/1). Shaun Sutton, Head of Drama Group, regretted this since it was the first time that Time-Life had expressed interest in a long-running series. The resulting constraints on budgets and technical services such as sets, design and special effects militated strongly against the scope of Nation's format for *Blake's 7*, whose requirements were much grander than the programme whose place it took. As a memo of March 1978 from Ian Scoones, visual effects designer for *Blake's 7*, reveals (BBC WAC T65/90/1), the programme was originally budgeted as if it were the police series *Softly, Softly: Task Force*, which it replaced, with only £50 per episode for effects. The specially constructed sets, props and model shots for this science fiction series were of course far more expensive than the conventional settings and sparse effects required for the contemporary police drama. Scoones notes that the audience was seeing *Star Wars* and *Close Encounters Of The Third Kind* at the cinema, and American science fiction on ITV, where much bigger effects budgets were available. The shortage of time and money meant that requirements for sets, props, models and effects kept changing, and effects were sometimes shot in one take. In April 1978 the visual effects organiser Ann Baugh sent a memo to Ronald Marsh (BBC WAC T65/90/1) saying that *Blake's 7* series one had used 1,898 more hours of labour and £4,433 worth of materials over and above what had been budgeted for. This was despite the fact that very fast production allowed just one or two takes for most shots, and the production team set and lit the studio in a single day, using another day to rehearse, then two days to record each episode. All this led to changes to some of Nation's scripts. For example, season one episode eight, 'Duel', was to include planet locations of a desert and caves. These were replaced by a forest, saving money on scenic backgrounds. There was going to be action on a bridge across a chasm, and a battering ram to penetrate a cave complex in Blake's fight against the Federation officer Travis. These action sequences were dropped. Even so, the actual cost of 'Duel' was £44,475 against a budget of £36,917. These details demonstrate how Nation's storylines and scripts were always subject to institutional constraints of budget and realisation, and that his work was always subject to intervention by producers and technical staff who were attempting to make his story ideas shootable. Yet despite the high cost and technical complexity of realising the scripts and ideas that Nation contributed, the BBC was aware of his asset value as someone who could assist the BBC as an institution.

## Audience and schedule

Audience response to programmes and their genres is important in examining the work credited to Nation, since that response was the primary reason why he was repeatedly invited to write for programmes and devise new formats. The key indicator of success within the television industry is the response of the audience, measured not only by total audience size, but also the share of the available audience watching one channel rather than another at a particular time. These numbers matter to channel controllers, commissioning editors, heads of network programming and department heads, who assume an authority function over how series progress, and determine which genres should be considered when new programmes are developed.

It was audience reaction that shifted *Doctor Who*'s science fiction format from explicitly educational historical stories to those futuristic stories that pitted the Doctor and his companions against alien creatures. For Whitaker, *Doctor Who* quickly became a series of science fiction serials, and he acknowledged this in a letter to a prospective scriptwriter in August 1964 (BBC WAC T5/649/1): 'we only regard the historical stories as necessary make-weights between the futuristic science fiction ones'. This shift was initiated by Nation's futuristic monster adventure, 'The Daleks', since its large audiences and the publicity it attracted lent legitimacy to those authority figures within the BBC who were prepared to argue for the change. Initially, *Doctor Who* had been devised to target a particular audience, and its scheduling partly determined how it was perceived by its audiences and thus contributed to the author function that organised its meanings. Sydney Newman created *Doctor Who* because of his concern with audience ratings in a schedule slot poised between different audience constituencies. As Newman pointed out (quoted in Bentham 1986: 38), 'there was a gap in the ratings on Saturday afternoons', a day associated with light entertainment, 'between BBC's vastly popular sports coverage, ending at 5.15 p.m., and the start at 5.45 p.m. of an equally popular pop music programme [*Juke Box Jury*]'. Newman continues:

> What was between them was, I vaguely recall, a children's classic drama serial, i.e. Charles Dickens dramatisations etc. This could be moved to Sunday if the Drama Department could come up with something more suitable. So we required a new programme that would reach the state of mind of sports fans, and the teenage pop music audience, while attracting and holding the children's audience ... The problem was, as I saw it, that it had to be a children's programme and still attract adults and teenagers.

Drama Department staff had already been discussing the format for their new programme based on assumptions about audiences. BBC staff writer C. E. 'Bunny' Webber considered the loyalty of the audience essential in a memo of 29 March 1963 to Donald Wilson (BBC WAC T5/647/1). Webber argued that the central characters could not be children because child viewers were thought to dislike characters younger than themselves. An older woman should be included and an older man. The older Doctor, the teenage child, the handsome young man and the attractive well-dressed woman of the first *Doctor Who* stories clearly retain many of the characteristics identified in Webber's memo. Newman was keen to provide a figure of identification for children, hence the central role of the Doctor's teenage companion Susan. The decision to make the TARDIS look like an everyday police box was to encourage audiences to question the world around them, and similarly the vast inside but small outside would surprise audiences in relation to conceptions of dimension and space. The Doctor himself was conceived as a grandfather figure. His wisdom and authority would be countered by his bad-temperedness and his terror of the advanced civilisation on a distant planet from which he was trying to escape. Keeping to serials that were not too long would reduce the risk of losing audiences if one story did not appeal to them. Newman indeed gave Verity Lambert a Cambridge University study on children's perceptions of television, which used Newman's *Pathfinders* series (see chapter 3) in its case-studies. *Doctor Who* had similarities with this programme and again the conclusions drawn by the study about the *Pathfinders* audience must have influenced the design of *Doctor Who*'s format for a similar 8 to 14 age group. The study argued that children's drama resembles drama for adults, but with the exclusion of violence and sexuality. It was a conception of the audience and its possible interest, then, which drove the planning for *Doctor Who*.

Nation's stories were highly successful from the outset. 'The Daleks' pushed *Doctor Who*'s ratings over 8 million and placed it in the top 20 programmes. The ratings and BBC audience appreciation indices for the first serial, 'An Unearthly Child', were good and above average for BBC children's programming, exceeding the performance of the 5.30 p.m. Sunday classic serial, and the first *Doctor Who* story was a worthy competitor for ITV's Saturday afternoon serial, *The Buccaneers*. But 'The Daleks' gained audiences nearer to the figures expected for peak viewing, allowing schedule planners to use *Doctor Who* to gather up audiences for the whole of BBC Saturday evening programmes. Information about audiences was gathered by the BBC's own Audience Research Department, which established a panel of around 250–300 viewers who kept records of what they watched, evaluated programmes on a scale from A+ to C–, and made brief comments on them. From this information, the BBC could calculate the number of viewers watching nationally by multiplying the sample audience size up, and could report to production staff and executives on viewers' interest and pleasure in particular programmes, as measured by a Reaction Index calculated by attaching numerical values to the A+ to C– scale. For the episodes of 'The Daleks' the figures were (BBC WAC T5/647/1):

*Episode one* (21st December 1963)
audience size: 14 per cent (7 million viewers), Reaction Index: 59.

*Episode two* (28th December 1963)
audience size: 13 per cent (6.5 million), Reaction Index: 58.
*Episode three* (4th January 1964)
audience size: 18 per cent (9 million), Reaction Index: 62.
*Episode four* (11th January 1964)
audience size: 20 per cent (10 million), Reaction Index: 63.
*Episode five* (18th January 1964)
audience size: 20 per cent (10 million), Reaction Index: 63.
*Episode six* (25th January 1964)
audience size: 21 per cent (10.5 million), Reaction Index: 63.
*Episode seven* (1st February 1964)
audience size: 21 per cent (10.5 million), Reaction Index: 65.

The story as a whole averaged just under 9 million viewers. As a result of this success, Nation was regarded as a writer who could supply large and enthusiastic audiences for the BBC, and this gave him significant status among the production team of *Doctor Who*. The script editor David Whitaker made this clear in his memo of April 1964 to Verity Lambert (BBC WAC T5/647/1), which began by noting the economies of time and effort available if only a small team of writers were contracted to write for the series. He then suggested: 'I recommend that we make Terry Nation the senior writer, insofar as future subjects are concerned. He has worked very well for us and his writing is obviously improving. His figures are certainly the highest so far of all the writers and my suggestion is that he be offered three serials in the new fifty-two weeks.' The success of 'The Daleks' overshadowed Newman's and Wilson's intentions for the educational aims of *Doctor Who*, but had the benefit of ensuring continuing publicity and public interest in the programme, and substantial audiences, once it focused on the monster adventure stories that Nation had initiated. Therefore, while Newman and Wilson had initially assumed author(ity) roles attempting to dictate the parameters of the programme, Nation's work and those who had commissioned it rose in status. 'The Dalek Invasion Of Earth' as a whole averaged just under 12 million viewers. Audience appreciation continued to be high during the early years of *Doctor Who* and Nation's later contribution, 'The Chase', where the Doctor and his companions flee the Daleks to a variety of locations, averaged over 9 million viewers. The BBC commissioned audience research reports (BBC WAC T5/1243/1) similar to that reported above, in which the viewers commented upon the first two episodes, 'Flight Through Eternity' and 'Journey Into Terror'. They felt that the story had ingenuity and imagination, although some adults feared that the mixing of science fiction adventure with horror (amusement park robots of Dracula and Frankenstein's monster threatened the Doctor and his companions in an old house, for example) may give children nightmares even though from their own adult perspective it was stupid and far-fetched. A report commissioned on the final episode of 'The Chase', 'The Planet Of Decision', where there is a final battle between the Daleks and the Mechanoid robots encountered in a futuristic city that gets destroyed, reveals how viewers thought the episode was exciting and dramatic. Adults enjoyed the story though many found some of it amusing (like the sequence set on the Marie Celeste where the ghostly abandonment of the sailing ship was explained by the Daleks' sudden appearance aboard it), and adults reported that children were enthralled by the science fiction aspects more than the historical stories in Doctor Who. Overall, the results of the audience research reports amply confirmed that Doctor Who was addressing the right audience sector.

The viewers' comments reported were all from adult viewers of 'The Chase', identified by occupation. A 'housewife' explained that her children 'sit fixed before the television as though hypnotised', while a 'salesman' said: 'I wouldn't miss it for anything and nor would the children'. Another 'housewife' said: 'I don't like it but if my grand-children are here it gives me a peaceful half hour or so as they sit enthralled' and a 'civil servant' reported that: 'Even the two year old twins recognise the Daleks'. A sizeable majority thought Doctor Who in general was ridiculous, this story disjointed, and fantasy rather than science fiction, but nevertheless found it compelling. Nation's 'The Chase' gained the BBC a significantly large audience, amounting in episode six to 19 per cent of the population (9.5 million viewers). This was not only important in itself as an index of Doctor Who's success at winning viewers for the channel, but also in relation to the BBC's com-petition with the then-dominant ITV channel. The BBC's audience share of 19 per cent was dramatically greater than ITV's in the same schedule slot, whose programmes attracted only 9 per cent of the popula-tion. Furthermore, the intention to bring both adult and child audiences to Doctor Who seemed to be working in practice, since it seems that adults watched with their children, and sometimes on their own. The social class of the audience is difficult to judge, but it is significant that the report notes the comments of the 'civil servant' and the 'salesman', who were likely to be the middle-class viewers that the BBC wished to address. Indeed, Nation's writing with its combination of science and time travel, fantasy, comedy (like the Marie Celeste sequence) and adventure offered pleasures to both children and adults alike, who were able to find elements in the story that were by turns entertaining, thrilling, comic, or indeed open to a sceptical reading when the adults found the story silly but enjoyed it anyway. Nation's writing offered the BBC a large audience composed of family groups from valuable class and social sectors, who could use *Doctor Who* as part of collective familial home life at weekend tea-time, and enjoy it both for its own textual qualities and for its role as a social cement between adults and children. Nation's following linked stories 'Mission To The Unknown' and 'The Daleks' Master Plan' about the Daleks' attempt to rule the cosmos, averaged over 8 and 9 million viewers respectively, while Nation's contributions in the 1970s – 'Planet Of The Daleks', 'Death To The Daleks' about the search for an antidote to a space plague on an alien planet, 'Genesis Of The Daleks' and 'Destiny Of The Daleks' – averaged between 9 and 10 million viewers, apart from the latter's colossal average of 13.5 million.

While our focus has been mainly on the genre drama that Nation wrote to bring in audiences including children, it is worth noting that because *Doctor Who*'s audience consisted of predominantly young people attracted by science fiction adventure, in dealing with Nation's draft scripts changes were sometimes requested because of the production staff's concern for children's reactions. In 'The Chase', for example, Verity Lambert (BBC WAC T5/1241/1) felt that in episode one while the protagonists were fleeing the Daleks 'the mire beast should be a mere suggestion of tentacles' not 'the whole thing', because 'if it works as well as it should, it will be too horrifying', and about episode two that 'Terry has gone too far in making the Aridians unpleasant looking', which 'does not serve any purpose in the script'. She regarded Nation's outline of their repulsive appearance as 'unpleasantness for the sake of unpleasantness' and to 'dehumanise them' the production team 'must find some less revolting way to do so'. In December 1973 when Nation had completed 'Death To The Daleks' and was invited to the studio recording by the script editor Terrance Dicks, Dicks needed to inform Nation that revisions had been required by the Head of Serials because of concerns over violence (BBC WAC T65/29/1). In episode one on page 22 of Nation's script, a 'raining of blows' by the alien Exxilons, the natives of the planet holding the space plague antidote, required the production team to monitor the way this was realised in case it could be upsetting to the audience. In episode two, a sacrificial ritual in which the Doctor's companion Sarah was threatened with death must not show her being restrained by ropes, and the part of the ritual where Sarah was forced to inhale a drug had to be conveyed by finding a means for administering the drug that did not show it being forcibly held under her nose.

This concern was sometimes corroborated by audience research reports, such as in a report (BBC WAC T5/1248/1) on the final episode, 'Destruction Of Time', of Nation's 'The Daleks' Master Plan' (1966). Members of the audience panel commented that in the battle against the Daleks, although they particularly enjoyed the rapid ageing of the Doctor's companion Sara Kingdom in this story (achieved through make-up effects and time-delay recording), many respondents thought this was too scary for children, especially when Sara disintegrates into dust and dies. Yet Verity Lambert commented in the *Radio Times Doctor Who 20th Anniversary Special* (1983: unpaginated) when referring to parents' complaints that *Doctor Who* was too frightening: 'But I believe children love being scared, provided they are in safe, protected circumstances, and not simply dumped on their own in front of the television'. She imagined the programme to be viewed by a family audience of both parents and children, attracted by its mix of genres and its different kinds of appeal to different audience groups.

Nation's next major project for BBC, *Survivors*, had its first episode transmitted on Wednesday 16 April 1975 at 8:10 p.m., preceded by *The Wednesday Film: The Lion And The Horse*. The position of the programme in the schedule and its relationships with other boundaries were significantly different from *Doctor Who*. The mid-evening period, known as prime-time, was scheduled by all three of the British television channels on a principle of a variety of generically coded formats and lengths of programme. The news broadcasts on BBC in the early evening and at 9.00 p.m. were fixed points in the schedule, and between them programmes were designed to be watched by viewers of any age, including children, and were not (as is now common) arranged in 'strips' or sequences of programmes of similar genre or kind (such as sitcoms or popular drama, or programmes aimed at particular audience groups such as younger adults). *Survivors* was announced as speculative and serious drama, in which a group of main characters would offer appeal to diverse audiences and provoke reflection and thought as well as entertainment. In relation to audiences and schedule position therefore, *Survivors* combined multiple forms of address to the audience, as speculative drama. It placed emphasis on reflective problem-solving, and dramatically challenging thriller components appropriate to a post-apocalyptic environment. But *Survivors'* viewing figures were of deep concern to its producer, Terence Dudley, when he attempted to plan the second series. Writing to Nation in July 1975 (BBC WAC RCONT21), he reported: 'We dropped two million after Number 3 and after No.7. The latter drop doesn't surprise me but the drop after 3 gives food for thought.' He told Nation that he was receiving many letters from viewers, and that he saw the most appealing feature of *Survivors* as 'family involvement. Without question viewers were identifying with the characters and their predicament.' He argued that unlike with the character of Garland, the aristocratic man of action: 'Viewers have taken to "Greg" [Preston, the main male character] because he's fallible and recognisable'. Dudley was at this point trying to persuade Nation to drop plans to keep Garland as a continuing character, and justified his ideas on the basis of his understanding of what the *Survivors* audience liked. The actual or perceived reactions of the audience functioned as a legitimation for the producer's authority and authorial intervention into Nation's writing, demonstrating a further strategy of institutional control.

*Blake's 7*'s success can be attributed partly to its scheduling, placed within boundaries not selected by Nation, and Nation's use of genres such as science fiction action adventure, which would appeal to a particular audience. The first episode of *Blake's 7* was screened on BBC1 on 2 January 1978 at 6.00 p.m. Its early evening slot in the Monday schedule showed that it was positioned to capture children who had been watching television prior to the early evening news, and also adults who were settling down to an evening's viewing after the news. The programmes before *Blake's 7* were the hugely popular children's magazine programme *Blue Peter*, then the *Evening News*, *Today's Sport* and a Tom and Jerry cartoon, which acted as a short filler before 6.00 p.m. The episodes later in the series and of subsequent series were scheduled slightly later, but still provided fare for children watching entertainment programming in the early evening as well as adults expected to remain with BBC during evening prime-time. The episode 'Redemption', which began the second series, was preceded by the light entertainment music programme *The Osmonds* and followed by the very popular US soap *Dallas*, on BBC1 on Tuesday 9 January 1979 at 7.20 p.m. Similarly, *Blake's 7* series three began on Monday 7 January 1980 on BBC1 at 7.15 p.m., when Nation's 'Aftermath' was preceded by the quiz *A Question of Sport* and followed by the prestigious current affairs series *Panorama*. The scheduling of *Blake's 7* demonstrates the BBC's confidence in Nation's format as a way of addressing a large audience of mixed age and gender, with a programme whose science fiction genre was deemed of interest to both children and adults.

In the 1970s BBC entertainment programming and popular drama were matching ITV output in terms of audience size and prestige, despite severe financial pressures on production due to the effects of inflation on production costs. As in the case of *Doctor Who*, the BBC was concerned about audience sizes and audience composition for *Blake's 7*, and the BBC's files contain statistical analysis on the subject. An audience research report on *Blake's 7* episodes 1 to 13 (BBC WAC T65/90/1) (2 January 1978 to 27 March 1978) showed that the lowest audience was 14.1 per cent of the British population with a viewing figure of 7.3 million (week two) and the highest audience was 20.9 per cent with a viewing figure of 10.9 million (week six), competing quite well with ITV's lowest and highest audiences during the period of 15.4 per cent to 29.7 per cent. The Reaction Index for the whole first series was the notably high 68, rising from 57 for episode one to 70 for episode 13. Clearly, Nation's new project was achieving good ratings, retained audiences across the series and attracted further viewers as its public profile rose during the run. Viewers reported that the most interesting characters were the ruthless Avon followed by the idealist Blake, and 73 per cent of the BBC's sample audience wanted a second series either a lot or quite a lot. As the scheduling position in early evening was clearly designed to achieve, many viewers reported that they watched *Blake's 7* because their children wanted to watch it, and this reinforced the BBC's aims to provide family viewing that we noted above in relation to *Doctor Who*. The age range of the audience sample was wide: 13 per cent were aged 12–19, 21 per cent were 20–29, 39 per cent were 30–49, 20 per cent were 50–64, and 7 per cent were aged over 65. Nearly half the sample watched with one or more children, and this again suggests that parents and children, as well as young adults, were the target audience. An audience research report (BBC WAC R9/7/158) on the second series of *Blake's 7* noted a Reaction Index for the whole series of 68, with audiences of between 12 per cent and 16 per cent of the UK population. As a relatively strong programme, *Blake's 7* could be scheduled against the landmark nature documentary series *Life On Earth* on BBC2, and the action drama series *Charlie's Angels* on ITV for some of its run, yet 52 per cent of the BBC's audience sample saw all or most of the 13 episodes; 35 per cent of the sample watched with children under 15, and 74 per cent said they would like another series to be made.

In addition, praise was given for the way in which the science fiction genre was delivered. Viewers commenting for the BBC's audience research report (BBC WAC T65/90/1) on episode eight of the first *Blake's 7* season, 'Duel', involving an alien planet and a physical fight, liked the characters and the special effects (discussed in detail in chapter 4), and a few viewers thought the effects 'made' the programme and were more imaginative than those on *Star Trek*. Furthermore, some viewers praised the inclusion of women as main characters, and it is clearly not the case that the audience consisted of predominantly young males as is sometimes assumed about science fiction television, and as we shall see in chapter 4 the programme dealt with issues of gender. Even though BBC programmes are not financed by commercials, where audience size needs to be measured so that potential advertisers can be aware of how many potential consumers their advertisements might reach, the BBC was clearly very interested in the size and composition of audiences for the programmes Nation contributed to, and in viewers' evaluation of those programmes. The prominent scheduling position of *Doctor Who*, *Survivors* and *Blake's 7*, and the broadly favourable responses to them in terms of ratings and evaluation, are very significant to an evaluation of Nation's own status as an author and an authority figure within British television culture. The attraction of significantly large audiences, composed of both adults and children, for series drama that could retain audiences across a number of episodes, was crucial to the BBC's claim to be the national broadcaster funded by a universally levied licence fee. Nation's involvement with the BBC was part of the institution's strategy to legitimate itself in this way, and to establish its own authority as a broadcaster by drawing on the authorship of Nation and the authority that the audiences commanded by programmes credited to him could provide.

## Nation's relationship with production staff: executives

From an elevated position in the institutional hierarchy, figures such as the controllers of BBC channels could exercise authority that was underwritten by audience reaction, setting boundaries to Nation's contributions and also opening up avenues for his authorship. As we have seen, Nation extended the boundaries of *Doctor Who* generically since he provided science fiction monster adventures, contrary to Newman's original aims for the series. Newman is quoted in the *Radio Times* 1983 (unpaginated) issue commemorating the twentieth anniversary of the programme, remembering 'The Daleks' story commissioned from Terry Nation: 'I had specifically said at the start that I didn't want any bug-eyed monsters in the series, so when Verity came up with the Daleks, I bawled her out. She protested that they weren't bug-eyed monsters, they were human brains whose bodies had atrophied, and therefore they needed those metal shells!' However, Nation's mixing of science fiction with the monster adventure was a success and contributed to the longevity of the programme, which would ultimately run on BBC terrestrial television for 26 years, becoming the longest continuing science fiction series in the world. Newman's institutional authority was effectively sidestepped because of the public acclaim and large audiences that Nation's story brought to *Doctor Who*.

The success of Nation's 'The Daleks' was therefore crucial to the survival of *Doctor Who*. The programme was unpopular with the BBC Children's Department, which resented the ownership of the series by the Drama Group rather than themselves. Newman had come from commercial television and been promoted over the heads of BBC staff, and brought many of his former ATV colleagues with him. Although the budget for the first *Doctor Who* stories was only £2,500, *Doctor Who* was seen as Newman's pet project on which excessive resources and attention were being lavished. In November 1963 Newman suggested that the Head of Serials Donald Wilson should go and see Donald Baverstock (Chief of Programmes BBC1) in person to convince him to extend *Doctor Who*'s run beyond 13 episodes. The intervention of an authority figure with much greater institutional power than either Nation, Lambert, Wilson or Newman was required in order to extend the boundaries set by the 13 episode limit, and the history of early *Doctor Who* is the history of the gradual widening out of these strict parameters, largely as a result of the popularity of the Daleks in the first story Nation was credited with writing. A memo from Baverstock to Newman dated 31 December 1963 (BBC WAC T5/647/1) agreed to another 10 episodes above an original 26, but criticised the scripts, including Nation's, which he thought lacked 'logic and inventiveness'. Referring in part to 'The Daleks', his memo noted that, 'In the episodes already recorded we have seen Dr. Who [*sic*] and his daughter [*sic*], though ageless and miraculously clever, reduced to helpless unscientific ordinariness once they left their spaceship … I suggest that you should make efforts in future episodes to reduce the amount of slow prosaic dialogue and to centre the dramatic movements'. While this was certainly a criticism of Nation's writing, the request for faster pace was also pushing *Doctor Who* towards the science fiction and action adventure genres that Nation would subsequently explore repeatedly, thus providing institutional authorisation for the science fiction in which Nation would specialise.

The saga of institutional authority figures imposing limits on *Doctor Who* but simultaneously widening out and extending its boundaries continued. The programme was under repeated threat of cancellation, but Baverstock allowed a further 13 episode runs to be made despite pressure to drop the programme (BBC WAC T5/647/1). While Nation's story 'The Dalek Invasion Of Earth' was already planned to run into 1965, there was doubt in summer 1964 about continuing after January 1965. Verity Lambert needed a decision in August 1964 so that script writers could be informed, especially Nation because she wanted to introduce a new companion to replace Susan (Carole Ann Ford) in

January 1965 after 'The Dalek Invasion Of Earth'. The presence of the companion was a further indication of the boundaries of the programme imposed by the stability of its format, and the intent to introduce a new companion illustrated how the limits originally placed on the series were being surpassed, as new companions and new performers to play the Doctor himself (as he regenerated into a new physical form) were introduced. A prime example of the success of the Daleks in extending the programme's boundaries and Nation's involvement was also the fact that a lengthy Dalek story was produced ('The Daleks' Master Plan' discussed in the next chapter). Not only did the success of the Daleks extend the boundaries of *Doctor Who*, but without them Nation's authorial status and reputation would have been confined and there may not have been opportunities for him to initiate programmes such as *Survivors* and *Blake's 7*.

## Promotional culture and authority: the 'star' system

Not only were programmes advertised generically as science fiction, as in the *Radio Times* features we have noted above, but promotional culture also drew programmes with which Nation was associated to the attention of audiences through promotion of their 'stars'. This promotional discourse therefore had an authority function itself, since it aimed to determine how programmes were perceived and understood by audiences, and the meanings of programmes could be inflected by the ways they were marketed. Promotional support for *Doctor Who* was consistently greater than for the other programmes that Nation worked on. This support was primarily intended to immerse children in the fictional world of the programme and revolved around the Daleks, which were elevated to 'star status' above the regular performers in the programme, functioning as a sign connoting excitement, threat and pleasure.

Both independently researched newspaper stories as well as BBC-initiated press releases and stunts repeatedly centred on the Daleks (BBC WAC T48/445). Newspapers are a significant form of media, which reach a mass audience and which work according to a process of selection, of inclusion and exclusion. Value judgements are evidently made about which stories to run, their appeal to the readership, and about how often a particular topic should be covered. Conventionally, world news would have greater news value than reportage revolving around a television programme, for example, but although 'quality' broadsheet newspapers have operated in this way, 'popular' tabloids have more crime-based or personality news, and media-related news stories and features. As *Doctor Who* fan Gary Gillatt (1998: 17) notes:

> The *Daily Mail* took a particular shine to the Daleks and in the first
> months of 1964 barely a week passed without some kind of Dalek-
> related story in its pages. If it wasn't a tale of how some eager enthusiast
> had assembled his own robot out of Austin Traveller hubcaps, it was a
> celebration of the donation by the BBC of two of the original props to a
> Dr Barnardo's children's home in Essex.

The *Daily Mail*, among many other newspapers, recognised that stories
revolving around *Doctor Who*'s Daleks would appeal to its readership
and thus increase newspaper sales. Furthermore, the *Daily Mail* saw the
Daleks' return in a second *Doctor Who* serial as an important event and
first broke the news about the comeback of the creatures (Gillatt 1998:
18), thereby stimulating audiences to tune in.

There was also support for *Doctor Who* and the Daleks where one
would expect to find it within particular television magazines. The
BBC's own listings magazine *Radio Times*, for example, was responsible
for a great deal of this support both on the cover and inside. After the
initial success of the Daleks in their first serial, the *Radio Times* featured
a *Doctor Who* Dalek cover for their second outing in 'The Dalek Invasion
Of Earth'. For a programme to be featured on the cover of the *Radio
Times* was a prestigious occasion and marked its importance. The cover
of the *Radio Times* occupied a central position in British culture and
served as an advertisement for the Daleks at the same time as
confirming their embeddedness in the British consciousness.

Such support continued into the 1970s, and the cover of the *Radio
Times* issue of 1–7 January 1972 was a cartoon in science fiction style
featuring Jon Pertwee and a Dalek, and trailed a feature on p. 10: 'Write
your own Dr Who adventure'. Nation's name was prominent: 'Below,
Terry Nation, inventor of the Daleks, starts a new adventure for RADIO
TIMES readers. Complete the story and you could win a unique Dalek
worth over £100 that talks and moves just like those on TV.' Readers
were invited to become immersed in the fictional world of the Daleks,
and also reminded of the BBC production context in which *Doctor Who*
was made by being rewarded if they won the competition with a chance
to see the programme recorded in the studio. In the following year, the
*Radio Times* of 13 December 1973 also had Pertwee on its cover, and ran
a feature by Liz Dickson, 'Who's who among Who's friends' (pp. 6–7), a
two-page spread about the popularity of *Doctor Who* and the Daleks. All
the interviewees mentioned Daleks, drawing attention to the ordinary
viewer's recognition of them, and the spread also advertised the *Radio
Times Doctor Who 10th Anniversary Special* of 1973. The *Special* contained

not only profiles of the three actors playing the Doctor, the companions since the start of the serial, a history of the programme, but also a Dalek story by Nation, 'We are the Daleks!', information on the making of the programme, and instructions on how to build your own full-size Dalek. The intimate connection between Nation, the Daleks and *Doctor Who* was a means of maintaining the public profile of the programme, and Nation himself co-operated often with the BBC's efforts to stimulate audience awareness of *Doctor Who* by acting as a 'brand name' that would signify easily the attractions of the series as a BBC property.

Other television programmes, both factual and entertainment, also fuelled Dalek-mania. These included *Points Of View*, where letters from viewers about various BBC television programmes were read out as a form of audience interaction. As Gillatt (1998: 17) notes, the BBC's own press releases stated that 'Eighty-five per cent of letters to the BBC's popular *Points Of View* TV programme concerned the Daleks'. *Junior Points Of View* also contained mention of *Doctor Who* and the Daleks. One young viewer, John Qualtrough (aged 14) wrote a spoof *Doctor Who* story, 'Doctor Who Strikes Again' and appeared on *Junior Points Of View* in December 1964 to talk about it.

Entertainment programming featuring the Daleks most notably included *The Black And White Minstrel Show* (Gillatt 1998: 19). Significantly, this was one of the most popular television series of the 1960s, and its 'crowd-pleasing mix of song-and-dance and variety' had 'won the first Golden Rose of Montreux television award for the BBC in 1961' (Gillatt 1998: 19). Again, value judgements were made about what to include in this popular programme and how often, and the Daleks appeared more than once. As Gillatt (1998: 19) goes on to point out, the Daleks made their second appearance on *The Black and White Minstrel Show* on the evening of 12 December 1964, hours after the broadcast of the fourth episode of 'The Dalek Invasion Of Earth', 'tap-dancing with Benny Garcia and had "This Can't Be Love" sung to them by Tony Mercer, before finally carrying Margaret Savage off set as she belted out "Whatever Lola Wants"'. The Daleks' appearance in such a playful environment had the effect of endearing the creatures, who were already the subject of school playground mimicking, to audiences and further maintained their position in the public eye, since *The Black And White Minstrel Show* was so widely watched. Daleks cropped up in unusual places, such as the outside broadcast light entertainment quiz programme *What's The Sense* in May 1970 for instance, and three Daleks appeared in David Climie's play (based on a story by Peter Phillips) 'Get Off My Cloud' (1 April 1969) for BBC2's science fiction anthology series *Out Of The Unknown* (Pixley 2001b: 28), which revolved around a science fiction writer psychologically living through his fantasies in hospital after having a nervous breakdown. The boundaries between programmes, genres and formats were permeable, and one programme could advertise the fictionality of another.

The association between *Doctor Who*, the Daleks and the youth culture that we have noted in the inclusion of the teenager Susan in the programme was furthered by the extension of Dalek-mania into the pop music arena. The Daleks were adopted by a pop culture that already emphasised modernity and fantasy, and the imagery associated with Nation's creatures lent itself to this. Johnny Worth and the Go-Gos wrote and performed a Daleks pop song in late 1964 for the Christmas market, and a beat group called The Daleks were also performing in December 1964.

The merchandising of children's toys also served to publicise *Doctor Who* as a programme and the Daleks more specifically. While initially slow to capitalise on the success of the Daleks through merchandising, turning down an offer by entrepreneur Walter Tuckwell to sell licences to produce Dalek merchandising because the Daleks would be finished off at the end of the first story (Gillatt 1998: 18), agreements were made with the BBC for third-party publishers to print a *Doctor Who* novel and an annual, *The Dalek Book*, for Christmas 1964. At this time 'two Dalek badges, available exclusively from Woolworths store, reportedly sold over a million units' and 'a PVC Dalek dressing-up costume was on sale for £8 15s 6d' (Gillatt 1998: 19). Merchandising also included inflatable Daleks for the beach, and small plastic toy Daleks. Dalek sweet cigarettes were produced by Paramount Confectionery with illustrated *Doctor Who* collector cards.

Furthermore, the production office of *Doctor Who* also co-operated with *TV Comic*, which was serialising *Doctor Who* adventures. Nation co-wrote *The Dalek Book* (1964) and *The Dalek World* (1965) with David Whitaker, which included comic strips, features and stories rather like an annual, and co-wrote *The Dalek Outer Space Book* (1966) with Brad Ashton. Nation compiled and wrote the preface for *The Dalek Pocketbook and Space Travellers Guide* (1965), a paperback collection of articles and features treating the Daleks as though they really existed. An attempt was also made to capitalise on the alien Voord from Nation's 'The Keys Of Marinus'. The first *Doctor Who* annual, issued in September 1965, presented the Voord on the cover and in the story 'The Fishmen Of Kandalinga'. The film company Amicus purchased the movie rights to 'The Keys Of Marinus' but did not pursue the project, and the Voord's success never equalled that of the Daleks.

There was also extensive interaction between the initial *Doctor Who* production team of Verity Lambert, David Whitaker and Dennis Spooner, and television viewers. They responded to numerous letters from viewers about the programme in this period, the majority being related to the Daleks. This indicated the popularity of the Daleks and by responding to these letters the production team maintained interest in the creatures. The BBC has kept a file of letters from viewers between 1963 and 1965 (BBC WAC T5/649/1). After 1965 the responsibility for replying to fan mail was given to Terry Nation, but prior to this the production office sent to the children who wrote to them photographs of the cast and of Daleks, do-it-yourself instructions to build a Dalek as shown on *Blue Peter*, and loaned Daleks to charity events and fetes at schools for the disabled, for example. The letters from adults pointed out factual inaccuracies and scientific errors, and offered suggestions for story ideas, with a few adults complaining about the violence in *Doctor Who* and the showing of dead bodies, but the letters from children demonstrated their wish to become immersed in the fictional Dalek universe of *Doctor Who*. This stimulation of interactivity, as a strategy to increase viewer involvement, was furthered by stunts organised by the BBC. Daleks roamed the streets of Birmingham in December 1964, and Daleks featured in the *Daily Mail* Boys and Girls Exhibition in late December and early January 1964–65. Daleks appeared in the Doctor Barnardo's student charity walk in December 1964, and at the London County Council children's party on Boxing Day 1964. The fortuitous combination of appeal to a child audience, newspaper publicity, appearances in other popular programmes, connections with the science fiction and fantasy imagery of 1960s pop culture, and active interaction with viewers through letters and stunts gave *Doctor Who* an extraordinary media profile that secondarily benefited Nation because of his copyright ownership of the Dalek concept (as did the use of the Daleks in the stage plays *The Curse of the Daleks* (1965) and *Doctor Who and the Daleks in Seven Keys to Doomsday* (1974).

This version of a commercial 'star system' was therefore different from that for both *Survivors*, pitched as 'serious' drama and aimed at a predominantly adult audience, with few opportunities for merchandising, and *Blake's 7*. For example, *Survivors* was publicised in the *Radio Times* in relation to the more traditional 'stars', the actors, as an ensemble piece involving several main characters, played by Carolyn Seymour (Abby Grant), Lucy Fleming (Jenny Richards) and Talfryn Thomas (Tom Price), with the audience offered the attraction of performers who had already gained repute in evening prime-time programmes and at the cinema. The programme was embedded in the discourses associated with seriousness and star power that British broadcasters had always attached to single plays and prime-time dramatic fiction. Seymour, for instance, (who had to fight for the part of Abby Grant, originally intended for Wanda Ventham) had featured as a regular character in the BBC's own drama series *Take Three Girls*, and in the feature films *Gumshoe*, *Steptoe And Son* and *Unman, Wittering And Zigo*, and Thomas was a Welsh character actor who appeared regularly as Mr Cheeseman in the hugely successful BBC sitcom *Dad's Army* as well as in two *Doctor Who* stories starring Jon Pertwee in the title role (see Alsop 1987).

In some respects *Blake's 7* represented a return to the merchandising strategies that succeeded well for *Doctor Who*, with the twin aims again being to generate revenue and to publicise the programme. Nation was asked as early as May 1977 to write a short presentation to marketing specialists presenting the logo and related visuals to be registered for copyright so they could be used on merchandise (BBC WAC T65/72/1). But there were not the same formidable monster stars as in *Doctor Who*, meaning that merchandise included transporter bracelets, space guns, action figures, models, annuals (as was common for programmes with an appeal to young audiences), a video shooting game, a board game, jigsaws, and even snack foods and sweets, but the lack of a high-profile central image to market, like that of the Daleks, meant that the promotion of *Blake's 7* did not result in the same type of mania.

## Conclusion

We have aimed in this chapter to demonstrate Nation's agency as an individual writer and deviser of formats for television programmes, focusing on the BBC science fiction series that he worked on. But we have also emphasised the boundaries and limits that circumscribed this agency, to underline the point that Nation's authorial role and authority within the programme-making contexts in which he worked were very significantly dependent on genre and form, and on a range of personnel, institutional arrangements and economic structures. These factors were either substantially outside Nation's control, or open to negotiations in which his own agency was only one of the contributing forces. This chapter's concentration on genre and form and on the multitude of author and authority figures provides grounding for later chapters, by moving from the focus of chapter 1's biographical outline of Nation's individual activity as a television writer to a broader framework in which Nation's writing, the texts that he originated or contributed to, and the forms and meanings of programmes for actual or possible audiences, will be discussed. In both of our subsequent chapters, we continue the emphasis on the necessary negotiation between Nation's individual authorial agency, the genres and forms in which he was writing, ideologies circulating in culture, and the contribution of other personnel, such as script editors, directors, designers and executives. We also examine how genres and forms were used as advertisements, building on the discussion of publicity in this chapter.

# Science fiction genre and form　　　3

## Introduction

In this chapter we continue our focus on the multiple author(ity) figures
involved in television production, and we introduce some of the
significant methodologies developed in the academic study of television
and of science fiction in order to explore the generic and formal
elements of the programmes Nation worked on, their form as popular
narrative television, and their address to television audiences. We note
that Nation's brand name became increasingly significant during his
career as a badge attached to science fiction and action adventure
programmes that were aimed at broad mass audiences. But we also
highlight the collaborative enterprise involved, since Nation was a
'craftsman', who spoke and wrote about himself in these terms in
interviews and newspaper profiles, when, for example, he admitted to
writing *Doctor Who*'s 'The Daleks' just for the money, and to making up
colourful creation stories about how the creatures got their name (*Radio
Times 10th Anniversary Special* 1973). The chapter will not only consider
the importance of multiple authorship but will also show how authorship is carved out intertextually, in relation to the genres of other works.
This happened when Nation adapted existing science fiction stories for
*Out Of This World* or *Out Of The Unknown*, for example, but also when
he scripted original stories and devised new programme formats.
Screenwriters have to accommodate their work to existing television
genres and forms, while these genres and forms also open up possibilities for the author. This issue extends our discussion of genre and
form in the previous chapter, for here we not only discuss Nation's
contributions, but also show how these fit in with conventions of storytelling for television and for science fiction television especially. The
chapter also considers how Nation, in collaboration with other production personnel, used genre, form and characters in ways that made

his works a success, and how genre, form and characters were extended subsequently as a result. Our work on genres and forms connects with the discussion of promotional discourses in the previous chapter since each was used to draw audiences to the programmes as products. While looking at questions of authorship, much of the analysis in this chapter will consist of our examination of programmes and what they reveal about science fiction genre and form.

The television medium has been theorised as an intimate medium that addresses a distracted viewer. This is primarily because of the television set's small screen and its usual positioning within the home. For this reason, academic work on television has placed little emphasis on the aesthetics of science fiction and fantasy television, preferring instead to consider its social contexts (Miller 1997; Kellner 1999a, 1999b; Wildermuth 1999; Barrett and Barrett 2001). The genre of science fiction television is known to address attentive viewers, some of whom are dedicated fans, and this has been a second strand of academic work (Bacon-Smith 1992; Jenkins 1992; Lewis 1992). Science fiction television has a large fan following where fans view their favourite series repeatedly, spawning both commercial publications like *Starburst*, *TV Zone* or *Doctor Who Magazine*, and also amateur fanzines, where fans write about how programmes are structured using production information and close readings. Nation worked on fantasy drama including *The Avengers*, *The Baron* and *The Champions*, as well as the science fiction programmes that we focus on here: *Doctor Who*, *Survivors* and *Blake's 7*. Both of these genres attract large fan audiences, and have attained the status of 'cult' television. They are collectively termed 'telefantasy' in the commercial publications that cater to their devotees, and telefantasy was first used as a generic label by the US magazine *Starlog* (1976–) and its British counterpart *Starburst* (1978–). These publications draw on the activity of viewers in becoming absorbed in the fictions, but also the fans' interest in stepping back from the work to analyse it and understand its production. As Henry Jenkins (1992: 65) points out, 'fans often display a desire to take the program apart and see how it works, to learn how it was made and why it looks the way it does'. We consider the ways that audiences were addressed and constituted by Nation's work at the end of this chapter, after discussing and analysing the genre and form of programme storylines in the main body of the chapter. Analysis of this type is especially important because it reveals how the programmes are dramatically constructed. Not all viewers will be consciously aware of the genres and structures of Nation's work but such analysis is important in seeing how programmes may function for viewers.

## Genre as an author function

We showed in the previous chapter that there are multiple personnel who can claim authorship and authority over television programmes, and we develop this here, but an author's work also operates in comparison with other works where genre assumes an authoring function. We looked at genre in the last chapter but only to show how a programme's genre exercised authority over a writer and we did not examine intertextuality. The concept of intertextuality refers to the permeable boundaries around programmes, which cannot be definitively established since programmes are authored by writers and other production personnel, either consciously or unconsciously, in relation to other programmes and other kinds of text. As we saw in chapter 2, while format aims to define uniqueness and therefore its boundaries need to be policed, genre works by establishing connections with other texts and programmes. As Jason Mittell (2001: 7) puts it, 'The boundaries between texts are too shifting and fluid to be reified', but each programme participates in a dominant genre. There has been historically a perception that genre applies most easily to mass audience popular texts, so that programmes which are firmly within genre boundaries are regarded as formulaic, and the features of a genre reveal the persistence of some kinds of storytelling and the issues it explores.

The theoretical study of genre has tended to begin from the assumption that individual popular television programmes are part of a larger generic group of relatively similar and undistinguished programmes. The study of genre has thus been based on the identification of the conventions and key features that distinguish one body of programme texts from another, such as the characteristics of television science fiction, news or situation comedy. The study of genre allows the linkage of conventions found in a group of texts with the expectations and understandings of audiences. In this respect, the study of genre aims to explain how audiences classify what they see and hear on television according to features of the text, generic cues that audiences identify, and the presence of performers associated with a particular genre, as well as supporting information in listings and advertising publications, for example. As Steve Neale (Neale and Turner 2001: 1) notes, 'Most theorists of genre argue that generic norms and conventions are recognised and shared not only by theorists themselves, but also by audiences, readers and viewers.' As Mittell (2001: 6) has argued, any individual television programme must be understood by audiences in relation to other programmes whose generic characteristics it may share, or from which the programme might distinguish itself: 'Genres are not found within one isolated text ... Genres emerge only from the intertextual relations between multiple texts, resulting in a common category ... Audiences link programs together all the time'. Drawing on a structuralist analytical method that aims to discover the shared patterns and structures animating texts and linking them together in a genre, theorists such as Mittell (2001: 7) have argued for the importance of genre study in understanding how television programmes and other kinds of text exhibit shared features. Genre is such a powerful concept that often texts are grouped together by genre rather than by author, so genre acquires a degree of pre-eminence over the writer.

### *Doctor Who*'s primary genre: science fiction, format and intertextuality

Science fiction has been seen by theoreticians such as Darko Suvin (1979: 7–8) as involving estrangement (the audience is taken to a different or transformed fictional world) and cognition (where the strange must be examined, using rational scientific methods), though the emphasis on scientific and rational investigation is much less central to television science fiction than in the literary texts that Suvin discusses, and television formats specify genre more loosely. *Doctor Who*'s format, as we explained in the previous chapter, was generically coded as science fiction by the production personnel who preceded Nation's involvement and was constructed intertextually, in relation to previous texts. Science fiction had been a successful genre in the cinema since the US film serials of the 1930s and 1940s, such as *Flash Gordon* (1936), based on a syndicated comic strip, and *Buck Rogers* (1939). One early television science fiction programme was the BBC's 1949 adaptation of H. G. Wells's *The Time Machine*, broadcast live as a single play from the Alexandra Palace studios. In 1953 BBC television broadcast the popular six-part serial *The Quatermass Experiment* by Nigel Kneale, and in 1959 Sydney Newman commissioned a seven-part children's serial for ITV, *Pathfinders In Space* (by Eric Paice and Malcolm Hulke), a space exploration story closely based on known scientific fact, with fast-moving action involving the British space explorer Professor Wedgewood and his children. Like the adult drama *Quatermass*, *Pathfinders* was followed by sequels, and the popularity of these programmes (among others) gave impetus to science fiction series and serials for both adult and child audiences.

Although elements of *Doctor Who*'s format were unique, in some ways it echoed these programmes since the Doctor was a scientist, like

Wells's character and Professors Quatermass and Wedgewood. He travelled in a time machine like Wells's protagonist, and like Wedgewood he was accompanied by younger travellers. *Doctor Who*'s genre is intertextual, relying on similarities with, and differences from, a history of television programmes, films and literary works. The planning for *Doctor Who* began in response to a report for the Head of Serial Drama (Television) in July 1962 by two of the staff of the Drama Department, John Braybon and Alice Frick (BBC WAC T5/647/1), who looked for ideas among science fiction short stories and recommended time travel and telepathy as suitable subjects. In the previous chapter we briefly noted the use of the *Radio Times* to advertise *Doctor Who* generically, and generic advertising can only succeed through the intertextuality of genre.

## Nation's *Doctor Who* and generic science fiction

Nation had to fit his stories within the overall generically coded format of *Doctor Who* and his work for the programme is coded primarily as science fiction. His stories are set on different worlds, or in changed versions of our own (like 'The Dalek Invasion Of Earth'). Several of his *Doctor Who* stories are premised on the misuse of scientific knowledge, and scientific and technological discourse and iconography are especially important in the creation of the evil machine-like Daleks in 'The Daleks', and even more explicitly in 'Genesis Of The Daleks' (see chapter 4). Indeed, 'The Daleks' has been seen by Howe *et al.* (1993: 31) as having close resemblances with Wells's novel *The Time Machine*, where the human race has evolved in a distant future into two distinct races. The evil Daleks in some respects parallel the carnivorous Morlocks and the peaceful Thals parallel the childlike Eloi in Wells's novel, and George Pal's film adaptation of the novel was released in 1960, shortly before Nation wrote 'The Daleks' (see Bignell 1999a). In Nation's later story 'Genesis Of The Daleks', argues Pixley (1997a: 36), where there is a war between two races and where Davros aims for the Kaled race to survive by turning it into Daleks, 'The notion of World War One trench warfare being fought with space-age weaponry was drawn from Nation's memories of William Cameron Menzies' 1936 movie "Things To Come", itself based on H. G. Wells' 1933 novel "The Shape Of Things To Come"'.

## *Survivors* and *Blake's 7*: science fiction, intertextuality and the advertisement

Title sequences border television programmes, distinguishing a programme from the one before it, and creating expectations in the viewer as to the genre in which the programme participates and the themes its storyline will develop. Title sequences are frequently presented as a series of images used to grab the viewer's attention. As John Ellis (1982: 120) puts it, a title sequence provides a type of 'narrative image for its programme' and usually 'a highly generalised ... conception of the programme'. This is a point also stressed by John Corner (1999: 32), who states that such sequences seek to convey 'the essence of a programme's identity through an associative strategy of imagery, sound, and music'. Nicholas Abercrombie (1996) and Graeme Burton (2000) similarly observe that title sequences suggest the identity of programmes, providing generic placing. In his section on genre, Abercrombie (1996: 42), looking at the Western, the soap opera and the police drama, writes that through the use of iconography 'the viewer is sure before even getting into the programme what kind of programme is being watched'. Similarly, Burton (2000: 76) remarks, 'Titles prepare the viewer for a certain mode of treatment, a certain set of conventions' of which '[t]he most familiar ... are realism and genre'. The title sequence, writes Burton (2000: 76), establishes 'a way of "talking" to ... and a kind of relationship with, the viewer'. Clearly, this kind of study requires close analysis of the individual meaningful elements in a short title sequence, in order to identify how they accomplish these functions. Close analysis using the methods of semiotics (see Bignell 2002a) to discuss the meanings of the visual signs in title sequences aims to show how these signs link together into structures of meaning, and it is this principle of analysis that we adopt here.

*Survivors'* title sequence establishes the science fiction genre intertextually and advertises the generic knowledge that viewers will need to make sense of the programme. The sequence was scripted by Nation although it was slightly altered, and represents an accident in a science laboratory leading to the escape of a deadly virus, spread through the international networks of aeroplane travel. This science fiction notion extrapolates from historical examples of serious epidemics, and in its final form it is more or less as Nation envisaged it, although 'the hand which drops the test tube was originally to have been mechanical, part of an automated laboratory apparatus' (Houldsworth, 1992: 14) while in the final version it is that of a Chinese scientist (see figure 1). 'The virus was to have been represented by small red dots, seen spreading over the images of people at the airport, and then over a map of the world' and '[t]he shot of the scientist, Chinese, collapsing at the airport was supposed to turn negative' (Houldsworth 1992: 14), while in the final version the scientist simply collapses at the airport and there are close-ups of passport stamps from different countries representing the plague's rapid spread.

There are science fiction stories with similar premises to *Survivors* both before and after it, such as Michael Crichton's film *The Andromeda Strain* (1971) in which a US space satellite crashes into a desert town releasing a virus. Television viewers today might note the more direct comparisons with John J. Nance's *Pandora's Clock* (1996) where a virus from a science lab is believed to be circulating on an aeroplane and political leaders try to arrest its spread. Key signifiers such as the virus, laboratory, airport and the airliner feature prominently in these examples, and show that *Survivors* connects intertextually with specific 1970s fears about scientific research and warfare (especially the danger posed by Communist China's scientists) and more current fears of disease explored in science fiction extrapolations from epidemiological research.

Furthermore, as we have explained in chapter 2, *Survivors* was advertised as science fiction in the *Radio Times* using quoted dialogue that positioned the series in relation to the Apollo space missions. The title sequence itself is a type of advertisement; it is in effect what Ellis (1982: 119) calls a 'commercial for the programme itself'. *Survivors* provides a science fiction scenario in order to offer the viewer the assurance of a main genre with which he or she is familiar, but the programme is best described as speculative fiction, since it is about what happens to individuals and groups of people after the scientific accident and how a new backward society contrasts with previous technological expertise.

*Blake's 7* is also advertised and coded as science fiction intertextually, with a title sequence prominently featuring images of space and a spaceship, images present in Nation's original idea for the opening (see chapter 4). As in *Survivors*, the sequence frames the programme, shaping and setting parameters for its concerns, and centres the series firmly within the boundaries of the science fiction genre. *Blake's 7*'s format, prescribing a setting largely in space where an oppressive future regime is combated, would have been either consciously or unconsciously influenced by other science fiction such as George Orwell's speculative novel set in the future, *Nineteen Eighty-four* (see chapter 4), where again an oppressive regime seeks to control its population, or the novel *Brave New World*, and can be read in relation to other films and programmes such as *Star Wars* (1977) and *Star Trek*. Nation's authorship, and that of the production team collaborating with him, was therefore established intertextually in relation to other texts, and is offered to audiences with prominent generic cues that shape how it can be understood.

## Science fiction and mixed genres: powers of authorship

This section not only examines the multiple personnel responsible for creating generic television but also how genre opens up possibilities for authorship. We have previously discussed the ways in which format plays a role in authorship by erecting boundaries around programmes, and how programmes are coded according to a dominant genre. The function of the format is to differentiate one programme from another, and by doing so that format can become a saleable and exchangeable product when it is offered for sale to another broadcaster, or defended against infringement of copyright. By contrast, genre works by connection and association. In this respect, genre itself might seem to have an authorship function, since the predominant genre of a programme effectively sets limits to what a programme may contain. It is as if, as Jacques Derrida (1980) has written in relation to literary genres, a 'law' of genre issues the commands 'Do' and 'Do Not', limiting the creativity of screenwriters and the interpretive activities of audiences. In fact, as Derrida recognises, this is not the case.

For while programmes are assimilated into a dominant genre, all texts necessarily participate in several genres simultaneously and this extends the boundaries of authorship. Programmes borrow intertextually from a variety of genres and blur the boundaries between them. Derrida (1980) proposed, in his work on written texts, that the law of genre is one of generic mixing where all texts participate in multiple genres and therefore belong to no one specific genre. This idea has been adopted in theoretical work on the media, and specifically television, by John Fiske (1987), Ulrike H. Meinhof and Jonathan Smith (2000), and Steve Neale (Neale and Turner 2001). As Neale (Neale and Turner 2001: 2) argues, 'The degree of hybridity and overlap between genres and areas has all too often been underplayed', and, 'Underplayed, too ... has been the degree to which texts of all kinds necessarily "participate" in genre ... and the extent to which they are likely to participate in more than one genre at once'. To make sense of the complexity of television, viewers become expert in recognising genre, and also derive pleasure from the manipulation of genre and from the ways that television plays with its boundaries. The study of genre is not only a way of pinning programmes down. Rather genres are fluid like water or, to use Meinhof and Smith's (2000) image, elastic.

Although the definition of science fiction as a genre has been the subject of much debate, it is therefore connected to, draws on and sometimes subsumes other genres. Some genres are mixed so frequently that sub-genres are produced such as science fiction Gothic. While programmes upon which Nation worked (*Doctor Who, Survivors, Blake's 7*) were primarily marketed to audiences as science fiction, as we have seen, these programmes still allowed the multiple author figures creativity where science fiction was mixed with other genres. Therefore the creator and screenwriter have some authorship and authority over genre by manipulating genres and mixing them. Because Nation was a 'craftsman' doing a job he returned to similar kinds of generic mixing in much of his science fiction work, as we now show, but we shall also demonstrate that these generic programmes were authored inter-textually and can be understood in this way, rather than being unitary and bounded texts.

## Nation's *Doctor Who* and mixed genres

Tulloch and Alvarado (1983: 5) seek to explain the popularity of *Doctor Who*, its 'complexity and variety', as arising from 'its use of a range of different genres – Science Fiction/Historical Romance/Comedy/Gothic Horror/Adventure, etc. which together with the regular phoenix-like reincarnation of the Doctor himself (allowing a range of different actors with different personalities and personae to play the role) make for another ... reason for its durability'. While Nation contributed similar types of story for *Doctor Who*, his works, realised by different production personnel, stretch genre boundaries. In chapter 2, we noted that a large degree of mystery was embedded in *Doctor Who*'s format, since the title character could not always control his ship's destination, and this meant that writers like Nation had the freedom to create unknown science fiction worlds, which would further extend the parameters of genre.

*Doctor Who*'s format mixes the genres of science fiction and mystery, since the Doctor's TARDIS, because it travels through space and time, is an object that does not have to bring its occupants to the start of a chain of events, but can land at any point on a time-line. The TARDIS can therefore land after significant events have already occurred, arriving in the midst of things that require exploration and explanation. Towards the end of the programme's history, however, there was often a cognitive gap between the Doctor (Sylvester McCoy), already aware of what was transpiring, and his companion (Ace) and the television viewer. The enigma of the Doctor was perpetually displaced in the early years of the programme by other more immediate mysteries concerning the environments and characters encountered in each episode. Similarly, *The Avengers*, for example, on which Nation also worked, displaced mystery from the enigmatic identities of the main characters on to individual episode stories, which often concerned the tortuous plotting of an evil mastermind. Steed (Patrick MacNee) and his female companion were required to unravel this mysterious plan and thus defeat its deviser. Nation's authorship can be read intertextually in relation to his work in other related television genres, as well as across his science fiction programmes and in relation to programmes, films and written texts authored by others. This occurs because the popular genres in which he worked had many shared structural features.

The result of the displacement of mystery from the main characters to specific puzzles within storylines is that the 'hermeneutic code', a term that refers to the setting and solution of puzzles and derives from the Greek word for interpretation, structures *Doctor Who*. As the television theorist John Fiske (1987: 143) observes in relation to television, drawing on Roland Barthes' (1990) discussion of written texts, this code 'sets and resolves the enigmas of the narrative and is motivated by the desire for closure and "truth"'. Fiske continues, 'It controls the pace and style of the narrative by controlling the flow of information that is desired' and is 'thus the motor of the narrative'. To play with Fiske's vocabulary, then, first the TARDIS and then the Doctor are the motors of the narrative. The Doctor is often driven by curiosity out of the ship's doors to a place he knows nothing about, and the Doctor's lack of knowledge parallels the television viewer's. For example, the original storyline for 'The Daleks' titled 'The Survivors' envisaged the TARDIS landing on the devastated planet Skaro in the distant future, and simply read: 'Dr Who's ship is unable to leave Skaro because of its liquid fuse which needs to be re-filled with water' (Pixley 2003: 30). But the flow of the transmitted story 'The Daleks' is initiated by the curiosity of the Doctor who at first aims to deduce what has occurred on Skaro by reading clues in his immediate environment. He is not being forced to remain, but wishes to explore the alien city that can be seen from afar (and turns out to be occupied by the Daleks), contrary to his fellow travellers' wishes. So he removes the fully operating Fluid Link from the TARDIS, which would enable the ship to leave, claiming that the travellers must enter the unknown city in order to find mercury to repair it. The TARDIS is a vehicle that can both initiate a new adventure and generate new narratives, but also, at the same time, facilitate escape and the cutting off of particular narratives. In 'The Daleks', the Doctor's pretence that the Fluid Link cannot flow and enable the TARDIS to move, means that the narrative cannot flow away from the planet.

The fact that the TARDIS can bring its occupants to any point on a time line facilitates mystery for the protagonists and for the television viewer. Stories like 'The Daleks', 'The Keys Of Marinus' where the oppressive Voord are attempting to seize control of a planet, 'The Dalek Invasion Of Earth', and 'Planet Of The Daleks' where the Daleks have invaded the planet Spiradon and are attempting to master invisibility, begin with something already having happened, and the Doctor and the television audience have to unravel things from the midst outwards. The inhabitants of story worlds have experienced events linearly from a starting point to the current time, whereas the Doctor, his fellow travellers and the audience have suddenly arrived later on the time-line.

*Doctor Who*'s format enables the mysteries set for the Doctor and his companions to push the genre of science fiction towards the epic. Science fiction is connected to the epic primarily in terms of scale, with the capability to develop storylines that concern great spans of time, extended wars and conflicts, and to represent entire planets and races by condensing these into a small number of characters and settings. The epic mode originated in oral and written texts, and has also been adopted in cinema where historical and mythological narratives have made use of widescreen, colour and special effects. The epic's extended spans of time are significant to some of Nation's storylines, which concern not only the current time of the story but also the revelation of beginnings that precede events on screen. For example, the events in Nation's first *Doctor Who* story 'The Daleks' occur over a number of days, but the notion of history and the way in which it can be repeated is important to the adventure. Events that occurred over 500 years previously, when there was a neutron war between two races, are referred to in the dialogue, and the repetition of this past conflict is one of the threats with which the Doctor and his allies deal. The events of 'The Dalek Invasion Of Earth' also occur across a number of days, but events that happened over a decade previously are explained. The audience learns that the Daleks have bombarded Earth with meteorites, a plague has decimated the planet, and Earth has been invaded. In 'Genesis Of The Daleks', the Doctor arrives after centuries of war between Kaleds and Thals that frame the present time of the story and provide an epic grandeur to its events. The story reveals this history and also begins at an appropriate dramatic point when Davros is putting the newly designed Daleks into action. This mystery and epic grandeur are partly signified by the use of characters within the fictions as narrators (for example, the Thal Alydon in 'The Daleks' and the London rebels in 'The Dalek Invasion Of Earth') who explain previous events to the regular characters. They are 'homodiegetic' narrators, within the story world, as opposed to 'heterodiegetic' narration (such as written captions) situated outside the story world. This grand epic scope can be seen in the literary epic and is present in later films such as *Star Wars* (1977). Its effect is to invite the audience to interpret the programmes in relation to other works and to regard the present time of the story as a fragment of a much larger fictional whole.

Nation's work further resembles the epic in that the central characters of the Doctor and his companions embody the assumptions and values of the television audience's culture and are presented as figures for audience identification. They are tested by frequently having to embark upon a long and perilous journey, like the heroes of literary epic. The division of 'The Daleks' into a relatively lengthy seven episodes (seven weeks of television time) parallels the epic grandeur of the story, and the journey undertaken in order to attack the Daleks' city is itself an extended epic journey that lasts from towards the end of the fourth episode until late in the final instalment. Geographically, the journey involves moving through a perilous swamp and through caverns. 'The Keys Of Marinus', structured as a picaresque narrative (a series of relatively self-contained adventures, which lacks substantial progression towards a resolution, although Nation's story is bound by a quest), sees the Doctor and his assistants moving from place to place to locate the keys that will enable the evil Voord to be defeated. This was Nation's idea although script editor Whitaker suggested landscapes such as the snowscape of the fourth episode. This is also a long journey in terms of screen time where most of the story concerns the voyage. In this case, however, the Doctor and his assistants are forced upon this quest by Arbitan in order to regain access to the TARDIS, rather than voluntarily undertaking it. In 'The Dalek Invasion Of Earth' the Doctor and his companions travel across Britain to the Dalek mine in Bedfordshire, encountering perils such as tunnels infested with alligators, in order to defeat the evil machines. In 'The Daleks' Master Plan', which Nation co-wrote with Dennis Spooner, the Doctor determines to journey to Earth, pursued by the Daleks, to warn the authorities of the Daleks' plan to use a weapon called the Time Destructor to seize control. This 12-part story has even greater length in terms of screentime, and a similar epic quality. In 'Planet Of The Daleks' the journey through caverns into the Dalek city to defeat the machines, resembling that in the first story 'The Daleks', recurs again. Only in 'The Chase' is the Doctor's and his companions' voyage through time and space in the TARDIS motivated by a need to flee from the Daleks, who initiate the journey rather than the narrative flow being initiated by a 'good' character. The epic scope of Nation's work was one of the reasons his scripts were so costly to realise visually, as we mentioned in chapter 2.

*Doctor Who*'s format enabled Nation and his collaborators to combine science fiction epic with the action adventure that was one of his particular strengths. 'The Chase', for instance, was signalled self-consciously as an adventure romp when the Doctor's fellow traveller, the schoolteacher Ian Chesterton, was discovered reading the book *Monsters From Outer Space* in the first episode, and the story becomes as 'far-fetched' as the book. A story such as 'Genesis Of The Daleks' involves action adventure both in the process of the protagonists trying to prevent the creation of the Daleks and in sub-plots such as a companion trying to escape her captors. In a conversation with us, Barry Letts praised the story for being a 'page-turner'. He remarked particularly on the scene in which the Doctor's companion Sarah Jane Smith, the Mutos and a group of Kaleds, who have been taken prisoner by the Thals in order to load a rocket with explosives that will be used against the Kaled dome, attempt to make their escape by climbing scaffolding to the top of the Thal dome while under fire from Thal soldiers, only to be recaptured. Letts told us that he initially felt the scene should develop the narrative by allowing the characters to escape, but the incoming producer Philip Hinchcliffe vetoed this and Letts confirms that it was the right decision. Although the scene did not advance the narrative, the physical action at this point in the adventure was used to create dramatic tension. Letts regarded action adventure as a significant part of the essence of *Doctor Who*, and Nation's writing, drawing on his skill in crafting scripts in this genre, could be accommodated within the parameters set by the programme format.

By the early 1970s the format of *Doctor Who* had evolved, since the Doctor (Jon Pertwee) acted in this period as scientific adviser for the paramilitary organisation UNIT (United Nations Intelligence Taskforce) to combat alien invasions. Science fiction was mixed with spy drama and action adventure, drawing the series closer to the action drama Nation had written in the 1960s in which intelligence operatives dealt with mysterious threats to national security under the authorisation of official or semi-official institutions (see Chapman 2002). Nation did not contribute to *Doctor Who* in the early 1970s, but his later story 'The Android Invasion' featured action adventure involving android replicas of UNIT personnel in the alien Kraals' plan to take over the Earth. Andrew Pixley (1992: 26) explains that this story was

> inspired by the idea of espionage training centres in different countries where agents were coached to the extent that KGB agents could become perfect Englishmen to infiltrate another country as 'sleepers'. This time though, the picturesque little English village would be constructed on an alien world ... and the trainees would be mechanical duplicates of real people.

The screenplay transposes these spy drama elements into a science-fictional setting. Pixley continues, 'the deserted village and seemingly hypnotised villagers in ... the story set against the realistic backdrop of Devesham evoked more of the offbeat adventure feeling associated with *The Avengers* and *Department S*', which would continue in this story's scenes involving physical action and combat. By this point in *Doctor Who*'s history, the main characters had been reduced in number and now consisted only of the Doctor and his female companion. This has structural parallels with the male and female team in the ITC action adventure programmes such as *The Avengers* and *The Baron* that Nation worked on. There are connections at the level of format and genre between these programmes, and science fiction and action adventure address their audiences in ways that invite viewers to make intertextual connections. Nation adapted his work as history shows.

There are further examples in the work credited to Nation where his authorship was affected by the intervention of other personnel, and where the mystery discussed above led to generically mixed worlds where the programmes depended on intertextual relationships that blurred genre boundaries. The *Doctor Who* story 'The Chase', where the Doctor and his companions flee from the Daleks, crossed the boundary between science fiction and fantasy, challenging the stability of the programme's format and earning the disapproval of the producer, Verity Lambert. In a script report on episode three (BBC WAC T5/1241/1), which contained a long sequence where the TARDIS crew arrives in a Gothic mansion occupied by Frankenstein's monster and Dracula, she complained that although *Doctor Who* might represent strange and alien characters and environments, these should always be plausibly realistic. She was concerned that drawing on characters from written fiction would open up the *Doctor Who* format to the extent that anything implausible and fantastic could then be included, thus undermining the conventions of realistic representation that the programme's version of science fiction had established. However, the Gothic characters in 'The Chase' turn out to be amusement park androids, thus providing a rational explanation for them that repositioned these fantasy figures within the realist conventions of the programme.

Science fiction epic was also mixed with the Gothic, to produce thrilling and terrifying effects by rendering something familiar unfamiliar, a disturbance of expectations that Freud (1955: 219) calls 'das Unheimlich' (the 'unhomely' or 'uncanny'). The use of the Gothic in Nation's later *Doctor Who* work was influenced by other production personnel and was the direction in which producer Philip Hinchcliffe and script editor Robert Holmes were steering the programme. By 1975, when Nation worked on 'Genesis Of The Daleks', the Daleks had become sufficiently familiar to be implausible as threats. The director David Maloney imbued the realisation of the story with familiar iconography (the trench warfare of the First World War, and military uniforms resembling those of British and German troops of the Second World War, for instance) in an unfamiliar science fiction setting, and this was regarded by the campaigner Mary Whitehouse as too frightening for children. Furthermore, the adoption of the Gothic was a response to the problem of how to present the Daleks, created out of one of the warring races, in a sufficiently menacing way. Tulloch and Alvarado (1983: 154–5) quote the producer Philip Hinchcliffe in relation to this:

> The great problem with those Daleks stories is not to make them silly. David Maloney directed that one, and he worked extremely hard to make the Daleks powerful – you know, so that they are not just idiots running around ... You can't dwell on those Daleks. You've really got to edit them together and make them more powerful and make them more menacing than they are by the way you shoot it.

The Daleks are, for instance, portrayed in dark night-time settings and their distorted shadows are thrown on to walls. Elements of the Gothic also appear in our discussion below of Nation's common motif of stalkers who resemble the monstrous creatures in Tod Browning's horror films. The Gothic continued to be significant to *Doctor Who*'s generic mix in stories that were scripted by other writers, such as the mixing of science fiction and the Gothic in the later story 'The Brain Of Morbius', where the Gothic motif of demonic possession is rendered in science fiction form when Solon, a perverted Frankenstein figure, can be regarded as a successor to the Dalek creator Davros, with the race in this former story being possessed by Daleks (see chapter 4). The intertextuality we have discussed here further complicates the assumption that the meanings of programme texts can be delimited by their authors.

In contrast to the uncanny and potentially frightening effects of mixing science fiction with the Gothic, the script editor of 'Destiny Of The Daleks', Douglas Adams, working with producer Graham Williams on his final season, oversaw the inclusion of comedy in the story's opening regeneration scene, and at the expense of the Daleks (Pixley 1999b: 16), highlighting a different generic blend. Comic moments had already been evident in the much earlier story 'The Chase', script-edited by Dennis Spooner who, like Nation, had a background in comedy writing. Nation wrote the seventh episode of 'The Daleks' Master Plan', 'The Feast Of Steven', which was transmitted on Christmas Day 1965. Its comic elements drew attention to its fictionality and led up to a striking ending that breached television conventions when the Doctor turned to the camera and wished all at home a Merry Christmas. In 'Destiny Of The Daleks', the Doctor is escaping from the Daleks by climbing a rope ladder, and turns to challenge his pursuers by asking why if they are going to be the masters of the universe they are unable to follow him up it. This was a scene that Nation felt diminished his creations somewhat (Pixley 1999b: 16) and contrasts with the aim of maintaining series continuity and plausibility in the earlier story 'Genesis Of The Daleks' (1975). The collaborative authorship common in these television forms is a way in which the genre experimentation undertaken by one collaborator can influence the work of another, just as the mixed generic science fiction television we have discussed opens up particular programmes to intertextual readings. For example, Adams's introduction of humour in *Doctor Who* can be related to his own work for his *The Hitch-Hiker's Guide To The Galaxy* science fiction spoof serial for BBC radio and television (Peel 1992).

### *Survivors* and mixed genres

The boundaries between genres in *Survivors*, set up by its format, are also permeable. Nation was responsible for the format as well as several of its episodes, and other personnel contributed to the programme and extended the boundaries of its component genres as well as altering the balance between them. *Survivors* mixes science fiction (the escaped virus) with the grand scale of epic, yet still homes in on localised domestic drama. For in *Survivors* there is a play between macrocosm (a whole world) and microcosm (a condensed representation of that world). The opening title sequence, scripted by Nation, reveals that the plague is spread across the world on an epic apocalyptic scale through the presentation of passport stamps from around the world. The final stamp is one from London, and the opening episodes then reveal the enormity of the crisis through dialogue, implying an epic scale that cannot be represented visually, and then home in even more specifically on a representative ensemble of British characters. In the early 1980s Terry Nation came close to resurrecting *Survivors* in the United States, proposing an epic journey across the country to find safety from the plague, but while a lot of interest was shown in the project the premise of the decimating plague was felt to be too unappealing to audiences aware of the coming of AIDS.

*Survivors* participates in the sub-genre of apocalyptic science fiction, and alludes to Biblical epic. The title of the first episode, 'The Fourth Horseman', invites an intertextual connection with the Biblical Book of Revelation and the four horsemen of the apocalypse, the fourth of whom represents plague or pestilence: 'And when he had opened the fourth seal, I heard the voice of the fourth beast say, Come and see./ And I looked, and behold a pale horse: and his name that sat on him was Death, and Hell followed with him. And power was given unto them over the fourth part of the earth, to kill with sword, and with hunger, and with death, and with the beasts of the earth' (Revelation 6: 7–8). The image of the fourth horseman has been a prominent one ever since, seen in medieval paintings (such as one by Beatus of Liebana), medieval manuscripts (such as the Douce, Trinity and Bamberg Apocalypse and MS Ludwig), and in books. Nation's title conjures up widespread cultural associations, just as do more recent programmes such as *Millennium*, which featured a 1998 episode concerning a plague, using the same title, and *Charmed*'s episode 'Apocalypse, Not' (2000) in which the fourth horseman becomes an on-screen character. Nation and the production team's authorship, as in these later series, includes allusions and references that invite cross-reference to, and seepage of meaning from, other texts from a range of cultural contexts, and invite their viewers to draw on these as interpretive generic frameworks.

*Survivors* contained elements of domestic drama as a new community is falteringly established in a country house. Various personnel contributed to this, but Nation wanted to tone down the domestic angle of the series. As Neil Alsop (1987: 14) points out, Nation's original version of *Survivors* saw the central characters as 'questing wanderers' (also a feature of epic), while another main writer Jack Ronder had the central characters operating from a fixed base. Following the first season and Nation's departure, the vision of the production team was more that of *The Good Life* (Alsop 1987: 17), a BBC sitcom about self-sufficiency whose title punned on the surname of its central married couple as well as connoting happy domesticity, and this was not the vision Nation wished to pursue (see chapters 1 and 2). Chapter 4 will consider the consequences of this increasing focus in *Survivors* on domestic drama, for the domestic is both associated with the running of a community where the structure of relationships in the home is conventionally seen as a microcosm of relationships in society at large, and is also important to considering issues of gender where the woman's place was at home. The contributions to authorship that were made by the different personnel working on *Survivors* had the effect of gradually shifting the generic boundaries of the series from the science fiction sub-genre of post-apocalyptic drama towards the domestic ensemble relationships characteristic of soap opera, together with an emphasis on interpersonal rivalries and romance, rather than the thriller and action components that Nation had planned. The effects of this shift in genre are to alter the kinds of generic intertextual references and interpretive frameworks that audiences and critics can bring to the series.

While combining science fiction, epic and domestic drama, *Survivors* was also noteworthy as an action adventure series, displaying some of the strengths of Nation's previous work, and this was Nation's contribution as Jack Ronder did not feel that the survivors of such a plague would resort to violence. The format allowed for conflicts between different communities as well as within the primary group of central characters, and this conflict with external groups is important in considering the way in which the programme could both involve the audience aesthetically, and also represent the political ideas and ideologies that we discuss in chapter 4. In the episode 'Gone Away' there is a shootout in which a paramilitary group under Arthur Wormley's authority shoot at the main characters, Abby Grant, Greg Preston and Jenny Richards, as they drive away from a supermarket with stocks of food. As well as being an example of the different ethics and tactics of the community of central characters in contrast to Wormley's gang, the sequence has the larger function within the unfolding series of introducing the threat that some groups of survivors will want control over resources and over other groups. In 'Garland's War', Garland is a man of action and there are shootouts between a group led by Knox that has seized control of the house inherited by Garland (under the now-collapsed law of the pre-plague society) and Garland himself. Garland is represented as a potential democratic leader, and Nation's choice of the name Knox for his opponent points generically to the episode's construction around a siege of the fortress (Fort Knox) into which Knox's henchmen have converted Garland's family residence. In 'The Future Hour', there is a shootout between Abby's community and a group led by Huxley, and in 'Something Of Value' there is a shootout reminiscent of the conventions of the film Western. The regular characters try to hold out in a barn until help arrives, fighting to defend a tanker of petrol against a group of itinerant thieves (like the Western genre's gang of outlaws). Again, these elements of action adventure exist in relation to other action adventure programmes such as television and film Westerns, and, less precisely, to the ITC action series in which gunplay and physical combat concretise the oppositional relationships between characters and groups of characters. Here again, relationships between texts and genres provide the means for audiences to interpret programmes by drawing on the codes of existing genres.

### *Blake's 7* and mixed genres

*Blake's 7*, marketed as an adventure series (see chapter 1), also displayed science fiction's epic and action adventure tendencies in its format, which involved collaboration between different personnel. In response to our questions about the series, the script editor Chris Boucher remembered that 'Terry Nation was a successful and long established professional and he never submitted anything less than good and complete scripts. Production constraints, however, meant that they were not always practical scripts since they were action and plot, rather than character, driven'. Nation's epic vision remains in the televised series, however, where the entirety of *Blake's 7* was structured around Blake, the heroic figure, involved in an unending journey on the Liberator from one point to another, not only fleeing from, but also attacking, the corrupt Earth Federation.

While the programme gradually became more character-driven, *Blake's 7* nevertheless featured conventional elements that clearly signify to its audience that its generic identity combined science fiction, epic and action adventure (and occasionally mystery as in 'Mission To Destiny'), regularly featuring spaceship battles and physical combat (in 'Duel', for example, see figure 2), and armed raids on enemy installations (for instance in 'Time Squad', 'Seek-Locate-Destroy', 'Project Avalon' and 'Pressure Point'). As early as the second episode 'Space Fall' there were even echoes of sea adventure where the oppressed prisoners aboard the spaceship London mount a mutiny against the officers guarding them, and are then sent to seize the super spacecraft Liberator in an act of piracy. This maritime motif recurs in a reversed form in the later first season episode 'Bounty', a story into which script editor Boucher and director Pennant Roberts had considerable input (see Stevens and Moore 2003: 50), in which a smuggler attempts to seize control of the Liberator from Blake and his crew.

Like Nation's *Doctor Who* and *Survivors* work, *Blake's 7* is read in relation to other texts, and indeed Nation had described its premise as '*The Dirty Dozen* in space' (see chapter 2). For example, in the *Radio Times* feature (Evans, 1977: 114–17) publicising *Blake's 7*, the producer David Maloney stressed its connections with, yet its dramatic superiority over, the film *Star Wars*, which happened to coincide with *Blake's 7*'s first transmitted episodes in 1978. *Star Wars* had already opened in the United States to huge popular acclaim, but had no connection with Nation's initial devising of the series. David Maloney is quoted in Evans' article (1977: 114): 'We've been in production in one way or another for about nine months. We were aware of *Star Wars* of course, and knew it had hit the jackpot, but we never saw its success as being anything but a good omen.' Maloney differentiates *Blake's 7* from the American film: '*Star Wars* is wide-screen, stereophonic sound, massive-budget stuff … we've got something *Star Wars* doesn't have – time to develop our plots, characters and action. They've got two hours, we've got 12.' (Evans 1977: 114–16). Additionally, in his comments to us, script editor Chris Boucher differentiated the requirements of television from film in relation to his view that Nation's scripts were not always practical because they were action- rather than character-driven: 'If you're making an action movie – *Star Wars* comes to mind – that's an acceptable approach'. Boucher's comparison of Nation's original scripts with *Star Wars* is interesting since George Lucas's film was an epic lasting over two hours and was planned as one episode in a longer mythic narrative. The film drew on the epic's conventions of establishing the hero before taking him on a long and perilous journey involving numerous set-piece action sequences, and centred on a hero who represented the ideologies of the society in which the film was made. While *Blake's 7* and *Star Wars* need to be differentiated according to the demands and production constraints of their respective media, their generic components were recognised by the production team and by their audiences as having a lot in common.

### Narrative form: the episodic serial, the suspended enigma and the advertisement

Form also imposed boundaries upon Nation's and other production personnel's contributions to these science fiction dramas yet simultaneously opened up avenues. Nation's contributions were designed to engage the television viewer as entertainment, and form played a vital role in this. The endings of episodes in episodic serials pose questions about what will happen next and are described by Tulloch and Alvarado (1983: xi) as 'suspended enigmas'. They often take the form of 'cliff-hangers' where a character is in immediate danger. Serial form in *Doctor Who* was an important constraint on Nation's writing and on other production personnel since episodes were required to end with a suspended enigma or cliffhanger (or both), which opened up a question whose answer was promised in the next episode. This set boundaries around authorship, but also created possibilities. The breaks between episodes of a *Doctor Who* story were clearly marked by the end titles of the programme and usually a gap of a week between transmissions, but each episode would flow on from the preceding one. The following episode of *Doctor Who* would begin with a brief reprise of the enigma from the end of the previous instalment, indicating that the narrative would recommence from that point. Nation's work, like that of other screenwriters, directors and production staff was accommodated to the episodic serial form devised by the production team, and his authorship cannot be considered apart from this context. Both series and serials involve audience loyalty being developed for the programmes, and the ends of episodes were an important way of building such devotion in *Doctor Who*. The suspended enigmas or dramatic moments concluding episodes not only force a break upon the viewer but also are designed to raise the viewer's curiosity so that he or she will return to the programme the following week. The break delays resolution of the narrative, controlling its pace, and enigmas are proposed, developed, resolved or deferred within episodes and also between them. The viewer assumes what Robert C. Allen (1992b) calls a 'wandering viewpoint', not knowing what lies around the next corner.

The *Doctor Who* production team's use of the serial's suspended enigma is nowhere better evident than at the end of the first episode of 'The Daleks', 'The Dead Planet'. The episode ends with Barbara, one of the Doctor's fellow travellers, forced up against a wall facing the camera, screaming in horror at something (which will turn out to be a Dalek) occupying the camera's position (see figure 3). Nation's script read: 'Barbara hears the sound behind her and turns in time to see the thing that is advancing on her. Only its arms are seen by the audience as they pin Barbara's arms to her side and she starts to scream' (quoted in Pixley 2003: 35).

Christopher Barry's directorial choices realised this aspect of the storyline very effectively. Only a suction cup is visible in the lower portion of the frame to indicate the identity of what Barbara sees. The camera (and thus the position of the viewer) takes the place of the unseen object, since the suction cup appears to be attached to the camera itself. This sets up a striking split identification between the threat (aligned with the camera and the viewer's position) and Barbara herself (a familiar character the viewer is also invited to identify with). The suction cup is a synecdoche (a part of a whole) representing the threatening object, thus both testifying to its presence but also deferring the viewer's realisation of what it might be. The fact that the suction cup is a synecdoche is interesting since each episode of a *Doctor Who* serial is also an incomplete part of a whole. Here the synecdoche of the suction cup works in tandem with the serial form, for the revelation of the whole of the threatening object is implicitly promised in the next episode, an episode that will itself contribute to the building of the whole story. As director Christopher Barry comments: 'Good thriller directors suggest terror ... rather than explicitly showing it' with the 'precept of allowing the audience's imagination to do the work by only showing one "arm" coming out' (quoted in Cook 2002: 10). While the object menacing Barbara could not be seen immediately when the second episode began, the revelation of its identity and the widening-out of the serial's fictional world was communicated by a wide shot of the Doctor, Susan and Ian surrounded by Daleks. The success of this ending in delaying revelation was attested to by the fact that, 'According to Terry Nation, after "The Dead Planet" went out, he was deluged with phone calls from friends and colleagues, all wanting to know "What was it?" Just what was the object of Barbara's terror that viewers had only seen so far as a suction cup visible through a circular lens cowl?' (Bentham 1986: 48). The suspended enigma, therefore, suspends narrative flow and the audience's experience of involvement. Nation was unhappy with the first Dalek film, based on 'The Daleks' storyline, and commented that the television version 'was good storytelling' where 'there was that nice feeling of coming up to a climax, and leaving a cliffhanger every week' (quoted in Nazzaro 1989: 20).

The endings in the first episodes of many of Nation's subsequent stories for *Doctor Who* differ from that in 'The Dead Planet' and play on the popularity of the evil Daleks in order to draw the television viewer back to the programme the following week, showing how Nation's authorship was governed not only by form but also by other forces. In Nation's stories of the 1970s (and even stories of the 1980s not written by Nation), the Daleks' presence was advertised in their titles: 'Planet Of The Daleks', 'Death To The Daleks', 'Genesis Of The Daleks' or 'Destiny Of The Daleks'. Therefore, unlike in the case of 'The Dead Planet', the viewer has foreknowledge of the monsters around which the stories will revolve. As a result, it comes as no surprise when the first episodes of these adventures conclude with the appearance of a Dalek or Daleks.

The deferral of the Daleks' appearance until the end of the first episodes kept the viewer in curiosity and anticipation as to when the dreaded creatures would appear (ceasing to be literally invisible at the end of the first part of 'Planet Of The Daleks', for instance). The break between episodes continued these emotions when viewers tuned in the following week to discover the Daleks' plan. For example, the first episode of 'Destiny Of The Daleks' was originally planned as a series of such moments leading to climactic revelation. This is indicated by producer Graham Williams's comments on the typed storyline (BBC WAC T65/79/1), where there is a question mark against the Doctor and Romana's discovery of a buried emaciated body shortly after their arrival, presumably because this is a loose end or red herring. Romana runs back in the dark to the trapped Doctor to get radiation drugs and hides briefly from her unseen pursuer in a ruined building where 'a green blob (a Dalek out of its casing) crawls onto her shoulder' leading Williams to write 'Too many threats!? (TO BUILD UP TO DALEK ENTRANCE)'. The episode was designed to lead towards the revelation of the Dalek, the high point at which the episode would end.

In chapter 2, we examined how television is a commercial industry whose programmes are advertised in similar ways to other products. The Daleks became a sign used to advertise *Doctor Who*, as revealed, for example, by their appearance on the cover of the BBC's listing magazine *Radio Times*, as well as by their inclusion in other popular programmes. These texts took on an author(ity) function that aimed to supervise and direct the programmes' meanings and the ways that audiences would engage with them. In *Doctor Who* stories themselves, the Daleks also become a sign to attract viewers, and to some extent it was the Daleks, rather than Nation, who 'wrote' the success of the adventures. The purpose of an advertisement is to draw people to a product, just as the purpose of an episode ending is to draw the audience to a product that will become available the following week: the next television episode. The episode ending is therefore not a definitive border marking the end, but rather a device that both separates and connects instalments. The cliffhanger in work credited to Nation began to take on a function not seen in many *Doctor Who* stories (except in the case of stories involving other 'regular' monsters like the Cybermen) where creatures within the cliffhanger blurred the boundaries of authorship and took on an authority function themselves.

We should briefly note that many other cliffhangers are used in more conventional ways by Nation. For instance, episode four of 'The Daleks', 'The Ambush', concludes with the Doctor's and his companions' horror when they realise they have no option but to return to the Dalek city to retrieve the Fluid Link needed to power the TARDIS, which has been accidentally left there. ECUs (Extreme Close Ups) are used by the director, Christopher Barry, to signify their emotions. In many cases there is extreme dissociation of plot time and viewer time, where the episode shows plot time running out for the protagonists, yet 'real' time slows down for the audience who must wait for the next instalment, and this combination creates suspense and anticipation. So, for example, characters are trapped while a bomb is ticking and there is a countdown to a bomb being launched, set in motion by the Daleks' scheming, at the ends of episodes three and five of 'The Dalek Invasion Of Earth': 'Day Of Reckoning' and 'The Waking Ally'. At the end of episode three of 'Planet Of The Daleks' the Doctor and his Thal allies attempt to escape the Daleks by rising up a ventilation shaft on a balloon made from a large plastic sheet. Indeed, Nation was later to write an entire *Blake's 7* episode 'Countdown' that revolved around attempts to defuse a bomb before it killed the entire population of a planet.

Nation's episode endings were sometimes changed by others for dramatic effect to accommodate them to the serial form, as in the case of 'Genesis Of The Daleks' (Pixley 1997a: 36). In the script the second episode ended with the Doctor and Harry escaping through an air-duct and encountering a huge monster, which was changed to Sarah Jane Smith falling from the scaffolding positioned by the Thal rocket in her attempt to escape. The third episode initially ended after the destruction of the Thal city rather than before it. The fourth episode had ended after, rather than before, the Doctor submitted to Davros because he was unable to bear his companion's torture. The fifth episode had ended with the Doctor worried about the morality of destroying the Daleks rather than with the Doctor leaving the creatures' incubation room with a Dalek mutant around his neck.

### Flexi-narrative combinations of series and serial and the advertising function

In television drama, episodic series that have new storylines each week as well as an ongoing storyline have been labelled 'flexi-narrative' by Robin Nelson (1997). As Jonathan Bignell (2002a: 158–9) remarks elsewhere, 'it is becoming increasingly common for television programmes to combine the single setting and new stories each episode which are components of series fiction with the ongoing development of characters and stories across episodes which are seen in serials'. Bignell writes that flexi-narrative mixes 'the perpetually new stories and challenges which occur each episode in television series' and the 'involvement in ongoing characters and stories associated with television soap opera' (2002a: 159). This notion of flexi-narrative shows how the medium of television differs from that of the novel and also the audiovisual medium of cinema, and John Ellis (1982: 99) asserts that normally, 'Television drama and fiction do not tend to use the self-contained narratives that are typical of entertainment cinema' except in series of films. Television programmes do not have the textual boundaries that are conventionally found in cinema films, and this is largely because of the institutional and economic structures of the television business, which we discuss further below.

In both *Survivors* and *Blake's 7*, flexi-narrative form aims to generate continued interest on the part of the audience so that viewers will return week after week to discover what will happen next, while also offering sufficiently self-contained stories in each episode for them to be understood as free-standing action adventure narratives. Furthermore, the flexi-narrative format is aesthetically important to these two series in establishing characters, atmosphere and developing strands of storyline that can extend across an entire season. For example, rather than *Survivors* beginning with a community already established in the aftermath of the plague, the audience sees dramatically how these scattered individuals cope gradually with being alone and searching out others. Their search is extended across separate episodes, so that the flexi-narrative form becomes a vehicle for epic breadth as well as for the representation of relatively self-contained storylines as their search takes them to different locations. The flexi-narrative form is dominant in the early episodes but continues as an ongoing serial element with Abby Grant's desire to find her son, who was away at boarding school when the plague struck. The storyline in which Tom Price, a member of the new community, unintentionally murders a young girl in an episode not written by Nation ('Law And Order') is referred back to in an episode Nation did write ('The Future Hour'). Flexi-narrative form opens up questions about what will occur in individual programmes and in the series as a whole, and also introduces possibilities for character development that will unfold across the series.

From its beginning, Nation's *Blake's 7* was an early example of flexi-narrative, and as its script editor Chris Boucher told us, Nation was responsible for the series' basic framework. The programme generally presents new stories and challenges in each episode, a characteristic of the episodic series form, but at the same time involves the television viewer with ongoing characters and running themes from week to week. This also contributes to the series' epic scope. Such a mixture of episodic series and serial is evident in the first four episodes ('The Way

Back', 'Space Fall', 'Cygnus Alpha' and 'Time Squad') and in the sixth instalment ('Seek-Locate-Destroy'), although there were changes to the ordering of episodes. While each episode has self-contained plots, the sequence establishes the regular characters: a group of people who escape from being taken to a penal colony, then become rebels aboard the spaceship Liberator, and who will be persistently pursued by their former captors. The end of each episode draws attention to the flexi-narrative form that enables the continuing mission, and therefore draws the viewer back to the programme each week. It is particularly important in the early episodes to arouse the viewer's interest, as well as introducing the continuing need to fight the oppressive Federation. Flexi-narrative form is also evident towards the end of the first season where the penultimate episode 'Deliverance' features a self-contained plot concerning a spaceship containing genetic banks of an ancient race, while introducing the story of the hunt for Orac, a sophisticated computer that the Federation wants, a storyline continued in the following final episode of that season, 'Orac'. It was this connectedness that enabled BBC Video to edit episodes together under the general headings 'The Beginning', 'Duel' and 'Orac' in the 1980s. In the second season of *Blake's 7*, Gan's death (in Nation's 'Pressure Point') and the resulting reactions to it (in Boucher's 'Trial'), linked episodes together, as did the hunt for the Federation Control Star One, which began in 'Pressure Point', was mentioned in Nation's 'Countdown', and ended in Boucher's 'Star One' with a war against aliens that was present in Nation's original outline for his aborted two-part season ending. In the third season, the forced departure from and need to return to the Liberator (in Nation's 'Aftermath' and 'Powerplay'), and the search for the supposed killer of Avon's lover (mentioned in the second season episode 'Countdown') were explored in linked episodes ('Children Of Auron' and 'Rumours Of Death', not by Nation). Indeed, as Stevens and Moore (2003: 108) point out, the original plan for the third season 'was to develop ongoing storylines' where 'Terry Nation was again given an option to ... decide the story threads for the year'.

> The first half of the season was initially planned to be taken up with the search for Blake (who would have gone missing during the intergalactic war) ... with the crew apparently finding his grave around the sixth episode. The other running storyline was to have been one revolving around a new character, the Captain ... who joined the crew after the war. His main interest would have been to turn in the Liberator for the sake of his own profit, and – following the usual Nation trope – he would have been revealed as a traitor in the end. (Stevens and Moore 2003: 108)

Co-ordination problems led to the ideas being shelved since the producer Maloney thought that the serial pattern was a trap (Stevens and Moore 2003: 108), and Paul Darrow felt that Avon would not wish to find Blake (Stevens and Moore 2003: 108–9). But the flexi-narrative form of *Blake's 7* also opened up possibilities and shares the functions of the cliffhangers concluding the first episodes of Nation's *Doctor Who* stories, for they are designed to bring viewers back to the programme the next week, and their effectiveness in retaining audiences was one reason for the success of the series.

### Storyline separation and parallel montage

Other forms are also important in engaging viewers. As is common in television fiction involving groups of characters whose experiences are represented separately, Nation's storylines often centre on characters whose initial unification as a group (as in *Doctor Who* and to an extent *Blake's 7*) gives way to separate strands of narrative as the characters become separated, or they begin separated (as in *Survivors*) and subsequently unite. 'Storyline separation' refers to the use of more than one strand of a story, with each strand occurring in a different location at the same point in plot time. Segments comprise brief sequences following developments with one character in one location, then cut to another character and location, and then back again. This establishes an alternation of 'meanwhiles' as the separate narrative strands are presented piecemeal one after another, and is known as 'parallel montage', since 'montage' means the piecing together of separate sections of cinema or television footage.

Nation adopted this technique, accommodating his writing to the type of 'thriller' programme that *Doctor Who* was designed to be. The question 'what will happen next?' is introduced within episodes by posing problems and challenges to characters and then cutting from one simultaneous storyline to another before that challenge or threat is resolved. In other words, an enigma is proposed but is suspended by storyline separation and parallel montage. The effect of this is to generate suspense, but it also further emphasises the characteristic narrative principle of deferred resolution that drives episodic serial form. Within episodes, as well as between them, the viewer of Nation's *Doctor Who* stories is perpetually suspended in a middle position between a proposed enigma and its likely solution. The viewer sees parts of sequences of events but not a whole (a version of synecdoche), and the viewing experience becomes one of anticipation, waiting and even anxiety. It is this experience, which can be both pleasurable and painful at the same time, that contributed to the success of Nation's work among the audience. In ordinary language, it is what viewers refer to as the feeling of 'being kept on the edge of one's seat', and in relation to *Doctor Who* especially, it is the reason that child viewers reputedly hid behind their sofas. It is not the revelation of something frightening or shocking that causes this reaction, but precisely the waiting for the revelation to occur. Suspended enigmas stretched out across multiple parallel storylines can be confusing or annoying, but they are also powerful devices for maintaining suspense, anxiety and anticipation.

As Nation himself noted (see Wiggins 1997: 8), in many of his *Doctor Who* scripts a separation is engineered between the Doctor and his relatively passive female companion who runs into a dangerous situation where the companion's physical and emotional separation from the Doctor makes her seem more vulnerable. As early as the second story, 'The Daleks' Nation paved the way for this dramatic device that would become a staple part of the *Doctor Who* format, and by the time of his later 1970s stories it seemed natural to the programme. In 'The Daleks', the separation is engineered by the fact that the Doctor's granddaughter Susan must make her way from the Dalek city through the alien forest to pick up anti-radiation drugs left outside the TARDIS, since the atmosphere is filled with radiation as a result of the neutron war and her comrades are too ill to make the journey themselves. A sequence of events is set up in 'The Daleks' so that Susan must journey through the jungle on her own to collect the drugs, and suspense is created with the feeling that she is being stalked (see below). As a young woman, Susan is not the automatic choice to make this journey. However, both the Doctor and Barbara are suffering from radiation sickness, while Ian has been temporarily paralysed by a burst from a Dalek gun while attempting to escape. By incapacitating the more conventionally adventurous and courageous characters in a parallel storyline, the script allowed Susan's storyline to offer challenges to her character and place considerable responsibility on her to save her companions. Much later, in 'Planet Of The Daleks', the Doctor's injury from the end of the preceding story, 'Frontier In Space', has rendered him unconscious and leaves Jo Grant with only a tape recorder into which to narrate her situation as she leaves the sanctuary of the TARDIS to seek help, an idea initiated by the script editor Dicks (Pixley 1993a: 26). In 'Genesis Of The Daleks', following a gas attack in a trench, the Doctor and Harry Sullivan are pulled inside a bunker by Kaled guards who miss the unconscious Sarah Jane Smith. When she regains consciousness she is left alone to traverse the hostile smoke-filled landscape, followed by mysterious pursuers (see below). After the mysterious creature is seen following Sarah, there is a cut to the Doctor and Harry back in the Kaled fortress being interrogated by the Kaled Nyder. The first three episodes are structured by two parallel and simultaneous storylines where the Doctor and Harry are separated from Sarah and so a digressive narrative deferral is created, which is only resolved when the trio are reunited at the end of the third episode in the Thal rocket area. Indeed through the use of storyline separation and parallel montage there is suspense not only about what befalls the Doctor's companion but also about what happens to the Doctor himself. In the first and second episodes of 'Planet Of The Daleks' there are cuts back and forth between Jo being stalked and the Doctor's predicament, leaving the viewer in anticipation as to what has befallen both sets of characters. In the first episode of 'Genesis Of The Daleks', the Doctor and Harry, who have escaped from the Kaled fortress back into the wasteland, are surrounded by Kaled troops with guns poised. At this crucial moment, there is a cut to Sarah being pursued by a mysterious creature, and the Doctor and Harry's storyline is temporarily suspended as another strand of the narrative is picked up.

Not only do these storylines continue until a dramatic turning point is reached and then the cuts defer resolution, but also they allow for ellipsis. Ellipsis is the omission of story-time, where dramatically dispensable incidents are left out, and clearly the use of parallel montage allows this to happen to an extreme extent. It becomes possible, using multiple parallel storylines and montage cuts, to compose an episode almost entirely out of dramatic turning points, using ellipsis to omit every other incident. To do this would threaten the narrative pace and mood of an episode, however, because the whole episode would seem to consist of enigmas, threats, dramatic turning points and physical action, rather like Nation's opening gambits to *MacGyver*, which are unrelated to the rest of the episode. The effect for the audience would be of a roller-coaster of action sequences or melodramatic scenes one after another. This is avoided in these stories through thematic comparisons and contrasts between incidents. For example, in 'Planet Of The Daleks' there are similarities between the scenes where Jo is stalked by a Spiradon, a native of the planet on which the story is set, and the Doctor and the Thals being pursued. In the second episode, a bush moves as the invisible Spiradon approaches Jo, and bushes move when the Spiradons are pursuing the Doctor and his group. An invisible Spiradon attacks Codal with a visible log, just as earlier, objects were seen moving in the spacecraft, carried by an invisible character. A mirroring effect is created where one scene parallels another. This visual identification between the two scenes carries over the interpretive frameworks proposed for one scene to the other, in this case that since the Doctor and the Thals are subsequently shown to be in danger, so Jo must be too. In the second episode of 'Genesis Of The Daleks' there is a scene in which Sarah is surrounded by Mutos, followed by a cut to Nyder bringing the Doctor and Harry as prisoners into an area of the bunker. Confinement and imprisonment thematically link the two storylines. Towards the end of the episode there are cuts between the Doctor and Harry making their way through the ventilation shaft into the perilous cave that contains Davros's mutations, and Sarah leading an escape attempt from the Thal dome. In this example, the Doctor and Harry are penetrating a space that contains a threat, while Sarah and her companions attempt to penetrate the dome in order to escape from the threats it contains.

These examples of parallel montage interweave characters from different scenes, but cutting back and forth between characters in the same physical space can have a similar effect. For instance, in 'The Daleks', where the protagonists are trapped in the Dalek city, there are cuts between Daleks attempting to break through a door and the Doctor's fellow traveller Ian Chesterton trying to escape from the room, and in a very similar scene from 'Planet Of The Daleks' there are cuts between Daleks cutting through the door of a refrigeration unit and the Doctor and the Thals trying to flee from it by ascending a shaft by balloon. This technique, like the others we have discussed above, aims to keep the television viewers watching by drawing their interest from shot to shot.

Nation also used storyline separation and parallel montage in his own series *Survivors* and *Blake's 7*. In the case of *Survivors'* opening episodes this enables flexi-narrative form to tell the stories of the two heroines, Abby and Jenny, in an extended series of parallel scenes before a more linear succession of scenes takes over as the main characters cohere into a group. In *Blake's 7*, storyline separation and parallel montage create thriller elements. Episodes sometimes involve a succession of scenes that build separate storylines centring on separated members of the central character group. For example, in 'Time Squad' two stories are told, both of which were in Nation's initial script: Blake, with Avon and Vila, engages in an attack on the Federation transceiver complex on the surface of the planet Saurian Major (the main plot), while on board the Liberator, Jenna and Gan are attacked by aliens who were taken on to the ship in a state of cryogenic suspension and who have awoken. In 'Deliverance' Avon, Jenna and Gan teleport to the planet Cephlon's surface to attempt a rescue of the crew who have escaped in life-pods after their ship was destroyed. One of the crew, the young Ensor, is teleported up to the Liberator where he takes Cally hostage and demands of Blake that he take the ship to save Ensor Senior, while on the planet's surface Avon encounters the beautiful Meegat and launches a ship containing genetic banks of the race that once existed on Cephlon to a suitable planet (in Nation's original draft script it was Blake and not Avon who went down to the planet (Stevens and Moore 2003: 54)). Very frequently, linear narrative and parallel montage are combined, creating dramatic structures emphasising repeated patterns of character separation and reunification.

### Aliens, stalkers and friends

The stalking of the Doctor's companion through the strange landscapes, by a mysterious creature either who ultimately befriends her itself or whose race becomes an ally against the story's primary threat, is a common motif in many of Nation's *Doctor Who* stories from his very first contribution 'The Daleks' to 'Planet Of The Daleks', 'Genesis Of The Daleks' and 'Destiny Of The Daleks'. This motif works with the episodic serial form and storyline separation discussed above, not only as a temporary threat enabling an internal enigma ('what is the creature?', 'how will the companion escape?') but also once the creature's identity as an ally is revealed, it permits the creature to become a vehicle for exposition. This idea of the creature as stalker is a structural point that has been made by *Doctor Who* fans Nicholas Briggs (1993: 50) and Philip MacDonald (1998: 28) in articles for *Doctor Who Magazine*.

Examples of this motif appear in 'The Daleks' where, in the petrified jungle in which the travellers have arrived, a mysterious creature touches Susan on the shoulder in the first episode. When Susan is sent back to the TARDIS in the second episode for anti-radiation drugs left outside, a figure follows her who turns out to be friendly, having earlier left the drugs for the travellers. In the first episode of 'The Keys Of Marinus', Susan is stalked by the vicious Voord. In 'Planet Of The Daleks', Jo Grant, who has left the sanctuary of the TARDIS to get help for the Doctor, is at first stalked by a native of the planet, the invisible Spiradon, Wester, who ultimately befriends her. In 'Genesis Of The Daleks', while Mutos menacingly pursue the wandering Sarah in the wasteland in the first episode, in the second episode, one of them, Sevrin, is revealed to be friendly, stopping one of his fellows from killing Sarah with a knife. Later, when Sarah tries to escape to the surface from capture in the Thal dome and falls from the rocket scaffolding, he moves back down to help her. The motif of the female companion being stalked appears in 'Death To The Daleks' where the stalker is not an ally, and much later in 'Destiny Of The Daleks' where a gaunt man advances on Romana and is later revealed to be Starship Engineer Tyssan from Earth brought in as a prisoner of the Daleks.

In 'The Daleks', 'Planet Of The Daleks' and 'Genesis Of The Daleks', dialogue anchors the notion of the creature as hostile and therefore the peril in which the Doctor's companion is placed. In 'The Daleks' and 'Genesis Of The Daleks' those creatures living in the open air are described as mutations. In 'Planet Of The Daleks' the Thals tell Jo that she is lucky a mysterious 'they' did not find her, that she will be safer inside the spacecraft, and that the Thals will lead the mysterious 'they' away from the craft. In the second episode, the Thals, who have rescued the Doctor from the TARDIS, reveal that the invisible Spiradons have been subjugated by the Daleks, which is reinforced by the fact that the Thal Codal is attacked and is next seen in a Dalek prison cell. It is after this scene that the viewer sees Jo lying down, and the fungus that has infected her being treated by the Spiradon Wester who assures her that he means no harm. The sense of menace followed by reassurance is extended across the first two episodes using the episodic serial format, and aims to keep viewers engaged in the drama.

### Aliens, stalkers and friends: the director's and composer's contribution

Directors, and sound and music composers, contribute to this repeated structural motif. In the latter part of 'The Daleks' second episode 'The Survivors', for instance, when Susan is traversing the forest in order to collect the anti-radiation drugs from the TARDIS, she is fleeing from an unseen potential terror. Nation's script specified that Susan was observed by 'an undefined shadow ... behind a bush' and continued: 'We see a pair of feet move into shot. They are swathed in furs, and are made to look as unattractive and non-human as possible' (quoted in Pixley 2003: 36). The director Christopher Barry shows Susan passing a cloaked figure. Susan moves through the forest with the camera sharing her point of view. The scene occurs at night, so the terrors that the forest may contain cannot be seen, and the stormy weather denoted by sound and lightning flashes adds to the scene's unsettling tone. The episode ends with Susan facing the opened TARDIS doors as lightning bursts.

In 'Planet Of The Daleks' this stalking motif is again realised through *mise en scène*. The invisibility of the Spiradons (a device also seen in 'The Daleks' Master Plan' with its invisible Visians, see Pixley 1993a: 26) adds to the initial assumption that Wester must be a threat, drawing on the convention that what is not seen, or only partially seen on camera, is more likely to be potentially terrifying than what can be seen by the characters and identified by the audience. When Jo is alone in the spacecraft, the main door opens from the inside, objects move by themselves, and the handle of the door behind which Jo is hiding can be seen moving. The camera repeatedly cuts back to Jo, offering an identification with her and with her fear. Since the Spiradon Wester cannot be presented visually because he is invisible, the sound of deep animalistic panting signifies his presence.

This common device in Nation's storylines is realised in the opening episodes of 'Genesis Of The Daleks' through director David Maloney's use of camera angles. The selection of shots made by the director conveys the subjective experience of menace that the viewer is encouraged to share with the fleeing Sarah, and withholds the identity of the pursuers from the viewer, to parallel the viewer's lack of knowledge about the creatures with Sarah's lack of knowledge. The camera both conceals and reveals. Pixley (1997a: 37) explains that Nation had commented on the desire of the Mutos to 'conceal their awful deformity with wrappings of any kind' and Nation's remark was picked up on by Maloney to create a threatening atmosphere. For instance, a shot shows only the feet of the creature moving forward, and there is then a cut to a shot from behind several creatures, covered in rags, as they move forward. Both shots suggest menace through partial revelation. Furthermore, the creature's stout legs are covered in rags and connote the repulsiveness of the body beneath (following a convention from Hollywood's horror films centred on Egyptian mummies). The scene near the start of the second episode when Sarah is being menaced by the Mutos is also important. Following a shot of Sarah's back, there is a shot of a hand moving from the left into an empty frame. Then a pan from left to right stops on Sarah looking around with fear, surrounded by Mutos. A pan is a connecting device, which in this case enables the viewer to see the hand in close proximity to Sarah. These interpretations will later be reversed, once the creatures' humanoid faces are revealed, and once the Muto Sevrin's friendly intentions are explained in dialogue.

Furthermore, eye-level shots, high-angle shots and low-angle shots often carry specific connotations. While an eye-level shot positions the television viewer as the equal of characters, and can invite involvement in a dramatic scene and especially in a dialogue between characters, a high-angle shot looking down at the character can connote the powerlessness of that character, and a low-angle shot can invite identification with a less powerful character dominated by characters looming above. 'Genesis Of The Daleks' mixes high- and low-angle shots to establish the powerlessness of characters being stalked. Such a mixture is at first apparent when high-angle shots are presented of the Doctor, Sarah and Harry proceeding to the minefield, with the suggestion that they are being watched communicated in dialogue. A low-angle shot of the cliff-face including a ragged creature atop it connotes the dominant vision and possible threat posed to them by the creature. Towards the end of the first episode a high-angle shot shows Sarah running from the creature, but the most notable use of this is when a high-angle shot of Sarah from the top of the cliff shows her running through the quarry. The mysterious creature is in the foreground of the frame at the viewer's eye level, while Sarah is in the background beneath the viewer's eye level. As a result, the camera and the audience share the creature's point of view and its dominance over her. Furthermore, a high-angle shot (though not from the top of the cliff) shows Sarah falling, and both Sarah's fall and the high-angle shot connote her vulnerability. The physical possibilities of the location, a quarry with a cliff top, are effectively used by the director to realise the emotional dynamics between stalker and stalked implied by the script.

Another important facet of shot composition is distance. The distance between characters can be employed to signify the quality of their relationship and to generate dramatic tension between them. Shot composition is inseparable from the issue of point of view. The high-angle shot of Sarah running through the quarry with the creature at the top of the cliff in the foreground is a visual mechanism for representing the narrative structural device at this point in the story, which establishes the creature as large, menacing and close, while Sarah is far below, small and vulnerable. The camera's distance from characters in the frame is itself a device connected to the contrasts between the two characters that are put in place by the narrative. Furthermore, the creature's legs are fully in focus while Sarah is not. This shot is followed by one showing Sarah falling, so that across the sequence as a whole, directorial choices follow a consistent pattern. The binary oppositions between not human/human, powerful/vulnerable, pursuer/pursued and (potentially, since the creature's gender is yet unspecified) masculine/feminine are enforced consistently by camera angle and shot size.

The tone and meaning of television sequences can be further enhanced by the use of sound and music. Not only is image used to create a sense of menace but so is the sound, created for this *Doctor Who* story by Dudley Simpson. In television drama as in other audiovisual media, sound and music play an important role in setting the mood of the narrative. During the first scene of Sarah walking, a breeze can be heard and the sound of Sarah moving over rocks. When the brief shot of the creature following Sarah appears at the very end of that scene, deep notes of incidental music can be heard on the soundtrack. The incidental music score intensifies the suspense around Sarah's predicament, and marks the culmination of this storyline at a dramatic moment just before a cut to a simultaneous scene involving the Doctor and Harry back in the Kaled room. The music accompanying the end of the scene with Sarah therefore functions to establish definitively a threat that is signified but which will not be followed up in a linear progression through that storyline, but must wait until a parallel storyline has been updated. The music, then, underlines a mood and an emotion but also marks a deferral, a minor suspended enigma, which the audience must wait to be resolved. The following scene involving Sarah begins with a rear shot of her with a breeze and the sound of her footsteps. However, when she starts to run, after looking behind her, incidental music dominates the scene. The incidental music is of deep haunting notes, repeated, matching the steady pacing of the creature as it follows her. The incidental music's mood and tonal structure match the mood and structure established in the preceding shot of Sarah, and have the effect of both binding the scenes with Sarah together as a unified storyline, and also distinguishing these scenes from the parallel storylines whose scenes are interposed into it. The interposed scenes from the storyline involving the Doctor and Harry have distinctively different music, or no music at all. Incidental music is not of course the creative product or responsibility of Terry Nation, but Dudley Simpson relied on the script's detailed scene breakdowns and dialogue in order to interpret the narrative pace and emotions suggested in it. As a matter of principle, then, no single element of a shot or sequence carries an intrinsic meaning, but attains its meaning by its interaction with the other elements of the programme in the context of a broader interpretation. Shot composition works in tandem with lighting (the shots of Sarah being pursued are very bleakly lit) and music. The tone and meaning of a shot or sequence can never be designed by mechanically following a set of rules, and depend on all the elements that contribute to *mise en scène*: shot composition, props and objects in frame, the lighting, sound and music.

## Form and characters: 'cult' Nation and the advertising function

Nation's authorship of character worked in tandem with form in other ways, for because *Doctor Who* was a long-running series of serials and *Blake's 7* was a flexi-narrative, they comprised both self-contained adventures and also recurring characters. This opened up possibilities for authorship. It meant that the antagonists (the 'villains') which Nation had created could reappear in numerous serials or episodes, just as the regular protagonists (the 'heroes') would. Each episode partly grows out of the previous one, and the programme and characters are intended to 'grow on' the television audience.

Nation is known for creating popular monsters and villains such as the Daleks and, much later on, Davros for *Doctor Who*. In *Doctor Who*, the Daleks had become cult figures whose return was demanded by television viewers, and the possibility of bringing the Daleks back in following serials was enabled by the programme's form. Nation structured the format of *Blake's 7* as one involving a continuing conflict between heroes and villains, and gave the faceless fascist Federation of the first four episodes personifications whose faces the audience could recognise from the episode 'Seek-Locate-Destroy' onwards, in the form of Supreme Commander Servalan (Jacqueline Pearce) and Space Commander Travis (Stephen Greif, later played by Brian Croucher). Like the Daleks these characters, especially Servalan, became cult figures among fans. The continual appearances of Servalan and Travis meant that they gained a familiar place in the public's consciousness, while Servalan was originally intended as a male character Shervalan (Stevens and Moore 2003: 18) only to appear in 'Seek-Locate-Destroy'. By contrast, the negative figure of Arthur Wormley in *Survivors*, for instance, only appeared in the first season's second episode 'Genesis', although he appears in Nation's novel *Survivors* and leads the paramilitary group in John Eyers' book *Genesis Of A Hero*. The kind of authorship required by the continuing forms of generic science fiction television produced cult figures. *Blake's 7*'s Servalan became more of a cult figure than Travis because in conjunction with Blake's departure a decision was made to write Travis out (Stevens and Moore 2003: 102). So Servalan, who had shared many scenes with Travis, was made Avon's main antagonist for seasons three and four (Stevens and Moore 2003: 109, 113). Servalan was unusual at the time in being a female character occupying the role of a melodramatically villainous woman, and this made her stick in the public consciousness to an unusual degree (see chapter 4) whereas the original intention to make Shervalan male may not have done. It was more customary to cast male actors in such roles, and a decision had been made that the character of a vicious IMC officer in the 1971 *Doctor Who* story 'Colony In Space', for example, would not be a woman (to be played by Susan Jameson) because, as producer Barry Letts reported, the Head of Serials thought that 'the public might find the notion of a female killer in a black, jack-booted uniform rather "kinky"' (quoted in Tulloch and Alvarado 1983: 209). The forms of the series of episodic serials in *Doctor Who* and the continuing flexi-narrative serial in *Blake's 7* privileged the roles of these continuing antagonists, and their presence was a significant factor in advertising the attractions of the programmes to audiences, and retaining these audiences from week to week.

## Breaks between television seasons: the cliffhanger and the advertisement

We have thus far examined the structure of individual stories and the linkage of episodes within series. Yet Nation's authorship, like that of other screenwriters, was also affected by the formal organisation of television programmes in seasons or 'runs' where connections between seasons created continued interest. This both imposed boundaries on Nation yet simultaneously widened writing parameters. These institutional arrangements further erode the notion that Nation's authorship was self-contained, and show that the forces blurring the boundaries of his authorship extended to the yearly patterns of television broadcasting. Television series were commonly divided into seasons that would run for a particular part of the calendar year, roughly matching the autumn, winter, spring or summer seasons, and it was very common for a programme's season to end on a cliffhanger in order to invite the audience to watch the following year's season. Cliffhanger season endings were not especially significant to *Doctor Who* or the first season of *Survivors*. But part of the continued viewer interest in *Blake's 7* and therefore part of its success derived from Nation's decision to use a cliffhanger at the end of the first season, leaving the viewer in suspense.

*Blake's 7*'s first three seasons began in January and lasted until late March or early April (2 January–27 March 1978, 9 January–3 April 1979, 7 January–31 March 1980) and the final fourth season was broadcast in the autumn of 1981 and ran from 28 September–21 December 1981. There was a considerable interval between seasons. As Chris Boucher told us, it was both Nation's idea to end the first season on a cliffhanger, and Nation who scripted the ending. This cliffhanger at the end of 'Orac' is of particular interest because it manipulates the relationship between plot time and the viewer's experience of time. We saw this operating in the episodic serial cliffhangers of *Doctor Who*, where the television viewer experiences both a suspenseful pause to the narrative but in many cases determined to watch the resolution the following week. The first season of *Blake's 7* ends with the newly acquired computer Orac predicting the destruction of the protagonists' ship the Liberator, and therefore the ending not only breaks a storyline but the very nature of prediction concerns something that will happen in the future. Stevens and Moore (2003: 69) write that this is 'a reworking of a familiar theme in ... mythology from Achilles through to Macbeth' but do not examine how the prediction functions aesthetically. Not only are the Liberator's crew left with a sense of desperation about what will occur, but the audience is also left in anticipation of something that is yet to happen in the next year's first episode, and this is the very purpose of the television cliffhanger. Prediction, even of the negative type, dictates that there will be a future of some kind both for the characters and for the television audience, and therefore the perpetuation of *Blake's 7* is assured. In some cases, programmes have ended on a season cliffhanger and for production reasons the series has been cancelled (for example, *The Tripods* season two), but such endings are never satisfying. The ending of the fourth and final season of *Blake's 7*, in which Avon raises his gun to fire at Federation guards, followed by the sound of a series of gunshots over the closing credits, seemed to declare that all of the series' protagonists were killed. But since Avon's death was not actually represented, this left the audience wondering what had transpired and gave rise to persistent requests for more *Blake's 7* adventures (see the conclusion to this book). The second season of *Blake's 7* also ended on a cliffhanger, though of a different type, but again aimed to persuade viewers to watch in the following year. It was originally planned as a two-part ending by Nation in which Jenna and Vila would be killed off, since Nation wished to convey threat by killing off regular characters (eventually Gan would be killed much earlier in the season) and it was rumoured that Nation wished to incorporate the Daleks (Stevens and Moore 2003: 64, 100). The eventual cliffhanger by Boucher, based on Nation's original outline for a two-part finale which was aborted in November 1978 (Stevens and Moore 2003: 100), was of the Liberator crew fending off an alien invasion. Nation's ending to the third season, planned to be the last, saw the Liberator destroyed and the crew stranded on the planet Terminal. The cliffhangers closing the first three seasons again took the place of the teasing revelations of narrative information that we paralleled with advertisements in our discussion of the endings of the first episodes in Nation's *Doctor Who* stories. Each has a similar purpose in engaging the audience's desire for succeeding episodes and the solving of narrative enigmas, and they partly explain the success of *Blake's 7*.

## Genre, form and Nation: institutional factors and audience address

So far, this chapter has offered a detailed analytical reading of the way Nation's science fiction stories work dramatically. However, Nation's televised science fictions are examples of popular television that were made for a mass audience to enjoy, even though *Doctor Who* sometimes had the potential to be educational at the same time. Programmes credited to Nation mix science fiction with other genres, which attracted large audiences both to *Doctor Who* and other programmes he was involved with. The diverse kinds of appeal in *Doctor Who* enabled the programme not only to aim to unify its audience but also to offer different audience constituencies something of particular interest to them. Tulloch and Alvarado (1983: 15) describe this aim as 'the "democratic" one of a sectional pluralism', and it was planted into the format of *Doctor Who* right from the start. Sydney Newman, who first proposed the idea for the programme, remembered: 'The problem was, as I saw it, that it had to be a children's programme and still attract adults and teenagers ... I also felt that no serial/story should last longer than between four and six episodes (I didn't want to risk losing audiences for longer, should one story not appeal). Each episode had to end with a cliffhanger and repeat this at the start of the next episode' (quoted in Bentham 1986: 38–40). The concerns mentioned in this quotation reveal the uncertainty among BBC staff about the audience addressed by this programme, and its possible success or failure as serial drama in attracting and holding audiences. Nation worked in the public service context of British broadcasting, which aims to entertain but also to inform and educate. Television is a mass medium, and broadcasters are concerned to satisfy the desires of a large audience, for both economic, regulatory and ethical reasons, and so can be attracted to science fiction and other modes of popular fiction because of their popularity with audiences. Although the science fiction work credited to Nation deals with 'serious' issues and therefore addressed multiple audience constituencies (see chapter 4), it was the fact that it was written in the adventure genre that proved to be successful and therefore paved the way, for instance, for the rest of *Doctor Who*, while series such as Nation's *Survivors* and particularly *Blake's 7* were also popular for this reason.

Watching television is an everyday domestic experience, which is offered in terms of Western societies' ideologies of leisure and entertainment. As Graeme Burton (2000: 72) notes, television fiction especially, but also documentary and other factual genres, involve 'the pleasure of suspending one's relationship with everyday reality and slipping on the garments of another world and other experiences'. This is particularly true of television science fiction since it deals with other realities and other worlds. As Jonathan Bignell (2002a: 133) has noted elsewhere, 'In Britain, the average person spends more than twenty-one hours per week watching television, so watching TV is evidently a very significant activity for most people'. The detailed analysis of television, and perhaps especially its most popular and apparently trivial genres such as science fiction or soap opera, is an essential part of the study of the culture. The understanding of how audiences are addressed by television, and information about audiences' responses to it, have become important in studies of culture and society.

Genre television such as Nation's science fiction work, but also police or hospital drama, for example, is attractive to television executives because a popular generic programme has a brand identity, and thus genre assumes an author(ity) function in directing or supervising the meanings of individual programmes. In the same way as casting a known television personality or performer, the recognition and familiarity of the forms and conventions of the programmes provide both security and appeal. Generic television also provides a sense of control and ownership to the viewers, who have a stake in the programmes rather than simply being offered another new product to consume. As well as being constrained by repetition, genre allows for innovation within and between genres, and programmes gain large audiences by manipulating conventions in new ways. This can sometimes suit broadcasters' policies to supervise the viewer's cultural education towards 'better' taste and informed citizenship as proposed by British television's public service ideals, though television institutions also offer mixed programme schedules to satisfy perceived desires and capture audiences through entertainment. Even schedules are planned generically on the basis of assumptions about the nature of the television audience and the ways audiences watch, and, as we saw in chapter 2, *Doctor Who*'s place in the schedule, positioned on early Saturday evenings, a day devoted to light entertainment, was designed largely to capture children as its audience, as *Blake's 7* was by being screened on a weekday before 9.00 p.m.

The television forms Nation adopted drew audiences back each week, and the television producer Irene Shubik (who worked for both the BBC and the Granada ITV company, producing drama from the 1960s to the 1980s) argued later in the mid-1970s that the best way to gain an audience and keep it was to adopt the conventions of the popular drama serial. Shubik (1975: 179) notes that 'the majority of people favour the familiar and expected over the new and unusual'. Broadcasters were encouraged to reduce spending on one-off prestige drama and to stimulate the growth of serials. It was this environment that gave rise to many entertainment programmes which are still to be seen as repeated 'classics' in today's schedules, and also to the adventure and science fiction programmes Nation wrote.

There are also other institutional reasons for the different forms we have discussed. While in the early years of television production the lengths of programmes and their interrelationships with each other were subject to little overall planning, by the 1960s standard programme lengths such as 30 minutes and one hour had produced grids of time slots such as were already common in the United States. The length and schedule position of many of the action adventure series that Nation wrote for were influenced by the requirements of American, rather than simply British, scheduling. We mentioned in the biographical sketch that Nation had been a contributor to the writing and production of several ITC series for the British ITV network that were also sold abroad, notably to the United States. In the mid-1960s, Lew Grade, the managing director of the ITV company ATV, also ran ITC and aimed to make programmes that would be attractive to the US networks (Bakewell and Garnham 1970). ITC was taken over by ATV in 1958, and acquired Elstree Studios (formerly named British National Studios) in 1961 in order to make television series on film (Osgerby and Gough-Yates, 2001). Filmed television drama series were the predominant component of US prime-time schedules, and the desire to sell into this market affected the content, genre and form of ITC's British-made programmes. The US programmes that British broadcasters bought were made in either 25 minute or 50 minute episodes, so that they could be scheduled according to the US practice of advertising programme starting times on the half-hour or on the hour, allowing for 5 minutes of advertising per 30 minutes. Because British television was showing these American programmes, and making programmes on film designed for sale to the United States, the standard lengths of 25 minutes and 50 minutes became the standard lengths of British-made programmes too, which was also the case of BBC work (*Doctor Who, Survivors, Blake's 7*). The effect of this on the form of programmes Nation wrote for was that it forced him and others to write scripts that would precisely fit these standard timings.

While we have examined the fact that Nation's *Doctor Who* work generally fits into the serial form, the original reason for Nation to write his single-episode *Doctor Who* story, 'Mission To The Unknown', broadcast on 9 October 1965, was a combination of budgetary and scheduling factors. This was the only story where the star was not the Doctor himself. Instead, Edward de Souza played Marc Cory, a stranded member of Space Security who has discovered that the Daleks are using the Planet Kembel as their base to invade Earth. The stories 'Planet Of

Giants' and Nation's own 'The Dalek Invasion Of Earth' were taken out of the first season and scheduled for the second. This gave the production staff a break, but because Verity Lambert had cut 'Planet Of Giants' from four episodes to three to make it more dramatic the second season was one episode short. Lambert realised that it would be contractually difficult and certainly expensive to require the regular cast to perform for another additional episode, so she decided to use this one episode as a teaser for the imminent Nation story 'The Daleks' Master Plan', and Nation was commissioned to write 'Mission To The Unknown'. It was radical for the format of *Doctor Who* to be altered in this way in a programme that had not been running for long, and this was indicated by the label 'cutaway' used by production staff to denote the episode. The way in which this situation was approached shows the enormous popularity of the Daleks, and Nation's remark, 'I used the episode as the central theme for the next big one I was going to do. I wanted to give a little trailer for that' (quoted in Pixley 1998a: 23) illuminates the way in which the episode was used as an advertisement in much the same way as the endings to first episodes noted earlier.

In the early years of *Doctor Who*, stories generally comprised a greater number of episodes than towards the end of the series' history, in order to attract viewers and retain them, and to reduce the costs of sets and props by spreading them across more episodes. The trend for the first two seasons was for more six- and seven-part stories than for the four-, three-, and occasionally two-part stories made in the 1980s. Following the seven-part 'The Daleks', the subsequent Dalek stories in the first two seasons were normally at least six episodes, and thus Nation contributed a huge number of episodes to the programme using the serial form, which, combined with the attractions of the Daleks, drew large audiences. Although originally planned as a six-part story, 'The Daleks' Master Plan' ultimately comprised 12 episodes jointly written by Nation with Dennis Spooner. Its increased length was suggested by Huw Wheldon whose mother was a fan of the Daleks, and demonstrates their popularity. Its average viewing figures were over 9 million.

We have also mentioned that programmes are divided into seasons, which had an effect on the aesthetic form of Nation's work. At the level of the year as a whole, new programmes are traditionally introduced around September or January, when the holiday season has finished and family routines get back to normal as school time begins. In the summer, people watch less television because they are more likely to be outside, so the summer period contains more repeats and fewer programmes that broadcasters have invested significant money in or attach importance to. *Blake's 7* began in January, while *Survivors* started in April, and starting the series at these times gave them relatively prominent places in yearly television schedules while their placing in mid-evening programming gave them prominence in the broadcasting day.


## Conclusion

In this chapter we have focused on Nation's science fiction work, where he acted in some cases as the deviser of a format or as a continuing contributor. As we have pointed out earlier in this book, however, we do not argue here that Nation was the sole, or even in some cases the predominant, creative figure in this work. Nation as a 'craftsman' sometimes fitted in with already established formats and was sometimes able to create his own, and the concept of format is useful in showing which features of a programme are regarded as distinctive, differentiating it from another. Format is coded generically and both format and genre have an authoring function in directing the ways in which programmes are written and can be interpreted. Not only have we seen how television authorship is multiple, composed by different personnel, but the study of genre shows how an individual programme attains meaning though its relationships of similarity and difference with others. Part of the discussion of programmes associated with Nation involves their relationship to generic codes that derive from audience understanding of the science fiction genre (in television and elsewhere). We have also seen that while genre has an author(ity) function, the individual contributor can stretch genre boundaries.

We moved gradually during the chapter to more detailed work on the specific audiovisual form and narrative structure of some of the programmes Nation worked on with other production personnel, where programme forms predetermined and also opened up possibilities for authorship. We have focused mainly on structural issues, but have not only discussed plot structures but also moments of aural and visual significance. Working in the genres of science fiction and fantasy television meant that the visuality of many of Nation's ideas was significant to their meaning and their appeal to audiences. The showing of a Dalek is a crucial moment in the storyline of *Doctor Who*, as is the revelation of a supposed stalker, for instance. These issues connect with audience address and the ways that audiences were invited to respond cognitively and emotionally. In relation to this issue of audience we have also argued that form is often used in a way similar to the advertisement, where specific programme features promote the attractions of programmes and encourage further viewing.

1 The scientist and the deadly virus, from the *Survivors* title sequence

2 A space battle in *Blake's 7* 'Duel'

3 Barbara (Jacqueline Hill) menaced by a Dalek, *Doctor Who* 'The Daleks'

**4** Pixillated image of Blake, from *Blake's 7*'s title sequence

**5** Tom Price (Talfryn Thomas) by a Rolls-Royce, from *Survivors* 'Genesis'

**6** The map, from *Doctor Who* 'Genesis Of The Daleks'

**7** Community, from *Survivors* 'A Beginning'

**8** Looking up at the Thal Alydon, from *Doctor Who* 'The Daleks'

**9** Looking down on Wormley's mob, from *Survivors* 'Genesis'

10 Drugged citizens, from
*Blake's 7* 'The Way Back'

11 Blake (Gareth Thomas) in frame, from
*Blake's 7* 'The Way Back'

12 The graveyard, from *Blake's 7* 'Duel'

13 Sinofar (Isla Blair) against the statue, from
*Blake's 7* 'Duel'

14 Sinofar (Isla Blair) and Giroc (Patsy Smart),
from *Blake's 7* 'Duel'

15 Portrait of Servalan (Jacqueline Pearce),
from *Blake's 7* 'Traitor'

# Nation, space and politics                                    4

## Introduction

The 'Golden Age' of British television (roughly 1960–75) is regarded as
a period when drama writers incorporated political ideas into their
work, but we believe Nation did not have such lofty ambitions. Even
though there is evidence that Nation did sometimes consciously
incorporate political ideas into his writing, he was first and foremost a
'craftsman'. This chapter will concern political readings of programmes
that Nation is credited with writing, and will discuss how political
meanings can derive from the screenplays themselves and also from the
contributions made by other members of the production team. The
issue of whether these meanings were intentional is not significant to
our analysis, since our aim is to show how the programmes open up
avenues of interpretation once they have been completed and screened,
and have broken away from the control of their makers. While the
emphasis is on Nation's writing for television, the approach adopted in
this chapter can be undertaken in analysis of programmes by other
writers. Our interpretations may not correspond with those that the
original viewers may have made, since Nation's work was marketed to
its audiences as entertaining action adventure drama. Gary Gillatt
(1998), for example, mentions the impact of *Doctor Who* on children,
who played Daleks in the school playground. The science fiction programmes that Nation worked on were not offered to their audiences as
contributions to social or political discourse, but like every television
programme, they drew on some of the taken-for-granted assumptions
and understandings that derive from the ideologies of their time.

As we argued in the introduction, our interpretations challenge a
narrow definition of 'quality' because they address the possibilities of
interpretation rather than claiming that Nation's authorial intent can be
praised for his incorporation of political 'messages' in the programmes.

Furthermore, our work in this chapter illustrates how Television Studies discourses do not translate neatly into one another since the issues of authorial intent and positions for audience decoding do not necessarily cohere. Indeed, we argue that audiences are able to take over, to a degree, the power of authorship. We have already argued that in the case of the popular television with which Nation is associated, clear-cut boundaries around authorship are very difficult to establish because they are 'crafted' collaboratively, and this chapter also challenges the notion that the production team, like the author, can be assumed to be the sole author(ity) figures in relation to the meanings of television programmes. In this chapter, we examine the potential effect of political television drama upon audiences and show how science fiction can have a marked political dimension, focusing on recurring ideas and ideologies across programmes that Nation worked on.

## Conceptions of political television drama

The term 'political television drama' can be used in three different ways (see Bignell 1994). Its first meaning would be drama that deals thematically with ideas recognised as political by the audience. Here the audience's ideological framework is a precondition for recognising situations, themes, references and relationships between characters as foregrounded political signs. Political television drama like this represents a comprehensible world and makes it available for political debate in the text. This form is the one with which the television audience is most familiar, providing a recognisable and 'realistic' environment into which characters are placed. But character can be seen as a vehicle for exploring ideas, not for its own sake and not only for the sake of involving the audience in a story. The story is often the most important aspect of a popular television drama, but we shall see how the apparently conventional characters in science fiction television can represent a return to the original purposes of naturalistic form, which has a heritage of exploring the contradictions of social issues.

The second sense of political drama describes an active relationship between television drama and the audience, where political television drama would aim to produce political effects in the lives of the audience. In order for such a relationship to be constructed, the audience needs to be able to decode a programme's dramatic form, and relate its concerns to their own experience and ideas. It is here that levels of competence are important, since the audience needs to recognise the way in which a fictional story (set in the future, or on an alien planet, for example) treats political issues that connect with the present time and place. The aim of this kind of political television drama is to mobilise the audience, and to engage viewers in a narrative that reflects on their own ideological assumptions. In the programmes that Nation worked on or devised we shall see at work the two types of political drama that we have identified so far.

Political television drama, in a third sense, can also denote drama in which the medium of television itself is foregrounded. The audience would be engaged in a self-conscious process of questioning their own modes of understanding dramatic representation, and questioning their assumptions about what the television medium might be. A high level of competence is required for this kind of political drama, and works that undertake to explore it are often those most valued by academic theorists of television drama (see Caughie 2000), and least watched by mass audiences. As Irene Shubik (1975: 179), producer of the BBC's high-profile drama anthology series *Play For Today* wrote, 'it has always been the straightforward documentary-type subject which gets the highest audiences, while the more adventurous a play is "stylistically", the smaller its audience is likely to be'. 'One can certainly conclude (if one did not know it already)', continues Shubik, 'that the majority of people favour the familiar and expected over the new and unusual'. We do not think, as we show below, that the science fiction work credited to Nation as writer exhibits many examples of this third kind of politics, although the format of some of the action adventure series that he wrote for, and especially *The Avengers*, did offer opportunities for this kind of self-conscious television representation (see Miller 1997; O'Day 2001). As popular television drama produced within the constraints of the series and serial forms, the contexts of Nation's science fiction work militated against formal experimentation and self-consciousness of performance.

## Science fiction: political origins

Generically coded science fiction television formats and individual stories can be read politically. Science fiction has long been seen as containing political messages, where the genre need not only rely on 'hard' sciences (such as physics or mathematics) but can also be a 'soft' rendering of the genre using discourses of anthropology or sociology, which enable the discussion of social and political ideas. A brief reference to critical approaches to science fiction as a literary genre can illustrate this. In H. G. Wells's *The Time Machine*, Wells, looking back on the social changes wrought by the Industrial Revolution, and influenced by the evolutionary theories of Darwin and their trans- ference into theories of social evolution, had established science fiction as a literary form devoted to the exploration of cultural change. This set the terms in which much of the genre has developed. Science fiction's atmosphere of seriousness derived from Wells whose work was a justification underlying the launch by Hugo Gernsback in the United States of the popular science fiction magazine *Amazing Stories* in 1926. The connection between technology and modernity, and the high profile and social power of scientific discourse through the twentieth century, were added to adventure and entertainment to turn 'pulp' science fiction into a form that converted its marginal, cultish and juvenile reputation into a badge of elitism. The low cultural status and alienation of science fiction writers and readers was recast as a claim for unusual imagination, breadth of vision and cultural leadership.

Literary theorists provide useful definitions of science fiction, which can be carried over to the study of television science fiction. A signi- ficant characterisation of science fiction is by Robert Scholes (1975), who regards fiction in general as constituted by cognition and sublima- tion, and sees science fiction as a particular expression of what all fiction does. Cognition is an analytical approach to the understanding of experience, and sublimation is the adaptation of real psychological anxiety into organised and meaningful fictional forms. Darko Suvin (1979) argues that science fiction does not have to rely on hard science, but only on the logical and rational extrapolation of scientific ideas, though they may derive from, for example, anthropology, sociology or linguistics rather than physics. For Suvin, science fiction is in effect a thought experiment. It begins with a 'novum' or new idea, which may or may not be in itself rational and logical. Science fiction differentiates this novum from the empirical observable environment of the author and subjects it to cognitive investigation. The science fiction story, for Suvin, explores the consequences and ramifications of this novum in a concretely specified, logical and consistent manner. Media critics Tulloch and Alvarado (1983: 141) then define science fiction in relation to realism: 'its emphasis on cognition and the belief that the universe is a knowable and natural phenomenon distinguishes it from fantasy', since fantasy lacks rigorously logical experimentation. 'Soft' science fiction concerning culture is often apparent in television renderings of the genre for a mass unscientifically educated public, and is important not only in attracting audiences to programmes (see chapter 3) but also because television science fiction often centres on social and political issues. Therefore, the first two types of political television drama

described above are often evident, since television science fiction represents ideas that the audience can recognise as political, and embeds
them in a real-seeming world. There are different sub-genres of science
fiction such as utopian and dystopian science fiction in the formats and
stories that we examine below.

## Science fiction, naturalism and Romanticism

Television formats and storylines express science fiction ideas through
settings and characters. While marking a deviation from reality, the
science fiction novum has connections with the viewer's empirical
world that enable the viewer to engage with the ideas in political science
fiction television. Naturalism and realism are particularly ambiguous
terms in the analysis of television. But generally, realism refers to
television's representation of recognisable and often contemporary
experience (for which a more accurate term than realism would be
verisimilitude), such as in the format's and individual storylines' representation of places and characters the audience can believe in, or
apparently likely chains of events. This relies on the familiarity of the
forms and conventions, the codes that represent a reality, and this kind
of realism is crucial to the dramatic form of science fiction programmes. As Neale (2000) has shown in a discussion of cinematic
science fiction, this produces a preoccupation with exposition so that
audiences can be provided with ways of fitting what they see and hear
into the expectations that they bring to the material.

The dominant form of realism in television, 'classic realism',
roughly coincides with the epoch of modern industrial society. It can be
seen in the majority of television fiction programmes, in formats and
storylines, and also affects the representation of people in television
factual programmes. In realist television programmes, individuals'
characters determine their choices and actions, and human nature is
seen as a pattern of character differences. This structured pattern of
differences allows for the binary structures we shall explore later, and it
permits the viewer to share the points of view of a wide range of
characters. The comparisons and judgements about identifiable human
figures represented on television refer back to a notion of 'normality',
which is the terrain on which the viewer's relationships with characters
can occur. Classic realism represents a world of psychologically consistent individual subjects, and its viewers are imagined as the same
kind of rational and psychologically consistent individuals. Television
programmes offer identification with the images and characters they

show, and promise intelligibility and significance. The viewer's varied and ordered pattern of identifications makes narrative crucial to classic realism, for the different kinds of look, point of view, sound and speech in narrative are the forms through which this communication between text and audience is produced.

Television realism is often labelled reactionary because it distances the viewer from the contradictory and ambiguous dynamics of reality. Tulloch and Alvarado (1983: 8–9) argue that *Doctor Who* rather unfortunately stays within the parameters of classic realism and the dominant television mode of naturalism, although its occasional self-reflexiveness or self-conscious parody have the potential to disturb this classic realist framework. Departures from television realism are not significantly important in discussion of Nation's work, but science fiction television can draw the viewer's attention to his or her relationship with the medium in order to make him or her recognise the social relations that this relationship involves. The strangeness or unrealistic nature of science fiction television might draw the viewer's attention to the fact that he or she is watching a representation and not a reality. This strategy would aim to reveal the work that forms of television representation do, so that they can be recognised as not natural but cultural and constructed.

The concept of the Romantic individual also underpins the formats and storylines of television science fiction. Romanticism stresses the differences between individuals' perception and experience of empirical reality. In an empiricist conception of individual perception, the external world acts in the same way upon the receptive senses of any person. By contrast, the Romantic individual is not regarded as a machine for registering impressions, but as having a much more dialectical relationship with the external world. If the Romantic individual is necessarily different from those around him or her and sees the world differently, there is scope not only for free will but also for failure, spontaneity, irrationality and arbitrariness. The Romantic hero resists conventional boundaries of behaviour and pursues a vision of an alternative world, but it is possible for the Romantic hero to become the Romantic villain very easily. Since the Romantic hero resists conventional boundaries, this allows for the manipulation of the binaries that we shall discuss below.

**Types of science fiction in Nation's work: dystopian Nations**

The science fiction novum outlined by Suvin is present as an aspect of programmes' settings in television credited to Nation, in their formats and in individual stories. The novum often relies on principles of 'hard' science. Not only is there the novum of time travel in the overall format of *Doctor Who*, but also in works credited to Nation such as the *Doctor Who* stories 'The Daleks' and 'Genesis Of The Daleks' there is nuclear war and genetic engineering on the planet Skaro (and the use of science fiction as a launching point for political ideas in the latter will be discussed in more detail below). In *Survivors* an accident in a science facility leads to the spreading of a plague that wipes out most of the Earth's population and requires new forms of social organisation to be developed, and in *Blake's 7*, although not set on a post-nuclear Earth, technological devices and drugs are used to keep the population of a future Earth subordinate. These notions of 'hard' science, however, serve solely as a launching point because, as Tulloch and Alvarado (1983: 41) put it, *Doctor Who* combines the socio-cultural scientific speculation associated with its Wellsian time travel model, with an 'investigation of different cultures through space and time'. All three programmes fit in with Wells's use of 'soft' science fiction, and indeed with Scholes and Suvin's definitions of the cultural potentials of the genre. In each of these three programmes, the political organisation of societies is drawn to the audience's attention, so that the programmes can be assimilated into Bignell's (1994) first kind of political television drama.

These formats and storylines, coded as science fiction through settings and characters, are dystopian in that they aim to represent a negative extrapolation from the television viewer's world, and they present strong contrasts with a tradition of utopian science fiction. The word 'utopia' (from the word 'ou-topia' meaning a 'no place' and 'eu-topia' meaning 'a good place') was first used in the sixteenth century by Sir Thomas More (1965), but the utopian tradition in science fiction has its roots in nineteenth-century thought. Its nineteenth-century forms were based on the assumption of continual technological progress and the associated progress of forms of social organisation. This progress would lead towards a utopian society that would be unified and ideal. But as Fredric Jameson (1982) argued in an essay on utopian science fiction, this nineteenth-century utopianism grew out of a specific moment in the history of Western culture, and the futures it imagined were those that could be extrapolated from a particular nineteenth-century present that is now in the past.

Liberal definitions of the self and of humankind are key components of this kind of utopian thought and setting. Differences of gender, race, geographical location and individual aim are regarded as local variations in a human essence that is essentially universal. The function of utopian thinking is to offer fictional environments that can serve as critiques of present day social arrangements or as models for the development of human culture. Whereas utopia has this function of suggesting a better future, its opposite, dystopia, the term for accounts of a 'bad place', uses the same principle of extrapolation to highlight the opposite features, of material scarcity, fragmentation and division among social groups, and the imposition of an oppressive unified political structure. Stylistically, dystopias conventionally open upon a vision of a nightmare world, as opposed to there being an educational journey from the normal world to the utopian locus followed by a return to the everyday world. The fact that the programmes we discuss here represent dystopian societies of different kinds militates surprisingly against the utopian function of television entertainment itself. As Richard Dyer has argued (1977), entertainment responds to the longings for abundance, community and pleasure that are only partially fulfilled by capitalist organisation and which are offered in fictional forms by popular television drama that is itself enabled by the capitalist system. The dystopian worlds in some of the programmes Nation worked on can be seen as potential political critiques of the Western society in which they were made and watched.

Drawing on the emerging social sciences of the nineteenth century, utopian thinking not only assumed increasing technological progress that could deliver better societies, but also assumed a social evolution of humankind which would lead the human race to forms of social and political organisation that would match its technological achievements. In the series we discuss in this chapter, the reverse is true. Progress in technology and in political organisation leads instead to imperialism, racism and ecological disaster, such as the creation of the Daleks in *Doctor Who*, the devastating results of experiments with genetics and the sophisticated global network of international air travel in *Survivors*, and technical devices and the medical technologies of drugs in *Blake's 7*. But the forces that would counter these dystopias are simply their binary opposites, the essential human characteristics identified in nineteenth-century utopianism that were then reversed in science fiction scenarios representing dystopias. Therefore there are only two differentiating factors that support the narratives' valorisation of these liberal humanistic qualities against the dystopic forces that derive from the same ideology. The first of these is the embodiment of liberal virtues in characters presented as attractive to the audience and as conduits for identification. The second is the design of storylines such that positive outcomes derive from the exercise of these liberal values in the course of the action. Effectiveness in resolving the enigma of the story, and in maintaining audience identification with the central characters, is the mechanism for justifying the liberal ideologies naturalised in the programmes. The dystopic scenarios are binary opposites of the liberal Western culture from which the programmes derive, and whose values they ultimately uphold. Internally, these dystopian fictions are constructed around binary oppositions consisting of opposed pairs of ideas.

**Binary Nations**

Binary oppositions are central to the television formats and individual science fiction stories we examine in this chapter. Establishing the structures of television narrative by noting opposed pairs of ideas, themes, characters or settings is a methodology deriving from structuralist and post-structuralist approaches to fictional narrative. Drama commonly sets up conflicts, and the way in which ideology is communicated by such oppositions in television drama has been the focus of numerous studies. Claude Lévi-Strauss (1970, for example) first argued in anthropological studies of oral and written myth that these stories are structured by binary oppositions, and such an approach has been adopted in television studies (see Bignell 2002a). Such oppositions structure not only the television news, which, as Hartley (1982) shows, is commonly structured by the binary of us/them, but also television fictions. Looking at the 1970s police series *The Sweeney*, Phillip Drummond (1976: 22) points out that the series has a binary opposition between police and criminals. Later, John Fiske (1987: 132), for instance, examines the American drama series *Hart To Hart* using Lévi-Strauss's notion of oppositions, identifying the principal binaries of good/evil and hero/villain.

Using a similar methodology we reveal the consistent patterns in the narrative organisation of work either credited to Nation as writer or devised by him, in formats and storylines. However, we also ultimately draw attention to the decisive contributions to meaning made by other production team members, including producers, script editors, directors and designers. The main binary structures we discuss are those that Fiske (1983) applies to the 1979 *Doctor Who* story 'The Creature From The Pit'. Fiske divides his reading into a series of discourses. The first of these is a general 'Discourse of Morality' featuring the opposing poles of good and evil, under which come more specific discourses corresponding to them. The next is the 'Discourse of Politics' divided into binaries such as the ruler or state/the individual, totalitarianism/democracy, and slavery/freedom. Fiske also identifies a 'Discourse of Economics', which he divides into binaries like state monopoly/free trade, scarcity/plenty, and imbalance/balance. The next discourse in Fiske's tabulation is the 'Discourse of Individualism', which is structured according to binaries such as conformity/individuality and eccentricity. Additionally, we shall see that these structures lead to a further binary in work credited to Nation: pacifism/militarism.

## Nation's people

Realist characters communicate these binary oppositions in the dystopian worlds of the formats and storylines Nation worked on, though as we noted, script editors such as Boucher for *Blake's 7* played a significant role in fleshing out character and dialogue. Programmes like these need to establish conventions of representation that connect what they show with the cultural understandings their audiences bring to them, even though they are in the science fiction genre. The alien creatures of *Doctor Who*, the pandemic of *Survivors* or the alien spacecraft of *Blake's 7* can conflict with cultural understandings of what can be believed to be true, but must also connect with these understandings. In Nation's *Doctor Who* story 'The Dalek Invasion Of Earth', especially, recognisably real contemporary buildings and locations in London (such as Westminster Bridge) draw on television's heritage of representing the familiar in order to contrast this with the fictional Daleks and the uncanny threat that they represent to human norms of civilisation.

All three of these series connect closely with the dominant television form of naturalism, which draws on discourses of evolution and inheritance: the *Doctor Who* stories 'The Daleks' and 'Genesis Of The Daleks' concern the evolution of the races living on the planet Skaro; in *Survivors* the inherited genes of certain characters allow them to fight off the plague; in the *Blake's 7* episode 'The Way Back' the past ultimately influences present psychology. In all three series the binary oppositions noted above are communicated through characters with free will and choice, and even in an episode such as 'Duel' where otherworldly mythological goddesses are presented, the regular characters are motivated psychologically. Furthermore, there are narrative logic and cause–effect structures that distinguish this type of classic realism from the action drama and melodrama genres with which Nation was associated at ABC and ITC. Characters in the ITC programmes tend towards types whose clearly identified characteristics differentiate them from each other. Nation was instructed to use more complex characters in some of his BBC work, for example when *Survivors'* producer Terence Dudley wrote to Nation (BBC WAC RCONT21) expressing his concern that 'Garland ... has limitations and that he will counter audience identification'. Dudley argued, referring to Nation's writing for ITC's *The Saint*, that 'the "Roger Moore" cardboard is ideal for the hokum series with the stylish tongue in cheek approach' where 'Audiences for this sort of thing escape in fantasy and are voyeurs of the antics of superman' but that while 'There's room for Garland ... he must be used in the context of "ordinary" characters'.

Tulloch and Alvarado (1983: 46–7) have argued that the format of *Doctor Who* established the central characters of this series as Romantic rather than rational. Illogicality, spontaneity and willingness to take risks are powerful weapons against the authoritarian Daleks, and against the Federation in the format and episodes of *Blake's 7*. While the Daleks and the Federation are cold and rational, rejecting individual difference in favour of the efficiency and order of mechanisation in physical and political terms, the Doctor and his companions, or Blake and his, are Romantic as opposed to rational. Since the Romantic hero can easily become the villain, in *Doctor Who*, for instance, the Doctor can appear to be an egotistical scientist, and in *Blake's 7* the refusal to accept norms of behaviour or social constraints is an advantage that allows Blake to pursue his vision of a better world, but also makes him somewhat ruthless and uncompromising.

## Microcosmic, allegorical Nations

Science fiction formats and storylines present microcosmic models of complex wholes, in which dystopian settings represent entire worlds, and an idea is explored consistently in a real-seeming environment that is meticulously and extensively described, using binaries expressed by realist characters. Therefore, these science fiction microcosms are also allegorical (meaning 'speaking otherwise') in that they have meanings that pertain to our own world, and Bernadette Casey *et al.* (2002: 208) argue that science fiction 'tends to deal in metaphors' that are 'often symbolic representations of something other than is manifest'. Science fiction (and fantasy) allow for allegorical expression since allegory involves the construction of different layers of symbolic meaning that enrich the text, just as science fiction invites its audience to understand alien worlds as symbolically parallel with their own. Wells's *The Time Machine* used microcosmic allegory to parallel future worlds with the industrial class-based society of his time, for example. Robert Scholes (1975) observed that structural fabulation becomes science fiction when it connects with, but represents a discontinuity from, a contemporary understanding of reality. This suggests that science fiction offers a microcosmic connection with, at the same time as a discontinuity from, the known world by presenting a 'novum' or new idea whose consequences the science fiction narrative will explore. Suvin (1979) also noted that science fiction had a theory of history in which future societies seem always to be cyclical returns to some earlier model from Earth, and although Suvin has a distinct predilection for science fiction that can be assimilated to high cultural literary models, and is at pains to distinguish 'true' science fiction from its mass media expressions, this notion of future societies as microcosmic returns to earlier Earth models is also evident in television science fiction. The microcosmic aesthetic in the science fiction works that Nation devised and/or scripted foregrounds dystopian science fiction's extrapolation of ideas and binaries from the audience's world through naturalistic characters and realist environments.

The connection between the audience and characters, and between microcosm and macrocosm, are implicit and allegorical in each of the formats and storylines credited to Nation as creator and/or writer. They counterpoise liberalism with autocratic tendencies through realist characters and settings, as Tulloch and Alvarado (1983: 41) have shown in the case of *Doctor Who*: 'Just as Wells's original *The Time Machine* was based in his own period, and was his projection of what he saw as unhealthy contemporary problems into a catastrophically divided and exploitative future society, so the original Daleks represented the extrapolation of contemporary militaristic, racist, and illiberal obsessions into a terrible future mutation'. 'The contrast in *Doctor Who*'s first "future-science" world, between the evilly warped intelligence of the Daleks and the Thals', they write, 'evoked a Nazi problematic which is familiar in popular science fiction, and which the creator of the Daleks, Terry Nation, has consciously pursued in the programme ever since'. Nation only realised retrospectively that his original story structure evolved from his own memory of Nazism during his childhood, and read this back into his work: 'By the time of "Genesis Of The Daleks", I had convinced myself that the Daleks were closer to the Nazis than to any other political group I could think of ... I grew up during the war, and was aware of the Nazis and their totalitarian state' (quoted by Howe *et al.* 1994: 86). 'If you look at this story', Nation continues, 'the Elite ...

seem to have echoes of what the Nazi regime was like'. The allegorical microcosms in the Dalek stories are represented implicitly but also explicitly, for example through Nazi imagery in 'Genesis Of The Daleks', and through the Daleks visually appearing like tanks, and *Survivors* and *Blake's* 7 also project contemporary concerns on to fictional societies.

In *Survivors*, for instance, the premise is that only 0.1 per cent of the world's population survive the plague. There is a process of condensation in the series, since the viewer is made aware that out of that 0.1 per cent, the programme focuses in on a microcosm of a small area of England and a particular group of representative characters, as noted in chapter 3. The characters of *Survivors* are metonymic of a much larger series of groups, and ultimately stand in for humanity in general and the tendencies of society in the viewer's present. Arthur Wormley says in the early *Survivors* episode 'Genesis' that people have to '*get back to the rudiments of government*' (our emphasis), and therefore what happens in this changed future world reflects microcosmically on the present macrocosm of the audience's public sphere and its different governmental forms. Present and past, and microcosm and macrocosm, are intertwined since the microcosm in *Survivors*' fictional present becomes a way to revisit the past macrocosm, which is, of course, still the television viewer's present. The past within the fiction becomes a way of reflecting on the audience's present, and the audience's present is extrapolated into a fictional future.

*Blake's* 7 also presents a microcosm of tendencies towards oppression or liberal democracy in the macrocosm of the audience's world, and the initial setting for oppression is a future Earth that thus alludes to Earth's past. There is also a series of metonymic condensations in *Blake's* 7 of microcosms and macrocosms, since the Earth dome represented in the first episode 'The Way Back' is a microcosm of what is transpiring all over Earth and on the outer planets. The oppression on the future Earth and these planets is a microcosm drawn from the audience's knowledge of European political regimes such as Soviet Russia and Nazi Germany, and from military technologies that were current in the 1970s. For example, in the second season episode 'Countdown' the populace of the planet Albian is kept in servitude to the Federation by the threat to use a thermonuclear device that will destroy all life but leave cities intact. The 'neutron bomb' with this capability was being developed when the episode was scripted, and as Stevens and Moore (2003: 90) note, the name 'Albian' recalls 'Albion', a legendary name for Britain. 'Countdown' extrapolated from the possibility of a Europe under Nazi rule and military technology that was being developed at the time.

## Format, character and political binaries

The dystopian television programmes we examine in this chapter are consistently structured around opposed binaries. In the tabulation noted above, Fiske (1983) recognises that *Doctor Who* generally features a 'Discourse of Morality' structured according to the opposition good/evil as well as containing 'Discourses of Politics and of Individualism'. The format of *Doctor Who*, not designed by Nation, which involved the TARDIS arriving on different worlds, made possible the exploration of these binary oppositions represented by the Doctor's humane and liberal individualism, which the viewer will accept, counterpoised with the monstrous creatures in individual stories. While the first incarnation of the Doctor (William Hartnell) was a tetchy, often selfish man (he endangers his companions' lives in 'The Daleks' by insisting that they need to go to the city to repair the Fluid Link, which is in reality in working order, and later needs the Thals' help to retrieve the Link from the Daleks), his moral code rejects violence except when his own life is threatened and he opposes enslavement (in 'The Dalek Invasion Of Earth', for example). Furthermore, the Doctor is marked by eccentricity rather than conformity. The fourth Doctor's (Tom Baker) eccentric dress and 'romantic echoes of Bohemia in his hat and coat and ... long scarf' served to individualise him (Fiske 1983: 76).

Both *Survivors'* and *Blake's 7*'s format lead to the discourses of politics and individuality. There are similarities between *Blake's 7*'s format, presented over a number of episodes through the flexi-narrative form, and *Star Trek*'s series format. Each focuses on a journeying spacecraft in the future with an ensemble bridge crew, a teleport system and an intergalactic Federation of planets. But the political institutions differ markedly in the two series. *Star Trek*'s Federation had an ambivalent role as both a military peacekeeping force (reminiscent of the United Nations' armed troops) and as a body undertaking scientific exploration. Historically, the problematic role of NASA as both a military and scientific organisation can be argued to underlie this television representation. But in the dystopian *Blake's 7*, the Earth Federation is an oppressive organisation that seeks to control not only the population of Earth (metonymically represented by the central character Blake himself) but also the outer worlds. So in contrast to the liberal utopianism of *Star Trek*'s Prime Directive of non-interference in other planetary cultures (often disregarded in the interests of creating storylines), *Blake's 7* begins from the dystopian assumption that the Federation is an imperial, colonial and militarist power. In the 'Discourse of Politics' and 'Discourse of Individualism' this leads in *Blake's 7* to the binaries of desire for liberty versus oppression. Again, the format of the programme relates to concerns in the viewer's world.

The dystopian format of *Blake's 7* is alluded to in the first set of images in each episode: the title sequence, which remained unchanged for the first two seasons. Not only does the title sequence serve as a generic 'advertisement' for a programme (Ellis 1982; Corner 1999), but also alerts the viewer to its themes. Originally, 'As envisioned by Nation, the title sequence would have involved a series of punch-cards bearing the portraits of the regulars coming out of a computer into a tray marked "Enemies of the State", plus a journey rushing through space (with portraits of the regulars overlaid) towards a planet, then the screen filling with fire and smoke' (Stevens and Moore 2003: 21). While this was changed, the final version retains the theme of the contest between oppression and liberty. The sequence begins with an image of the Federation dome, which is a virtual prison for citizens like Blake. Over this image, a pixillated eye begins to form and then the whole pixillated image of Blake's head. The image of Blake's head moves from side to side, signifying writhing in pain, then becomes a surveillance camera moving from side to side. Following this, a uniformed guard fires a gun, and the word 'ELIMINATE' appears under a pixillated profile of Blake, which then turns to face the viewer (see figure 4) (not dissimilar to Nation's original idea for the title sequence). Blake's head appears to recede in space as planets move towards the screen, and the spaceship Liberator moves towards the viewer and then away in a reverse angle shot as the series logo appears. The image of the camera is reminiscent of the idea of Big Brother's surveillance in George Orwell's novel *Nineteen Eighty-four*, signifying oppression, and the pixillated image of the tortured Blake signifies the Federation's aggression against the body. The space background represents freedom from the oppressive Earth state represented by the camera, pixillation, and the futuristic guard and his gun. The Liberator begins to connote both the space journey and the freedom desired.

In Nation's format, characters' control of this super-spacecraft, called 'Liberator One' in draft scripts (Stevens and Moore 2003: 17), highlights this dystopian binary opposition in the 'Discourse of Politics' of oppression/freedom. In 'Space Fall', Blake, Jenna and Avon are sent from the prison ship to explore a craft drifting in space, which they take for themselves, and which is used for the first three seasons of the programme until its destruction in 'Terminal'. The ship's final title, 'The Liberator', is explicitly connected with the protagonists' goal since the ship's computer Zen scans Jenna's thoughts for a possible name (in 'Cygnus Alpha').

Structural elements were still being set up in *Blake's 7* in the sixth episode, 'Seek-Locate-Destroy', which develops the dystopian binary oppression/freedom and conformity/individuality in the 'Discourses of Politics and Individualism'. It is here that the hitherto largely faceless Federation is personified by the introduction of Supreme Commander Servalan (Jacqueline Pearce). Her title denotes a holder of institutional military power, and, unlike when the character was planned to be a male named Shervalan (noted in Stevens and Moore 2003: 18), the name Servalan's association with 'serve' hints at her embodiment of the oppressiveness of the regime Nation created, and also recalls 'the Scarlet Pimpernel's nemesis Chauvelin' (Stevens and Moore 2003: 38). Servalan embodies the principle that the Federation is a God-like power that must be served, although she also often acts in her own interest (as in 'Orac' where she may keep the computer for a time before delivering it to the Federation). At first answerable to the President, Servalan assumes narrative authority over the direction *Blake's 7* will follow by appointing Space Commander Travis (Stephen Greif, later played by Brian Croucher) to eliminate Blake, since Blake's rebellion stirs up discontent among Federation citizens. Travis is coded as evil through his constant appearance in black and his physical deformities (he has an eye-patch and an artificial arm), and was originally to be introduced in the first episode.

The ideology of democratic freedom embedded in *Blake's 7*'s format is not represented through the main characters' simplistic moral heroism. They are individuated, and draw on the naturalistic tradition of individual difference as a signifier of psychological realism. They are not the emblematic moral types in much science fiction including *Doctor Who*. The central figure of Roj Blake, who eventually comes closest to the conventional crusading hero by waging war on the Federation, is at first counterpoised by Kerr Avon (Paul Darrow). Avon 'is an amalgam of two … figures in the original draft scripts: Arco, who plots against Blake but develops a grudging respect for him after Blake saves his life' (killed in the actual third episode 'Cygnus Alpha') 'and Avon, a self-serving, treacherous coward who follows Arco' (Stevens and Moore 2003: 19). In the transmitted series, Avon sees Blake as a crusader who cannot win against the Federation, and for Avon freedom instead means immense wealth (he had previously been an avaricious and unprincipled computer fraudster), so he is prepared to leave Blake stranded on Cygnus Alpha. But Darrow's often witty and sarcastic performance attracted the audience. Out of the two remaining male characters, Vila Restal (Michael Keating) 'was originally depicted as an urbane, wise-cracking criminal' and it seems 'a slippery, devious character with a harder edge' (Stevens and Moore 2003: 19). He is portrayed as a thief and a coward (as opposed to Avon) whose desire to run from trouble neatly counters Blake's bravery (in 'Cygnus Alpha' Vila hides from a fight and teleports to safety). Olag Gan (David Jackson), a convicted murderer and the physically strong 'heavy' in the crew (see 'Space Fall'), has had a limiter (seen in close-up in 'Time Squad') placed in his brain by the Federation because he murdered a security guard. This stops him from killing, but signifies that the Federation's ideology of obedience must be enforced repressively, and the audience is invited to sympathise with Gan since the guard killed his partner. Gan's ability to kill in 'Cygnus Alpha' was probably an oversight. Of the two female characters, 'the original conception of Jenna' (Sally Knyvette), a smuggler, 'appears to have been as something of a gangster's moll, being strongly tempted by Avon's offer of wealth in "Cygnus Alpha"', while Cally (Jan Chappell), conceived much later as an alien from the planet Saurian Major (Stevens and Moore 2003: 19), is introduced in the fourth episode 'Time Squad'. In early drafts of the episode 'she was explicitly described as being like 'an Israeli terrorist girl' and her name echoes *Kali*, the Hindu goddess of death (Stevens and Moore 2003: 19). In the final televised version she is the only survivor of a guerrilla force that attacked the Federation, and comes closest to paralleling Blake's political aims. Therefore, these are not the conventionally insubordinate members of an institution who use their individual and Romantically attractive talents to change or undermine it from within. Instead, they are definitively outsiders, outlaws, and seem at first to have no political aims except in the case of Blake himself, and later Cally. However, their talents will be employed to wage war on the Federation. Nation's format reverses the values conventionally attached to the binaries of citizen/criminal, insider/ outlaw, and also proposes that war and terrorism are justifiable responses to the Federation's stultifying peace. There are parallels between *Blake's 7* and the Robin Hood legend, each of which feature the dystopian oppression of a populace and the fight against this by a leader and his companions. Robin steals from the rich to give to the poor, leading a band of outlaws against the Sheriff Of Nottingham (equivalent to Travis), lackey of the oppressive King John (equivalent to Servalan). But script editor Chris Boucher told us that he does not see *Blake's 7* as presenting issues in such a black and white way. Indeed, following Blake's departure, under Avon the crew became more self-seeking and concerned with their survival.

### *Survivors, Blake's 7* and political binary oppositions: individual and community

There is a repeated distinction between the individual and the community in Nation's formats for *Survivors* and *Blake's 7* (seen in *Doctor Who* only within specific stories, as with the Thals in 'The Daleks'). Since assembling a group occurs across several episodes, it is important to view the programmes as unified wholes. Nation had been thinking about the format for *Survivors* for some time, and explained that living in a 'big house in the country' he was 'becoming more and more aware of the difficulties in just surviving in such a house with running water' and electricity and was aware also of 'how little' he knew, realising that he and his 'whole generation were virtual victims of a tremendous industry' (quoted in Nazzaro 1992b: 28). While writing this series, Nation and his wife Kate attempted to live self-sufficiently at their Lynstead Park house, baking their own bread, and raising chickens, sheep and other animals in the grounds.

Starting from Nation's own experiences and developing the concerns he had explored in his own life, *Survivors'* format sees a group of characters surviving the plague in a small area of England, and presents the binary opposition between 'tremendous industry' and self-sufficiency. In proposing a fictional scenario in which almost all of the Earth's population is wiped out by disease through an accident in a scientific lab (a science fiction novum), the format devised by Nation necessitates the isolation of individuals from the 'tremendous industry' of modern capitalism that renders individuals dependent on it. Without explicitly opposing capitalism as a form of political and social organisation, *Survivors* requires its audience to consider what individual agency and community might mean when these two apparently opposed ideas have to be reinvented. *Survivors*, in fact, connects individual agency and community by dramatically demonstrating their interdependence. Individuals simply cannot survive on their own in the post-plague world, and must reinvent forms of society that in different ways articulate the opposed terms, individual and community, together.

The initial binary between being alone and being part of a group was developed in the opening episodes of the series as each of the main characters, Abby Grant, Jenny Richards and Greg Preston, broke away from his or her previous relationships with family members, friends and communities, now killed by the plague. Each character is initially preoccupied with lone survival but ultimately seeks new bonds with other survivors. For example, the first episode 'The Fourth Horseman' begins with Abby Grant practising tennis shots on her own, prefiguring her imminent isolation as the plague takes hold. After the death of her husband and her own survival, Abby's determination to rebuild her life independently is signified by cutting her hair short, and setting fire to her house with the body of her dead husband inside, connoting her exile from familial relationships. However, Abby Grant's aim is to find her son, and therefore re-establish a familial bond, and also on a more general level not to be alone. For as she explores the devastated village in which she lives, finding the dead in the local church, signifying the now devastated community, she looks up to the sky and exclaims: 'Dear God, don't let me be the only one!' At this point a high-angle shot presents her in the midst of the whole deserted village and, as is conventional, the use of this type of shot (see chapter 3 on stalkers) connotes the character's vulnerability and isolation. Jenny Richards is persuaded to save herself, and she leaves her dead flatmate and boyfriend to wander out of London into the country, but seeks other survivors as she gradually becomes desperate for company. Greg Preston arrives from Holland by helicopter and similarly leaves his home and dead partner, but joins forces with the other survivors, first Jenny and later Abby. The initial dramatic structure of the series rests on the opposition between, on one hand, lost familial or romantic relationships leading to a focus on the self, and on the other hand the need for community. The characters' desire is not only to survive but also to find company and gradually rebuild a dead world with others. While the first episode is titled 'The Fourth Horseman', connoting destruction, the second episode is titled 'Genesis', suggesting that from the ending comes a new beginning.

Characters who are concerned only with the self and not with establishing new relationships with others in this dystopian micro-cosmic world are shown to be flawed. For instance, in 'Genesis' Anne Tranter aims to maintain her high-class status, signified by her fur coat, and is concerned only with herself, leaving the crippled Vic Thatcher for dead. Again a high-angle shot connotes Vic's physical and symbolic powerlessness, surrounded by the steep walls of a quarry, as he screams 'Help me!' Also, the Welsh labourer Tom Price is not depicted moving away from any type of familial relationship, desires others to keep away from him in case they give him the plague, and sees the dismantling of society as beneficial since he can rise in status, putting on a suit that does not fit him and taking a Rolls-Royce to drive around in (see figure 5). But both characters' concern with the self is shown to be wrong, and indeed Price (and for a while, the absent Anne) is later incorporated into a societal model devised by Abby and the other main characters.

The dystopian format of Blake's 7 provides a similar contrast between self and community, and the series begins with its central character isolated (in a prison cell) before he initiates the formation of a group (in another cell). The 'heroic' characters again display individual traits (individuality does not appeal to the Federation). Like Abby Grant, Blake is an idealist. Like Greg Preston initially, Avon is motivated largely by self-interest. Like Tom Price, Vila is a thief and a coward. But to function effectively each character must remain part of a group. Questions of individual liberation (by using wealth to procure liberty in Avon's case, for example) are counterpoised with collective liberation (the creation of the Liberator crew as a team with shared political aims). The title of the series introduces the significance of group identity through the number '7' (originally Blake was to be accompanied by seven other humanoids), yet although the collectivity of the '7' is cemented by its leader, Blake, his authority is frequently challenged and he is eventually replaced by Avon. The name of the spacecraft, 'Liberator', at first has different meanings for different members of the crew. At the end of 'Cygnus Alpha', Blake argues that in future the Liberator must be used to fight the Federation, but the prospects of using one ship and a small crew to overthrow the Federation are always unrealistic, and appear so to other characters. 'Liberator' signifies potential riches for Avon (the ship contains a huge store of wealth), and personal liberty for Vila, for instance. Interestingly, as Stevens and Moore (2003: 148) point out, the Liberator is eventually destroyed in Nation's 'Terminal' when, after Blake's departure, Avon dispenses with a largely democratic aim and takes the ship to the artificially constructed planet Terminal. The sign 'Liberator' becomes a key signifier in Nation's series, whose many meanings enable the narrative to dramatise the differences and relationships between main characters and to debate the possible storyline trajectories that the series could take. This contest of interpretation is based in binaries including personal/collective and selfish/altruistic.

### Doctor Who, Survivors, Blake's 7 and epic political activism

In *Doctor Who* and *Survivors*, political activism occurs within specific stories and episodes. But *Blake's 7*'s flexi-narrative form, as well as specifying the programme's format and drawing the television audience back to the series each week to discover the next plot development, thematically highlights the dystopian conflict in the 'Discourse of Politics' between resignation and militancy in response to the oppressive force, making it again important to view the programme's episodes as a unified whole. For active militancy rather than passive resignation is needed among the main characters for the flexi-narrative to progress, and it is largely Blake who actively takes control of it. The ends of episodes represent pauses until the following week when the over-arching linear storyline will continue, and Blake sounds a militant chord at the end of episodes such as 'The Way Back' where he vows to return one day to Earth, 'Space Fall' and 'Cygnus Alpha' where he vows to use the ship to fight the Federation ('With a ship like this and a full crew then we can start fighting back', 'When we can handle this ship properly we'll stop running. Then we'll fight'). The forward movement of the Liberator under Blake's control drives the programme onwards, charting the progress of a continuing epic battle against the Federation.

Paradoxically, the expression of the binary of militancy versus resignation and Blake and his crew's resolve to seize agency for themselves as subjects of action rather than the objects of the Federation's gaze and power, makes them into fleeing quarries in a pursuit narrative, for which Nation provided the structure, where Travis aims to destroy Blake. Blake's attempt to become a subject therefore leads him into the role of object (indeed, the same is true of Robin Hood), and this narrative strand continues from episode to episode. Again, the ending of the episode is important in setting up a narrative of pursuit, devised by Nation, that will continue, as Travis says: 'Run Blake. Run. As far and as fast as you like. I'll find you. You can't hide from me. I am your death. Blake'. Blake's heroic rebellion opens up the possibility that he will in the end be killed, although ironically, at the end of the fourth season this is at the hands of Avon, not the Federation.

Episodes such as 'The Web' and 'Mission To Destiny' stand out since apart from a mention at the end of 'The Web' that the Liberator must avoid Federation pursuit ships, the Federation is conspicuous by its absence. Even these episodes, however, deal with the theme of oppression/liberty, for example in the conflict in 'The Web' between Lost (a late addition to the script) and the Decimas race, deemed the socially inferior. They are caught in a literal and allegorical web, and the episode's antagonists, a woman and a man, foreshadow Servalan and Travis introduced in the following episode (Stevens and Moore 2003: 34). In 'Mission To Destiny' possession of the 'neutrotope', a cure for the planet Destiny's fungal plague, is of great value, and the ship, 'the Ortega', conjures up the twentieth-century Spanish philosopher Jose Ortega y Gasset who opposed dictatorship and supported Republicans, showing what the planet's 'destiny' ought to be (Stevens and Moore 2003: 40). Narrative carefully orders things ideologically.

## *Doctor Who:* 'The Daleks' and political binary oppositions

Specific analysis of some of Nation's works highlights the dystopian binary structures that reflect on tendencies in our world. Nation's first story for *Doctor Who*, 'The Daleks', displays what became an authorial 'signature' when the protagonists arrive on a 'dead planet' (the title of the first episode), Skaro, which phonetically suggests 'scar' (see Bentham 1986). Skaro (spelt Skara once in a rehearsal script for the fourth episode) and its inhabitants have literally been scarred by the use of atomic technology some 500 years previously when two races (now called the Daleks and the Thals) were at war and had a disrespect for each other and for the planet on which they lived. At the current time of the story, the dystopian categories identified by Fiske (1983) of autocratic rule (in the 'Discourse of Politics') and racism (in the 'Discourse of Individualism'), microcosmic of tendencies existing in the viewer's world, are expressed through the Daleks' perpetuation of the war and continued lack of respect for the environment, counterpoised by the Thals' sympathy with nature and the protagonists' liberalism and tolerance.

The Daleks' autocratic, racist nature is, for example, given expression when the Doctor's fellow traveller Ian Chesterton says to the Thals that the Daleks have, 'A dislike for the unlike ... They're afraid of you because you're different from them'. Chesterton is a schoolteacher, and a representative of the tolerant attitudes of the urban educated middle class that are thus transplanted from 1960s London on to Skaro, just as he has himself been literally uprooted from his own time and space by the TARDIS into this future society. Therefore an opposition between 'us' and 'them' is set up.

Indeed, the Daleks' autocratic opposition to difference is suggested throughout *Doctor Who*'s history, and is represented for the first time in this story through the Daleks' speech and movement in unison, rather than as individuals. The creatures can dominate scenes through the force of their united cries, sometimes literally drowning other characters out. Difference is represented in this first Dalek story by the Thals, who are not only distinguished by difference from the Daleks, but also from each other in a more democratic and tolerant model of society. Although the Thals have a leader, individuals express different points of view during the course of the story, and unlike the Daleks, the Thals speak by turns and listen to what each has to contribute to the debate about the organisation of their society. Individual tolerance metonymically and microcosmically reflects the tolerance of their race, and the protagonists' epic quest to defeat the Daleks validates their ideologies by its success.

Nation's original storyline for 'The Daleks', at first titled 'The Survivors', however, saw the Daleks believing that the Thals had started the initial neutron war and aiming to destroy them completely in order to end all wars. The storyline ended with the Thals treating the vanquished Daleks with compassion when talks are held to agree how the two races will live together peacefully. Invader rockets from another race approach Skaro and it transpires that the new arrivals are from the planet that actually fired neutron bombs on Skaro 2000 years before, but now the civilisation has come to make reparations. By the time the story was called 'Beyond The Sun', 'Nation's story had eliminated the race of aliens who arrived at the conclusion, and now climaxed with the Daleks preparing to detonate another neutron bomb to destroy the Thals', making 'the Daleks ... the clear villians of the piece' (Pixley 2003: 33). Because of the changes made, there was more potential for the Daleks to return in future serials as clear-cut villains. Similar representations of oppression/liberty can also be found in Nation's other 1960s *Doctor Who* stories, 'The Keys Of Marinus' in which the oppressive Voord are defeated, 'The Dalek Invasion Of Earth', and 'The Daleks' Master Plan' where Mavic Chen, Guardian of the Solar System, prefigures *Blake's 7*'s power-hungry Servalan.

## *Doctor Who*: 'Genesis Of The Daleks' and political binary oppositions

Nation's 1970s *Doctor Who* story 'Genesis Of The Daleks' offers a revisionist approach to the Daleks' history yet also offers a cyclical model of history where origins and subsequent events are intertwined. Rereading 'The Daleks', Nation saw ideas in the original that he then transplanted into this story. The story also exists in dialogue with the earlier non-Dalek story 'The Keys Of Marinus'. Nation (quoted by Howe *et al.*, 1994: 87), claims that 'Genesis Of The Daleks', a dystopian story, is structured around an opposition; on Skaro there are 'two different cities ... two different races of people' and 'highly complex political manoeuvring going on', and Fiske's binary discourses are evident in it. Nation recalled that the story was 'always intended to be a kind of anti-war piece' and 'a highly moral tale' (quoted by Howe *et al.*, 1994: 86), thus microcosmically reflecting upon tendencies in the viewer's world. While Nation could not claim that he was sole creator, he did assert that 'the Elite ... and the general idea' were, he believed, his, though it is likely that script editor Robert Holmes built significantly on these ideas. *Doctor Who* fans have read the story as political: Philip MacDonald (1998) made such a reading for *Doctor Who Magazine* when it was voted by readers their favourite *Doctor Who* television story of all, but he did not draw out its binary structures.

'Genesis Of The Daleks' exploits the potential of the science fiction genre to use 'hard' science as a catalyst for presenting political binaries far more fully than 'The Daleks'. Science fiction enables a contrast to be made between science being employed negatively as a tool of power and science being used in a positive manner. Fiske (1983: 74) writes that: 'In story after story in *Dr Who*, "pure" or "cold" science is used to maintain or establish a totalitarian political order. Science is a means of power ... The Doctor typically defeats a totalitarian, scientific antagonist and replaces him or her with a liberal democratic humane scientist to take over and bring justice and freedom'. While Fiske's subsequent discussion revolves around the way in which science is used in communist and capitalist ways, his points are relevant to its uses in Nation's story.

On the one hand, Davros uses cold science in order to establish an autocratic regime, by creating the Daleks to exterminate any individual or group that threatens it. Science and war merge, and indeed Davros himself is a two-sided character embodying both. He is described as the Kaled's 'greatest scientist' and is using scientific methods to create the Dalek army (mentioned in chapter 3, above, and discussed later). The first scene in which Davros appears, at the end of the first episode, involves Dalek weaponry being tested. His embodiment of these dual qualities is further expressed when the Doctor asks him whether he would use a bacterium that had the capacity to kill every living being if he had created one in his laboratory (this question prefigures the science lab accident in *Survivors*, as Brown (1993) has noted). Davros, who sees such a potential scientific creation as a means of power, replies in the affirmative. Also significantly, the creation of the Daleks occurs within the Kaled bunker in which these dual characteristics of science and war are manifested. The bunker is occupied by an elite group of the finest Kaled scientific minds, a type of 'think tank' assembled to work on the Dalek project, and is protected by the military. But Davros's scientific aims are revealed as evil in the lines spoken by various scientists during the story. They share the Doctor's humane view of science, and indeed assist him in trying to bring an end to Davros's experiments, voicing the view that Davros has perverted their work. The mission on which the Time Lords send the Doctor is to prevent the development of the fascist Dalek regime either by making them evolve into 'less aggressive creatures' or by completely preventing their development.

'Hard' science acts as a launching point for the binary structures that fall under the most general 'Discourse of Morality', identified by Fiske

(1983). In the overall binary of good versus evil, the heroic Doctor represents good in relation to the evil creatures he encounters: the Daleks are 'evil ... creatures of hate' from whom he wants to distinguish himself. As in 'The Daleks', the 'Discourse of Politics' is apparent. The ruler of the dystopian state (Davros) stands against democracy. Davros plans the deaths of the Kaled government which threatens the develop-ment of the Daleks. In the final episode, Davros makes a pretence of allowing a debate in which cases are put forward for and against the development of the Daleks, and allows a vote to decide the issue, which could lead to 'a new democratically elected leader'. But when the vote goes against Davros, at his orchestration Daleks enter the room and exterminate the Kaled protesters. Using the combination of science and the military (the two groupings of Kaleds represented in the story), Davros aims to create the Daleks by excluding notions of liberalism and conscience. Gharman, for example, stands against Davros because he is creating the Daleks without a conscience, and this marks him for destruction. The Doctor also opposes Davros, since he, of course, is rooted on the side of liberalism. Nation's storyline returns to the idea of conscience seen in his earlier story 'The Keys of Marinus', in which a 'Conscience Machine' could forcibly eliminate crime on Marinus and obviate the situation in which Ian Chesterton is suspected of murder and put on trial. Lack of conscience is partly what makes Davros and the Daleks monstrous and 'other'.

The 'Discourse of Individualism' appears again in the dystopian 'Genesis Of The Daleks' through the theme of racism. Like 'The Daleks', 'Genesis Of The Daleks' echoes Nazi policies of racial puri-fication. The desire for conformity and elimination of individualism is specifically represented when 'Genesis Of The Daleks' debates the question of what belongs within the Kaled system and what does not. Even 'impure' Kaleds, mutants who do not conform, are exiled to the wasteland literally to waste away, but are shown to have more value and to be more sympathetic characters than the Kaled officer Nyder. As Gary K. Wolfe (1979) has argued, science fiction narratives present structural patterns based on distinctions between the familiar and the unfamiliar (spaceships voyaging into the unknown, or humans' encounters with alien monsters or mutants, for example). But the Thals are the main group whom the Kaleds seek to eliminate, and the Kaled and Thal nations are at war. The war in 'Genesis Of The Daleks' is represented through the recurrent image of a map, which shows the two identical city domes of the Kaleds and Thals, with a mountain ridge separating them and empty wasteland around them (see figure 6). The symmetry of the map and the identical domes of the two cities demonstrate the simplification of the story into a struggle between two binarily opposed forces that are potentially interchangeable. What marks them as separate is that the Kaled state has an ideology of racial purity, and the Daleks (an anagram of Kaleds) are tools of this ideology, although many Kaleds stand against the Daleks.

Davros, however, further works against individualism by creating the Daleks to continue the Kaled aim to eliminate non-Kaleds, especially the Thals. Davros treacherously gives the Thals the chemical formula to enable them to penetrate the protective dome of the Kaled city so that the Thals kill most of the Kaleds who were planning to halt the Dalek project, and the Daleks then kill most of the Thals in turn. The first discourse we therefore hear a Dalek use (referring to the necessity to exterminate the Doctor) is a racist one, with Davros exclaiming: 'Brilliant. Brilliant. It has detected the non-conformity'. In this orgy of destruction of the other, however, the Daleks refuse to accept the authority of the 'imperfect' Davros, and he appears to be killed. The binary of racism versus tolerance is pushed further and further so that each opposing race or faction eliminates the group it has identified as 'other', until finally the scientist who orchestrated the whole sequence, Davros himself, becomes the victim of his own ideology of purity. By contrast, the Doctor is aligned with liberalism, tolerance and democracy, and is marked in the programme's format as eccentric (see above) and at the beginning of this story as rebellious against his own race, and thus Davros's opposite.

### *Survivors* and binary oppositions: the nature of communities

Since *Survivors* favours the idea of the self fitting into a community, this leads to the emergence of new sets of binaries as one proto-community contrasts with another, and members of each community engage in dramatic conflicts with each other. The question arises of what the new or restored society should be like, and this is clearly a political issue. Again, the dystopian binary of autocratic rule and democratic rule, noted by Fiske (1983), is manifest in *Survivors'* various systems of government, as is a 'Discourse of Economics'. Since Abby Grant is the lead character who is offered as the primary figure of identification for the viewer, the systems of government proposed by other characters are seen from her perspective. Her structural role is to encounter and work through the implications of binarily opposed systems and to test these systems as potential models for the community she wishes to develop. As the term 'model' suggests, the systems of social organisation represented in the series are ultimately for her to judge and learn from, and for her to align herself with or to oppose. While she is not the only character who occupies such a role, she functions as a 'litmus test' for the series' point of view.

The first microcosmic system of government that the lone Abby and the audience encounter is autocratic: a community set up by former union leader Arthur Wormley in *Survivors*' second episode 'Genesis'. As well as suggesting a new beginning, the title 'Genesis' connotes that the new world contains the seeds of its own potential undoing, and a choice between temptation and instinct (as in the Biblical Book of Genesis). A 'worm' is a snake in a pastoral setting. Wormley's community is, he claims, the beginnings of a new government that would gather resources and distribute them in exchange for labour. This system broadly follows the Marxist principle expressed in Marx and Engels' nineteenth-century political tract *The Communist Manifesto* (2002) in which each person would be required to contribute according to his or her abilities, and be rewarded according to his or her needs. As a former union leader, Wormley's espousal of this arrangement derives from the discourses of labour power and nationalisation that were current in the 1970s. However, as Abby soon learns, this apparent socialist form of government is being perverted by Wormley, with the 'worm' in his name suggesting his unpleasantness, into an autocratic system (in the 'Discourse of Politics') in which he dispenses violent justice and oversees the seizure of resources from other survivors in his neighbourhood (in the 'Discourse of Economics'). Rather than a society in which collective good is overseen by a benevolent state to the benefit of its people, Wormley's community is a Stalinist one in which the miniature command economy is run by an autocratic elite, backed up by violence and intimidation. Abby becomes Wormley's antithesis and opposes his position in the binary structure that animates the episode.

This system of government is to an extent opposed with a second system that Abby Grant (but none of the other regular characters) and the audience encounter. Abby experiences and judges this model too. This second possible model is represented in the sixth episode 'Garland's War' by Jimmy Garland, whose name, unlike Wormley's, connotes something natural and beautiful. His rambling country manor house, of which he has become the heir after the death of his family, had been taken over by a substantial group of survivors, and 'Garland's War' is initially presented as a struggle to take back his property from Knox. Garland's aim to rule seems to conflict with the liberal democratic ideology of the series, and places Garland instead as an autocrat somewhat similar to Wormley. However, two significant differences between the two characters are gradually revealed in the episode. First, Garland is youthful, charming and attractive to Abby. He has a background in the Army, but this is explained as an opportunity for him to explore distant and inhospitable places rather than as evidence of militaristic impulses. His survival skills enable him to feed and protect Abby, and they begin a cautious romantic relationship based not only on mutual support but also on their sharing of upper-middle-class values and tastes.

When Garland is captured by the usurpers of his house after a truce violated by the community living in it, he is beaten up and seems destined to be executed. But Garland's intentions are significantly softened as he claims that he plans to act as a benevolent advisor and leader, whose survival skills, local knowledge and innate ability to lead give him a 'natural' authority. On the basis of this, Abby continues to support him, and he emerges alive as the eventual victor and lynchpin of the community in his house, whose leaders are overthrown. So Garland represents a class with inherited personal charm, good taste, leadership skills and charisma, an enlightened aristocracy in the post-plague world. By casting Garland as an attractive man of action, this class-based authority is naturalised dramatically, and Garland persists in the series as a recurring character with whom Abby later forms a romantic partnership, and who assists her in her quest for her missing son. In contrast to Wormley's Stalinism, Garland's role is to establish authority hegemonically, by consent rather than by violence. Garland's role is structurally very similar to Wormley's. Like Wormley, Garland leads a diverse community, heads a stratified society that organises labour, produces food and distributes goods among a subordinate population. The difference between them is the means by which these ends are achieved. Wormley rules through dictatorial power enforced by violence, whereas Garland rules by 'natural' charisma and consent. That Garland's position is favoured is interesting since in the 1960s the assumption of cultural consensus had been widely challenged, and the BBC itself moved from regarding its audience as a unified or potentially unified group, to addressing different audiences with different needs. The role of the BBC was no longer imagined as paternal, leading its audience towards better citizenship, in parallel with Garland's initial assumption of 'natural' authority. Instead, the BBC would be an efficient mediating and managing institution that would channel resources in an effective and responsible way (just as it turns out that the community wants and needs Garland). Therefore, it is appropriate that Garland's ideology is the right one. Abby largely becomes aligned with Garland, thus giving significant structural and narrative weight to his position among the binarily opposed systems represented at this early point in the series.

After encountering these microcosmic models of government, Abby, Greg Preston and Jenny Richards set up a society in a democratically-run household whose relationships replace the familial ones that the main characters have long since lost (see figure 7). But as we noted in the previous chapter, Nation's original version of *Survivors* saw the characters as questing wanderers while Jack Ronder's vision was of the characters operating from a fixed base (Alsop 1987: 14). The mixing of science fiction and domestic drama discussed in chapter 3 is important to political readings of *Survivors*, since the negotiation of personal relationships becomes increasingly significant to the series. There are parallels between Wormley's execution of a man to maintain law and order and the similar decision made by Abby's community in 'Law And Order' (written by Clive Exton), when the young woman Wendy is found dead at the hands of an unknown killer among the survivors. But while Wormley has no reservations about execution, there is a painstaking decision-making process in Abby's community involving a democratic vote. Abby has the deciding vote and reaches it with difficulty and sadness. The fact that the wrong man is executed (the killer was not the mentally disabled Barney but in fact Tom Price) draws further attention to the necessity for humane and democratic organisa-tion in the post-plague world. The danger for the survivors is that their precarious situation leads all too easily to rough justice, oppression and violence. Abby's democratic system matches Garland's more closely, making their meeting and their relationship structurally important to the series as a whole.

## *Blake's 7*: 'The Way Back' and political binary oppositions

The opening *Blake's 7* episode, 'The Way Back', scripted mainly by Nation with little input from Chris Boucher (Stevens and Moore 2003: 22), is set on Earth before the introduction of all the main characters and the assembling of the Liberator crew, and thus may appear unrepresentative of the programme. But it is representative in steering the series in a political direction and this and other episodes must be seen as part of a unified whole. Often in television production, the first episode of a programme is known as the 'pilot episode', the success or failure of which will determine whether the show will be picked up for an entire season's run. While this was not the case with *Blake's 7*, the term 'pilot' is a particularly apt one since a pilot steers a vehicle, and this episode demonstrates how the series will be steered forwards. The episode is structured by the 'Discourses of Politics and Individualism' noted by Fiske (1983), for democracy is opposed by an autocracy established through medical science, and individual identity is discovered and restored. The storyline mirrors tendencies from the television viewer's world, for example as Stevens and Moore (2003: 22) note, the Earth dome has connections with the drabness and stratification of Soviet Russia. The episode dramatises the distinction between passive resignation (remaining still with no goal) and active militance (moving forwards), and uses ideas of the labyrinth to convey this. *Blake's 7*, as a whole, begins as a didactic project: this episode dramatises the move from the citizen Blake's oppressed state to his confrontation of the society in acts of militance set up by the format and by flexi-narrative. The series title alludes to Blake's assembly of a group and his role in leading attacks.

Labyrinths are common metaphors for spatial imprisonment, for states of mind, and for a type of narrative progression. The autocratic and actively militant Federation has taken control over events on Earth and beyond, and Blake is a passive resigned object of its actions with his individuality removed. The episode begins *in medias res* where spatially Blake, like other citizens, is imprisoned within a dome. Additionally, the Federation has had Blake strapped to a brainwashing machine, in order to remove the memory of his active militance against the regime, and has dosed his food and drink with suppressants to induce passive mental acceptance of his state. Inside a labyrinth, Blake therefore lacks knowledge of the design of the whole of the Federation's regime, and lacks control over narrative progression. The Federation's attempts to keep its citizens in a psychological maze is further evident in a scene between Blake and the psychiatrist, Doctor Havant, where instead of encouraging Blake to reflect on his memories and help him, Havant attempts to make Blake believe that he is out of touch with reality and that a massacre of rebellious civilians did not occur. Correctly seeing reality versus being disengaged from it is a pivotal opposition in this scene. The psychiatrist makes Blake question his sanity and his hold on reality, encouraging him to repudiate the evidence of his own eyes so that he cannot react to the massacre actively. We have noted that surveillance cameras are used by the Federation to police its citizens, and this motif of control through vision is developed in the scene in relation to evidence and memory. As in George Orwell's *Nineteen Eighty-four*, the Federation aims to control what is perceived to be real by demanding that its citizens disbelieve their own senses and memories, represented here by images from Blake's point of view.

But witnessing the massacre breaks down Blake's conditioning and he perceives the autocracy of the Federation and its removal of individuality. Blake's sanity allows him to take control of his life and the narrative to the point where he will become an outlaw, seizing a super-spacecraft, assembling a group to replace the massacred resistance fighters, and moving the action forwards as the format requires. Being sane involves seeing the truth of events and acting in response to them, thereby leaving a mental labyrinth, and in this drama of perception Blake sees the design of the whole and embarks upon active militance. The title 'The Way Back' alludes both to Blake's determination to return to Earth when he is transported to the penal colony at the end of the episode, and also signifies his mental journey from a resigned present state to knowledge of his active militant past. 'The way back' is thus the means forward. In 'Space Fall', the society on board the prison ship London is, as the name suggests, a microcosmic city replicating the Earth dome where in a small confined area prisoners' food and water are dosed with suppressants (Stevens and Moore 2003: 25) and where the disobedient find themselves restrained in their seats on the way to the further restraint of the penal colony of Cygnus Alpha. But with Blake's newly found awareness of the Federation's horrific regime, the Liberator offers mobility away from symbolic and physical stasis.

### *Blake's 7*: 'Duel' and political binary oppositions

The *Star Trek* episode 'Arena' involves the alien Metrons settling a conflict in their area of space between the Enterprise and the Gorn species through a single combat between the respective captains, in which Kirk ultimately refuses to kill his opponent. Similarly 'Duel' involves aliens setting up a physical duel between Blake and the Federation officer Travis whose war has intruded upon a planet, and Blake finally refuses to kill Travis. But despite its intertextual relationship with *Star Trek*, 'Duel' is again a highly representative *Blake's 7* episode, and is representa-tive of Nation's work. It is a dystopian fiction, which returns to some of the plots and binary structures outlined above, such as militance versus pacifism, which are also found in the aborted script 'Locate And Destroy' (Stevens and Moore 2003: 42), and the state versus the individual. It further reflects microcosmically upon tendencies in the television viewer's world, as well as on the Federation's means of suppression, and on the programme's continuing space battle between Blake and Travis.

Nation's authorial signature of a dystopian world made barren by atomic war, seen in 'The Daleks' episode 'The Dead Planet', reappears in the first draft script of 'Duel'. The unnamed planet potentially stands for Earth since a new more powerful weapon was developed to end the war when one side refused to surrender, recalling America's use of the hydrogen bomb in 1945 against Japanese cities for similar reasons. The episode reflects on the Federation's oppressive nature generally, where framing format and story link as well as specifically through the Federation's threat to use a thermonuclear device in 'Countdown'. The planet in 'Duel' is now a planet of the dead, as well as a dead (uninhabited) planet. One of the first shots in the episode is of a burial ground that is not the traditional isolated area but is 'a memorial to the dead' (as Blake later notes) with grave markers 'as far as the eye can see' (as Gan asserts). Conventional tombstones are often shaped in the symbolic design of the cross signifying Christ's and humankind's resurrection, and contain an inscription to the deceased individual carved upon them, but in 'Duel' the graves are not individual memorials but a collective remembrance of the destructiveness of war.

The binary of pacifism versus militarism is condensed into a concrete visual form where the episode is framed symbolically, building on Nation's original idea. The gravestones are smaller versions of the larger statue of a man, with a broken weapon in each of his hands, which is all that remains of this barren world, and repeats and emphasises the meaning of the grave markers. Both serve as a critique of war. The statue's multiple interpretations are later highlighted: the broken weapons could signify peace (as Jenna remarks), or defeat (as Blake, it turns out, concludes correctly), but both readings are critiques of war since the prospect of defeat makes suing for peace attractive.

'Duel' becomes an allegory about war and peace, and also reflects on the programme as a whole where Blake, having seized the Liberator, needs to attack the Federation as a militant rather than a pacifist. Like the statue, Sinofar, the younger guardian (whose name is composed of the words 'sin' and 'afar'), wishes to teach a lesson about the perils of widespread war that are represented largely by the older keeper Giroc's savage instincts ('gyre' means a circular path leading nowhere, and 'rock' suggests harshness). Sinofar orchestrates the duel, but can only teach about the exclusion of war with the inclusion of Giroc and there is a contest for narrative control between the two. With Giroc, Sinofar arrests the narrative during the space combat between Travis and Blake, the director choosing to represent this visually by events on the ships going into slow-motion. The women remove the two men from their spaceships and outline to them and to the other characters via the viewscreens how the narrative will progress, aligning the television viewer with the other observers. Shots of the women watching the duel are superimposed on to the forest, coding them as all powerful, all seeing, and in full control of the narrative. But while Giroc at first assumes narrative authority, placing Travis in the forest right by Blake, whose vision becomes impaired, so that she can enjoy the sight of the Federation officer cutting Blake's throat, her narrative authority is usurped by Sinofar who literally freezes the action (conveyed by television freeze-frame), and repositions Travis and Blake apart from each other so that Blake will have a fair chance. It is Sinofar, arguing for pacifism, who finally frees the main characters when Blake refuses to kill Travis at the end of the fight on the grounds that such an act would serve no purpose but enjoyment.

The dystopian brutality of war and the concomitant need for peace (even though there is sometimes a necessity for battle) are enforced through the use of physical touch as the medium of aggression. Contrasting with the broken weapons in the statue's hands, the original war on the planet involved a weapon that did not require bodily contact. On being brought to the planet by Sinofar, Travis and Blake are frozen like statues but then restored to motion, and can function in opposition to the statue's message. Travis attempts to use his hands to destroy; he tries to fire his artificial hand's in-built weapon at Blake (but it is rendered useless), and he prepares to cut his temporarily blinded opponent's throat in the forest. Later, Blake prepares to ram a wooden spear into Travis, paralleling his earlier plan to ram the Liberator into Travis's pursuit ship, but at the final moment Blake throws the spear away, paralleling the breakage of the weapon in the statue's hand. Blake fights only for justice and survival.

'Duel' also reflects on the 'Discourse of Individualism' present in *Blake's 7* as a whole. The dystopian Federation's lack of concern for the individual, and the law that it must be served blindly, is represented in the format through Servalan's character and is later alluded to in 'Pressure Point'. The Federation destroyed all churches, thus establishing its own ideology as the only system of ideas and values for its citizens, and the power of religion as a means of control was attested to earlier in 'Cygnus Alpha' by the corrupt leader (unconnected to the Federation) of the planet's penal colony. The devaluation of individuality is countered by Blake and the Liberator crew who assemble for political ends as outlaws rather than conventional heroes, and drive the narrative forwards. In order to communicate the horror of war, the duel aims to teach a lesson about the death of a friend when Travis's Mutoid Pilot and Blake's companion Jenna are brought into the forest. As Stevens and Moore (2003: 43) note, Travis's and the Mutoid Pilot's functions are to serve the Federation blindly, creating an identification between them.

The Mutoid Pilot claims she has no other purpose, even her identity has been erased from her mind (recalling the Federation's brainwashing techniques in 'The Way Back'), and she has no desire to find 'the way back' to her former self. Significantly, Travis has to reveal her name, Keera, to her, highlighting this lack of selfhood. Travis, who, as Blake observes, has no friends, has no regard for the Mutoid Pilot's life once she has failed him. Blake and Jenna are both sympathetic characters believing in the worth of the individual and are structurally opposed to the Federation, Travis and his Mutoid Pilot. Blake already stands in opposition to the Mutoid Pilot since in 'The Way Back' it was established that Blake was kept under control by being sent faked tapes of his family and he ultimately seeks a way back to his past. Blake risks walking into a trap in order to save Jenna since he values his friend's life, and the worth of the individual and Blake's compassion as well as Gan's is again highlighted in the second season episode 'Pressure Point'. Gan dies during a raid on a Federation complex while saving his comrades by holding up a door. The incident is based, as Stevens and Moore note (2003: 80–1), on the song 'Big John' about a strong man saving his friends in a mining disaster by holding up the roof. This contrasts with the original storyline in which Gan kills Veron when his limiter malfunctions and is in turn killed by Blake.

### Binaries and disavowals of binaries: the body and doubled bodies

Having set up a series of dystopian binary oppositions, these programmes are as much concerned with the challenges to their binary structures by autocratic and homogeneous systems of government as with the binaries themselves. This preoccupation is expressed by using the humanoid body as a microcosmic representation of the body politic, as seen in *Beowulf*. The term 'body politic' derives from the Anglo-Saxon notion of a man's governance of himself being microcosmic of his rule over the developing macrocosms of family and state. The terms 'head of the family' and 'head of state' derive from the bodily head (containing the brain and suggesting superiority). Since the body politic received its name from the idea of a man's body as a microcosm of rule, it is apt that the body is microcosmic of the body politic in some of Nation's work.

Doubling of bodies in literature and media can sometimes straightforwardly signify an identification. But doubling can be more complex. For literal doubling has long been examined by literary critics, such as Ralph Tymms (1949), Sandra Gilbert and Susan Gubar (1979), Fred Botting (1996) Antonio Ballesteros Gonzàlez (1998) and Helen

Hanson (2000), and, to a lesser extent, by television critics such as Lenora Ledwon (1993) and Helen Wheatley (2002), who each tend to focus on the psychological double in the Gothic, where, as Tymms (1949: 115) notes, a character might project repressed desires as an image, or project an aspect of the soul from which he or she struggles to be free. Concerned with division and unification, the double can function in two ways. First, it can signify a desire to unify two parts as one. Conversely, as the comment above suggests, it can signify an attempt to separate the one into two and be left with a 'pure' one, a process that again involves division and unification. In both of these instances there is an obvious concern with homogeneity.

The 'body politic' can therefore be represented by the physical body, where an attempt to join two bodies into one may represent its unification. Splitting off the unworthy part of the self in order to leave a unified body may also stand for the perfectability of the body politic. Our discussion is therefore a development of the common theoretical principle of creating unity by eliminating the double's duality. However, the connection between the body politic and doubling does not displace the realistic texture of characters in programmes associated with Nation.

The *Doctor Who* story 'Genesis Of The Daleks' outlines the history of the Daleks, thereby providing a creation story for them, and the narration of this creation story connects the ideas of physical doubling, the unified body politic, and the 'essence' of the Dalek species. Davros's autocratic aim is to wipe out one side of a binary structure and make the body politic unified in its destructive aims through scientifically reinventing the Kaleds as one unitary force, the Daleks, whose physical bodies will be combined into one creature comprising a mechanical and a biological component that cannot exist independently. This is also a science fiction Gothic parody of the Christian notion of death and rebirth since it aims to prevent the extinction of the Kaled race residing in a tomb-like underground bunker, by recreating them as 'vampires' from beneath the ground who will drain the life from the Thals. Davros is a perverted Frankenstein figure constructing physical and mechanical bodies by misuse of science, and the literary Gothic commonly echoed an ambivalence about the values of the past and the scientific present (see Kilgour 1995). Not only do the literal dead bodies play a part in the war against the Thals, propped up to make trenches appear fully manned, but Davros also aims through genetic engineering to turn the Kaleds into Daleks using bodily metamorphosis. Significantly, in the first episode, even though he is not a Dalek, Ravon uses what will become the Daleks' customary discourse, stating that 'the Kaled battlecry will be total extermination of the Thals'. Davros attempts to take this to extremes by creating new unified bodies, as the word 'genesis' in the story's title underlines to act like a raven. The microcosm of the 'monstrous' body politic where the body of Skaro's race is replaced by one 'monster' can be read allegorically as a recognition of the threat that humanoids will become 'monsters' in political terms. Therefore, the monster does not only function aesthetically but the etymological origin of the word 'monster', *monstrare*, 'to show forth', is put into effect.

In 'Genesis Of The Daleks' the desire of Davros and some of the Kaleds to create this unified and autocratic body politic depends on a second use of the double whereby there is a splitting off of the unworthy element of the race, dividing the one into two as a means of perfecting it. This requires the physically deformed Mutos, 'scarred relics' of the Kaleds, to be cast out into the wasteland surrounding the city (the name of the Muto Sevrin suggests this 'severing' off of an unworthy part of the self), and Davros intends that surgery on Gharman's brain will eliminate his wayward leanings caused by conscience. The story presents a reversal of 'The Keys Of Marinus', which played with the connection between brain and body rather than literal body doubling: Arbitan (whose name suggests 'arbiter' or 'judge') intended to use the 'Conscience Machine' (appearing like a mechanical brain) to bring all literal bodies under one rule by splitting off leanings towards crime (where the brain governs the actions of the human body). The 'Conscience Machine' stands for the body politic, and Yartek, leader of the Voord, wished to employ it to dominate the populace as one entity.

*Survivors* and the *Blake's 7* episode 'The Way Back' express the idea of political assimilation but not through body doubling. However, the notion of the body politic symbolised through doubling appears again in the *Blake's 7* episode 'Duel' and reflects on the programme's Federation. Sinofar and Giroc do not simply exist in the text to supply narrative exposition of the catastrophe that has befallen their dead planet. We know from Boucher's comment to us that the relationship between Sinofar and Giroc was changed from Nation's original script. But the overall idea of war and peace and of the duel was Nation's, and the relationship between the two women develops the thematic structures that we have identified in the episode and in the series as a whole. Sinofar and Giroc are one (as illustrated by their similar titles 'The Guardian' and 'The Keeper') yet are two sides. The original autocratic unity of the planet's body politic, which parallels the autocratic homogeneity of the Federation and its belief in military power, is apparent when Giroc, allegorically representing war, attempts to act independently of Sinofar, allegorically representing the desire for peace. Giroc has Blake temporarily blinded in the forest in order that Travis can gain the advantage and cut Blake's throat before Sinofar intervenes. The planet's original autocratic unity is therefore symbolised by Giroc's attempt to act alone and dispense with her 'other'.

## Dissolving binaries and blurring categories

Dystopian formats and storylines also raise challenges to the binary structures that animate them, by thematising rigid autocratic categorisation in relation to the 'hero' figures. Binary oppositions, often presented in critical texts by listing the terms in grids or charts (such as those used by Fiske 1987), involve a process of categorisation, labelling and defining one thing in relation to another. The autocratic and racist side of the structure is concerned with unity whereas the structure itself must necessarily recognise difference, multiplicity and a place for opposition. This is evident from an examination of *Doctor Who*'s Daleks and *Blake's 7*'s Federation, whose respective watchwords are 'Exterminate' (which eventually emerged as the prime Dalek battle-cry) and 'Eliminate' (seen across the screen in the title sequence of *Blake's 7*'s first two seasons, though not scripted by Nation). Both are concerned with a unitary process of labelling and a denial of the other. These autocratic regimes are characterised by recognising the two sides of the binary structure, but since they are autocratic and often racist regimes they aim for unity as opposed to multiplicity, and rather than seeking out relationships with their opposites they seek literally and symbolically to exterminate them. Binary structures involve the fluidity of categorisation, which we recognise here, and this can be seen as a 'signature' running throughout Nation's television science fiction work.

Both *Doctor Who*'s Davros and his creations the Daleks are autocratic and racist figures who stand against binarily opposed categories involving democracy and tolerance, and seek to exterminate these in a process of exclusion. In the 'Discourse of Politics' in the final episode of 'Genesis Of The Daleks', Davros calls a vote with the approval of the 'heroic' Doctor to determine whether Davros continues as leader. The vote implies democracy and a choice between two categories, but because autocratic rule is concerned with a unitary power, which does not take other viewpoints into account, Davros renders the vote meaningless by ordering the Daleks to exterminate all those who oppose him. In the 'Discourse of Individualism' the first step in the destruction of the other is the identification of the other as different. Racism can be understood as the internalisation of a binary structure (us and them) and a desire to abolish 'them' and end up only with 'us'. Racism refuses to acknowledge the rights of the different and desires the same, thereby exterminating the binary structure: 'a dislike for the unlike' as Ian Chesterton puts it in 'The Daleks'. The Doctor himself is labelled as non-conforming by Davros who takes satisfaction from the fact that this is recognised by his new creation, the Dalek, which prepares to exterminate this deviant.

*Blake's 7*'s Federation is analogous to both Davros and the Daleks in its recognition of a binary structure, and its concern to exterminate one side of it. Notions of categorisation, labelling and containment are indeed thematised in the first episode 'The Way Back' as the Federation aims to keep the 'hero' figure Blake and his allies within specific categories as well as behind prison bars, but Blake refuses to be contained and labelled and puts a series of binary oppositions into operation. In order to dispose of Blake, the Federation is intent on having him categorised as an insane 'child molester' and firmly framed in this category, an idea that in Nation's original drafts corresponded with the fact that, as Stevens and Moore (2003: 23) note, Blake was a schoolteacher, an idea abandoned due to the costs of hiring child actors. But the idea of child molestation contained in the final televised version is still significant. The Federation does not want to advertise the resistance displayed at the meeting outside the dome and so Blake is not charged for this. The Federation, therefore, is not drawing attention to a binary structure since it wants only itself to be recognised and indeed one of the complaints made to Servalan in the later episode 'Seek-Locate-Destroy' is that Blake is becoming a notorious figurehead for rebellious activities. By having Blake labelled a 'child molester', he is categorised as an enemy of the people according to the Federation's chosen discourse, and this also discredits Blake's position in the series' structure of binary oppositions. Blake, like the Doctor, however, aims to introduce opposing categories and to dissolve these principles of categorisation in an act of militance. He refuses resignation and refuses the Federation's label 'insane', instead fighting against the Federation, which he knows has massacred a group of innocent civilians. The series is premised on Blake's perception of the horrific truth about the oppressive Federation and dramatises his effort to bring about justice and oppose its rigid labels.

## A Nation divided: geographical and symbolic space

The programmes' dystopian binaries and the attempts to collapse them are further expressed through the use of geographical space. Binary oppositions involve a gap between categories and this can be realised spatially. Autocratic racist forms of government are interested in control over all space, making it homogenous. The dystopian binaries of autocracy/freedom and racism/tolerance are commonly realised in Nation's work in terms of divisions of geographical space, specifically inside versus outside, but these distinctions are blurred. This use of space is evident in both *Doctor Who* stories 'The Daleks' and 'Genesis Of The Daleks'. Nation's original story outline for 'The Daleks' specified that the Daleks dwelt underground and that 'the city below ground was prepared before the war to ensure the survival of a select group' (quoted in Pixley 2003: 30), with outcasts left outside it on the surface. In the transmitted story 'The Daleks' the Daleks plan to control the entire planet. In 'Genesis Of The Daleks', 'impure' Kaleds are banished into the wasteland by the 'pure' Kaleds who control space, and while literal monsters were traditionally exiled from community, here it is those who create the monstrous who exile the deformed segment of the race. By contrast, uncommonly, in 'The Keys Of Marinus' Arbitan attempts to keep the oppressive Voord outside the city that protects the brain, with the city located on an island surrounded by acid sea ('Marinus' is a Latin word meaning 'belonging to the sea').

In *Survivors*, Wormley's group sees itself as a centre and while there is a return to the symbolic division between inside/outside seen in the Dalek stories (Tom Price is briefly brought 'inside' the system at the end of 'Gone Away'), this is not expressed geographically and Wormley's group prowls the countryside to prevent looting. Symbolic uses of geographical space can also, however, be seen in the first *Blake's 7* episode 'The Way Back' where the oppressive Federation controls citizens in the dome with surveillance cameras, and Blake calls the people at the secret resistance meeting 'outsiders', saying that 'it's illegal to have contact with anyone who lives *outside* the city' (our emphasis). Inside, water is 'dosed with suppressants' to create a 'drug induced tranquillity', but the outside is associated with nature through the presence of a flowing stream. The boundary between inside and outside is permeable, however, and each region is contaminated by elements that do not belong there. The Federation's city is itself contaminated by the active presence of anti-Federation resistance, presumably allowed there, as Stevens and Moore (2003: 24) note, to get them to betray other rebels, and in episodes such as the second season's 'Voice From The Past' (by Roger Parkes) there are Federation officers who betray their position. Federation agents still engage in surveillance outside the city and the resistance meeting is contaminated by the presence of one of them.

The series as a whole ultimately develops the binary of autocratic systems versus democracy where the main character Blake, who represents a more liberal stance, is progressively removed spatially and thematically from inside the system. Leaving Earth on a prison ship at first contains the main character within the Federation's jurisdiction, repeating themes from 'The Way Back', while the penal colony Cygnus Alpha in the episode of that title is a savage outside chosen by the Federation to contain the prisoners. However, seizing control of the Liberator involves a flight from containment, first from this penal colony and later from the Federation. The science fiction setting of 'outer space' is defined in opposition to what is known and controlled and is also used to realise the binary. The rebels wish to infiltrate Federation space on their terms (as seen in 'Pressure Point') but always move back into outer space, using the Liberator's teleport system to penetrate Federation space and to return to the Liberator and leave orbit.

Outer space is traditionally seen as boundless yet the Federation aims to set boundaries around it, just as it did with inner space in 'The Way Back'. Indeed, the Federation want to capture not only Blake and his band of rebels but also the super-spacecraft the Liberator, which will give them more control over outer space (and this provides potential to engineer narratives). The idea builds on 'Space Fall', and is conveyed in Nation's 'Duel' where Travis wishes to take the Liberator, in 'Project Avalon' where a trap is set to eliminate Blake and his crew while leaving the Liberator intact, and in 'Terminal' where Servalan aims to seize the ship, although by this point, as Stevens and Moore (2003: 147) point out, she may be acting in self-interest and not for the Federation. By attempting to seize the Liberator, the Federation is attempting to eliminate the very freedom for which the ship stands, and therefore also the series' binary structure. The binary of autocracy/freedom is expressed geographically and spatially, and in Nation's episodes 'Orac' and 'Aftermath' Federation exiles (Ensor Senior and Hal Mellanby) reside in under-sea bases, representing a fragile and temporary separation from the Federation system and also protection from the planet's primitive inhabitants.

## Post-structuralist interdependence of binaries

While dystopian autocratic systems of government are concerned with homogeneity and are opposed by characters espousing the values of liberalism, post-structuralist theoretical discourse highlights the importance of binary structures but recognises the dependence of one side of a binary on the other, and sometimes the boundaries between the terms are blurred (see Kristeva 1984, for example). Characters such as the Doctor, Abby Grant and Roj Blake stand for democracy and tolerance in the 'Discourses of Politics and Individualism', yet recognise that these discourses' binary structures are interdependent and see the value of their opponents.

In 'The Daleks', for example, the Thals have chosen to be pacifists after seeing the destruction that their forebears' war brought to Skaro. But the Doctor recognises the need for combat as well as pacifism. In a development of an apparently obvious binary divide between masculine and feminine, the Thal men's blond hair gives them a feminine quality, as does their pacifism, which becomes an obstacle to their survival against the Daleks. This is what provoked the comment (see chapter 2) that the Thals were 'faeries', a derogative term often used to describe homosexuals with feminine qualities. Attaining a conventional mas- culine willingness to fight for survival, prompted by the Doctor's intervention, enables the Thals to resist the Daleks so that a constructive way of life becomes possible for them.

In 'Genesis Of The Daleks', the Doctor recognises that good can come out of the Daleks' evil, since they prompt other races to band together in resistance, thereby highlighting the interconnectedness of binary terms. This is not only indicated by the Doctor's final line of dialogue in the story but also through the very presence of the Doctor in it. For without the Genesis of Evil (the Daleks), the Time Lords would not have brought the Doctor (representing good) to Skaro. If the Doctor's mission to destroy the Daleks were successful, the evil against which good is measured would disappear.

In *Survivors* Abby and her companions must be aware of autocratic systems of government to ensure that they do not replicate them. In the *Blake's 7* episode 'Duel', only through understanding and experiencing war can characters choose peace. Militarism, for example, is both repudiated since the grave markers and the statue each have a broken weapon in their hands, but incorporated since the weapon alludes to the planet's warlike past. Furthermore, there is no clear division between the visitors, Blake and Travis as representatives of violence, versus the women on the planet standing for peace. Although Blake is more identified with Sinofar's awareness of the horror of war, while Travis's violent instincts are more in keeping with Giroc's, even Blake, like Sinofar, sees the necessity and the seductiveness of war (as the Thals eventually do), in line with the rebels' combat against the Federation embedded in *Blake's 7*'s format, and even Giroc realises the peril that war involves.

The notion of the double is not only important for what it reveals about the unified body politic but is also significant in representing the interconnectedness of binaries. For the double implies a connection where the two comprise one, as well as a separation of one into two. Binaries consist of two separate categories, yet they are connected since they are to be read together and in opposition. The principle of doubling is evident in 'Genesis Of The Daleks' encapsulation of the Dalek myth as a whole. Many Kaleds actually wish to remain separate from the Daleks, and to stop the autocratic Dalek project, but this requires them to recognise one side of the binary structure in order to reject it.

The separated but unified double in 'Duel' highlights the separation and interdependence in the binaries of militarism/pacifism that run throughout *Blake's 7*. Sinofar and Giroc, like the binaries of pacifism/ militarism, which they respectively stand for as doubles, are separated but also connected. The boundaries around these characters, and between binaries, are not clearly defined. While Giroc (with savage instincts) can attempt to function independently, Sinofar needs and uses Giroc to teach a lesson about the perils of war because peace can only be known as the opposite of war. The understanding and rejection of war is involved in peace, and the boundaries between them are permeable. The exclusion of war is represented mainly by Sinofar yet Sinofar's connection to Giroc includes it. Indeed, the episode begins with Sinofar calling out to Giroc that she is needed, therefore implying not only a separation between the characters but a doubling connection. As noted, their two titles 'The Guardian' (Sinofar) and 'The Keeper' (Giroc) actually mean the same thing, again suggesting both the separation between the two figures and also their connection.

### Giving birth: the birth and death of a Nation

Survival or lack of survival and the resulting positive or negative implications are a common theme in Nation's work (the Daleks are, as the title of the second episode makes explicit, 'The Survivors', autocratic beings; in *Survivors*, characters can be autocratic or democratic). This theme is also sometimes conjured up by the potential to give birth to physical bodies, or the lack of this potential, which is a representation in microcosm of the birth of a new body politic and illustrates the importance of the values of the hero team. We argued that *Doctor Who's* Davros is a creator figure seeking the Kaleds' rebirth and hence survival, and two of Nation's *Blake's 7* episodes also display a preoccupation with the macrocosmic formation or destruction of the body politic as a result of the binaries we have noted. The importance of democratic peaceful societies is illustrated in the *Blake's 7* episode 'Duel' by developing the creation story of 'Genesis Of The Daleks' in a different way. A unified body politic cannot be created in 'Duel' since the planet's whole population has been wiped out and there are no physical bodies left and thus no survival. This symbolises the dangers inherent in the Federation's political strategies, which aim to eliminate opponents. The tombstones in 'Duel' are, as we suggested earlier, parodies of Christian tombstones, which are associated with the resurrection of the body. Sinofar and Giroc, as Stevens and Moore (2003: 42) observe, 'represent two-thirds of the Celtic maiden-mother-crone triad, but with the mother ... the fertile third ... missing'. Sinofar states that on the devastated planet in 'Duel', children were born monsters or were never born, so the womb became a tomb. Birth and reproduction become means for the episode to comment on the death and sterility associated with war and the Federation's warlike political order.

The importance of democracy and of the fight against autocratic systems is also expressed in the later *Blake's 7* first season episode 'Deliverance'. Because of an atomic war, the original population of the planet Cephlon were wiped out (lack of survival) but their genetic material is contained in a rocket, guarded by Meegat (leading to the potential for survival). Stevens and Moore (2003: 54–5) note that 'Meegat (whose name is an anagram of "gamete", a sexual reproductive cell) is a woman, dressed in a ... vestal-virgin outfit, who is waiting for a man to come along and fire off a rocket full of genetic matter' (the implication being that this is a symbolic phallus). This turns out to be Avon, and not Blake as originally planned. But Stevens and Moore do not connect the ideas of microcosmic 'bodies' and the macrocosmic body politic or note the parallels with 'Duel'. In 'Duel', Sinofar is labelled as 'The Guardian' but is a guardian over a completely dead world, whereas in 'Deliverance' Meegat is also a guardian, but she guards the rocket full of genetic matter that can lead to new life and a new body politic. Indeed 'deliverance' not only means escape but also plays on the 'delivery' of birth where a baby is first guarded by the mother and literally released into the world. Read side by side, the life/death binary in the two episodes suggests an allegorical dialogue between them. While 'Duel' sees the body politic completely destroyed, 'Deliverance' considers possibilities for a constructive body politic arising out of its planet's devastation. However, 'Terminal', an egg, pessimistically sees evolution causing bodily and national bestiality, represented by the ape Links (Stevens and Moore 2003: 147), whose name suggests a doubling connection, in this case with humankind.

## Mythology of a Nation

Dystopian science fiction presents political 'myths' through binaries that are microcosmic of tendencies in the viewer's world. H. J. Rose (1958: 12–14) has defined myth (from the Greek *mythos* meaning 'word', 'speech' or 'story') as 'the result of the working of naïve imagination upon the facts of experience', and it is therefore distinguished not only from history, but also, as Mark P. O. Morford and Robert J. Lenardon (1991: 2) observe, from saga and legend, which 'however fanciful and imaginative, is rooted in historical fact', and from folktale, 'whose major function is', conversely, 'to present a story primarily for the sake of entertainment'. Claude Lévi-Strauss (1970) argued that mythology provides in its fictional forms structures of thought that both illustrate, teach and reinforce the deep binarily opposed structures animating a culture. Myth therefore serves to blur the distinctions between fiction and reality. Work credited to Nation connects with Rose's and Lévi-Strauss's conceptions of myth, rather than saga or legend, since these programmes work on widely shared components of late twentieth-century thought by presenting in fictional worlds binary oppositions that result from significant ideological tensions and contradictions in it. Our analysis of Nation's stories therefore connects with the political mythologies of science fiction, and science fiction television in particular. Repetition, of the kind we discuss below, is not only interesting in itself as a mode of working that Nation employed for economic reasons to make the prolific production of television storylines and scripts possible. Repetition of dystopian binary structures reveals how cultural components of the ideologies current in the later twentieth century are manifested in television drama, especially the liberal ideologies that sought to narrativise and comment upon conflict, agency, institutions and political arrangements.

The idea of Nation's storylines being binarily structured myths is made doubly resonant by the inclusion of narrative structures and allusions deriving from Ancient Greek myth. This use of myth extends to the narration within episodes of historical back-stories that explain the present time of the plot, even though that plot may be set in a distant future. These allusions are 'history' to characters within the plots, but they highlight the myth-like fiction's reflection on twentieth-century culture. Characters within the fictions read the past as history and it informs their actions in the present. Conversely, audiences are invited to interpret these fictions' pasts and presents as mythological narratives that might inform their own present. Mythological narration in these Nation-credited stories therefore combines realism and symbolism and addresses contemporary ideologies.

For example, Nation's first contribution to *Doctor Who*, 'The Daleks', does not draw on a single myth (unlike 'The Keys Of Marinus' where not only is Arbitan adorned in classical robes but where the story is indebted to that of Hercules undergoing various physical labours). Yet, it relies heavily on mythological elements, as noted by Bentham (1986: 68), and the divide between past and present. Details of the history of Skaro and of the Daleks and Thals, from characters' perspectives, are represented through interpretations of the visual evidence left from the past. This is a past that the present Thals have learnt from, witnessing the destructiveness and futility of war and changing their way of life. Just as the Thals are 'readers' of history, the television viewers are 'readers' of this binarily structured didactic myth. The Thals themselves are cast and costumed in order to appear like classical images of gods and heroes, and Susan is in awe of them, giving the story a further aura of myth. The later story 'Genesis Of The Daleks' does not rely heavily on traditional mythological images but is in effect a reinvention of 'The Daleks', which had attained the status of myth in the history of *Doctor Who* and for some members of its audience, as well as representing a past that the audience is invited to learn from.

The *Blake's 7* episode 'Duel', like 'The Daleks', draws on mythological elements and its dystopian binaries connect with historical narratives about the audience's world. Its mythological elements reflect the history of the planet as contained within the fiction, but just as Blake is a 'reader' of this history, the viewers are positioned as 'readers' of this myth. Past and present are therefore intertwined differently for characters in the episode and for the television viewer. For example, the statue in the episode resembles a sculpture of a mythological god of peace (such mythological statues being seen in works such as Geoffrey Chaucer's *The Knight's Tale*), and is part of the planet's history to the characters but is myth to television viewers. Similarly, Sinofar and Giroc resemble goddesses of peace and war respectively and are characters who teach about history to those within the story and about myth to the television viewers. Myth and science fiction frequently concern beings who are superhuman or immortal. Sinofar and Giroc are not ordinary mortals, having survived the holocaust that left the unnamed planet 'dead', and they have the power to appear and disappear at will. This is evident when Sinofar first appears out of nowhere in the cavern as lightning strikes, when Gan first sees the pair only for them promptly to vanish, and when they watch the duel in the forest, which their powers have brought about. Sinofar and Giroc orchestrate the contest between Blake and Travis, just as in Greek myth the gods orchestrate contests, sometimes between mortals, whose purpose can be didactic. Just as

Blake and Travis are being taught a lesson, the episode's mythologies can be regarded as didactic 'lessons' for the television audience about its own culture.

## Questions of authorship: the blurring of Nations

The structure of this chapter has emphasised the similarities between Nation's works both within and between programmes, showing, as in chapter 3, that they are characterised not only by their connections with established genres, but also by their connections with one another. The borders between works are erected yet are simultaneously collapsed. As production staff and fans have observed, Nation repeated similar plots, motifs and character names. For example, *Doctor Who* producer Barry Letts told us that when asking Nation to write 'Genesis Of The Daleks' he told him to come up with a new story rather than reworking 'The Daleks' and 'Planet Of The Daleks', and in the *Blake's 7* episode 'Powerplay' Avon repeats Sara's plan in 'Mission To Destiny' to launch a life capsule so it seems that someone has escaped from the ship (Stevens and Moore 2003: 115). The name Tarrant occurs frequently (in *Doctor Who*'s 'Death To The Daleks', and in *Blake's 7*'s 'The Way Back', as well as for the regular character from the third season), and names recur in draft and final scripts between the *Doctor Who* stories 'The Dalek Invasion Of Earth' (Sonheim, Dortmun), and 'The Daleks' Master Plan' (Sara) with *Blake's 7*'s 'Mission To Destiny' (Stevens and Moore 2003: 39–40).

More significantly, repetition occurs because of programmes' generic similarities. Fiske (1990), examining the Western, argued that individual Westerns are 'specific versions of the same myth of the Western' with 'the same deep structure of binarily opposed concepts', and his work on the *Doctor Who* story 'The Creature From The Pit' demonstrated shared mythic structures in science fiction. Our analysis has shown that this is also the case with programmes credited to Nation, once characters have assembled into political groups since all cities are one (represented by symbolic names). Indeed, the analysis above shows that while producer Barry Letts suggested that Nation come up with a new story about the genesis of the Daleks, that new story was structurally composed of the same binaries as 'The Daleks'. Furthermore, 'Genesis Of The Daleks' shares the same binaries as the earlier 'The Keys Of Marinus' while reversing its scenario by featuring machines without a conscience. The premise of *Survivors* differs, yet an episode such as 'Genesis' revolves around similar binaries to the *Doctor Who* and *Blake's*

7 stories that Nation is credited with writing. *Blake's 7*'s 'The Way Back' seems to differ in plot and tone from 'The Daleks' and another *Blake's 7* episode, 'Duel', but it shares the similar binary oppositions of autocracy versus democracy, and resignation versus militancy. The *Blake's 7* episode 'Countdown' also resembles 'Duel': autocratic tendencies in both lead to the attempted detonation of a weapon of mass destruction, successful (before the episode's present time) in 'Duel' but defused in 'Countdown'. These binaries are also communicated using similar techniques (for example, doubling, uses of symbolic space).

Boundaries are also established and collapsed between the characters who embody the repeated binary structures we have identified, producing doubled characters between the works credited to Nation. These characters can connect with one another and also be differentiated. We have noted similar character traits in the 'hero teams' of *Survivors* and *Blake's 7* where, for instance, both Abby Grant and Roj Blake are the idealistic 'leads' concerned with democracy. We noted the connections between Mavic Chen in 'The Daleks' Master Plan' and Servalan from *Blake's 7*, and between Arthur Wormley from the *Survivors* episode 'Genesis' and (in a far more extreme form) *Blake's 7*'s Federation. Davros, Sinofar and Meegat play similar roles in representing aspects of the perpetuation or destruction of the body politic, resulting from the binaries we have identified, expressed through the creation, or lack of creation, of microcosmic physical bodies. Sinofar and Meegat are particular and differentiated, separated by their appearance in different episodes that express this idea differently, yet they serve the same structural role. Allegorical texts dealing with shared themes often have blurred boundaries in this way; for example, in literature, Edmund Spenser's epic narrative *The Faerie Queene* is divided into different books that relate to each other, and in cinema, the *Star Wars* films repeat structures and themes.

### Other author(ity) figures: *mise en scène* and the realisation of political binaries

An analysis of *mise en scène* shows how the contributions of the director, designer, and other members of the production team actualised dystopian oppositions in the television episodes' final transmitted form, in some cases realising similar plots in differing ways. The binary oppositions of autocracy/democracy and racism/tolerance in the dystopian storyline of 'The Daleks' are transformed into further structural binaries through the use of *mise en scène*. Fiske (1987: 132) argued that in the American series *Hart To Hart* the oppositions of good/evil and hero/villain were represented by structural binaries including American/non-American, middle class/lower class, attractive/unattractive, light/dark and humorous/humourless. The effect, Fiske demonstrated, was to present a series of ideological contradictions, and a similar outcome occurs in 'The Daleks'. The central binary oppositions are realised by the oppositions of machines/humanoids, cold/warm, unattractive/attractive and dark/light.

The Daleks' 'otherness' is conveyed by their representation as cold machines, whereas the Thals are humanoids. A change was made from the rehearsal script where 'The Daleks' dialogue was written in a 'more human, less mechanised way' and 'they would comment "Very puzzling", "You may sit down" and "No, no ... that won't do"' (Pixley 2003: 38). The contribution of Raymond Cusick's design, and the eventual tonelessness of the Dalek voices, is essential to this coding system, dissuading audience sympathy with the Daleks, and making Cusick and those performers providing the Dalek voices author(ity) figures along with Nation. The Daleks' grey metal casings and their loud monotonous voices signify their totalitarianism, while the Thals' humanity emphasised by their soft and sympathetic speech signifies their structural position in the narrative as figures offered for audience identification.

These oppositions are further realised through the concrete binary representations of unattractiveness/attractiveness and, corresponding to this, dark/light. The Daleks are unattractive, while the Thals are presented as if they were mythological gods of beauty. As Howe *et al.* (1993: 31) note, the Thals have turned 'from a race of warriors into Aryan visions of physical perfection'. The Thals, mostly exemplars of masculine and feminine attractiveness, are predominantly youthful. As Pixley (2003: 33) notes, 'All the Thals had been written by Nation as being male', but he was asked 'to make one of them "a gorgeous woman" to emphasise the race's grace and beauty'. The young men are well built with their chests visible, attributes that are conventionally coded as sexually attractive (though the Thal men also possess feminine qualities), and the visible flesh of the women's arms and legs code them as attractive too in relation to the cultural expectations of the 1960s. Furthermore, unattractiveness/attractiveness is suggested through the binary of dark/light. The Daleks are grey while the Thals generally have light blond hair. In a story shot in black and white, colour coding is systematically used by transforming it into easily readable differences between light and dark.

In what would be the start of the third episode 'The Escape' in Nation's original storyline for 'The Daleks', titled 'The Survivors', Susan was sent to the TARDIS to collect anti-radiation drugs. Hearing tapping outside, and after 'taking her courage in one hand and a large spanner in the other', she saw 'a half circle of figures (standing) back in the shadows, lit sometimes by the flickering light'. 'Susan moves ... and a flash of lightning reveals that they are identical to the human race, "but perhaps even more beautiful"' (Pixley 2003: 31). This was changed but the physical perfection of the Thals by contrast with the Daleks, and its links with mythology, is still foregrounded at the start of the transmitted episode, where Susan is on her knees with just one Thal, Alydon, above her eye level wrapped in an other-worldly cloak. Mythological gods are commonly worshipped and looked up to, often in the forms of statues. The scene in 'The Escape' begins with Susan being frightened of Alydon who appears to dominate her (see chapter 3's discussion of the stalked female companion), but this domination becomes a relationship akin to worship in which Susan is overawed by what seems to her a mythological god-like figure of beauty (see figure 8). The use of a point-of-view shot aligns the television viewer with her position, and the meaning of the shot is anchored by Susan's remarks on Alydon's physical perfection, whereas the Daleks had told her that the Thals were horrible mutations.

In 'Genesis Of The Daleks', the director, David Maloney, another author(ity) figure, realised the first side of the binary of war/peace caused by autocratic desires. Originally, the story was to open with a garden scene but 'the director found the planned garden setting too pastoral and rewrote it to open instead on a brutal massacre in the wastelands' (Pixley 1997a: 37). Following a shot of mist, the camera zooms in on a Thal soldier, then two more. After the Thal soldiers have stood up, the sound of gunfire is heard and they fall to the ground in slow-motion. This was a decision that rested solely with the director since Nation was not pleased with this portrayal, regarding it as too horrific (see Howe *et al.* 1993: 87; Hearn 1993: 15). Slow motion requires the viewer to focus on selected details, and the use of slow motion here signals the significance of anonymous death, war and futile destruction through its allusion to the codes used in representing the First World War in particular, and twentieth-century wars in general, recalling our discussion of how iconography from the audience's world is transplanted to Skaro. Slow-motion shots of soldiers rising from the trenches, shots of bodies lying in trenches, the wearing of gas masks, and clouds of smoke or gas drifting across a ravaged no-man's land are conventional signifiers of the First World War, seen in television documentary programmes (and originally in cinema newsreel). The dominant understanding of the First World War is of a static and largely futile conflict that resulted in the deaths of huge numbers of soldiers led by incompetent generals. By signalling this set of myths and televisual and cinematic codes at the start of 'Genesis Of The Daleks', the audience is already prepared for the narrative themes of the futility of war, which are developed further by the allusions to representations of Nazism and the Second World War, which we have already pointed out. Furthermore, the tone of the opening sequence is established by colour and sound as well as by the choice of shot. The first side of the binary of war/peace is represented by literal and metaphoric coldness, signified, unlike in the first Dalek story, by dense mist carried on a breeze whose whistling can be heard in the absence of any sound made by living creatures. The light grey mist belongs to the colour coding based on grey that dominates the Kaled trench into which the Doctor, Sarah and Harry wander in the first episode. The corridors in the Kaled bunker are also grey, and Davros himself has skin and clothing that are a mixture of beige and grey while he wears a black tunic. Grey was the colour of German army uniforms in both world wars, thus connecting its conventional cultural signification as cold, uncomfortable, lifeless, etc. with the more specific allusions to war that we have been discussing. The grey and black uniforms of the Kaleds (recalling the black uniforms of the German SS), together with the grey Dalek casings, contrast with the green combat jackets of the Thal soldiers, perhaps recalling the olive green and khaki uniforms of British and American troops. Coldness is also signified by texture, where the metallic grey corridors of the Kaled bunker mirror the casings of the Daleks, coding the creatures as cold and ruthless.

In *Survivors*, too, the binary opposition between autocracy/democracy and the 'heroic' characters' separation and connectedness to these categories is expressed through *mise en scène*. In this dystopian fiction, binary oppositions between microcosmic forms of government evidently involve a gap between categories and between those who represent these categories, even though in a post-structuralist fashion one side of a binary opposition depends on knowledge of the other. In *Survivors*, then, there is a gap between Abby's favouring of democracy and Wormley's autocratic system of rule and seizure of goods, and a connection between Abby's and Garland's viewpoints. These gaps and relationships are expressed in both the 'Genesis' and 'Garland's War' episodes through directorial technique. In 'Genesis', Abby, who has been enjoying Wormley's warm hospitality by eating and drinking with him and having a hot bath, glimpses the effects of Wormley's model of government when she witnesses the shooting of people who arrive at Wormley's house to protest at the usurpation of their goods. Warmth turns to coldness and Abby's distancing from proceedings is represented spatially through her positioning above the hallway, behind the bars of the banisters (see figure 9). She peeps out at the ensuing action unseen, with a high-angle shot offering her point of view to the audience. Importantly, Abby is positioned in this way after a brick has been thrown through the bathroom window and so her position is based on the psychological assumption that she is cautious about descending the stairs. But the shots in this sequence come to represent the gap between herself and Wormley rather than connectedness. The camerawork, which is naturalistic as well as symbolic, further reinforces the audience's identification with Abby (already established as a continuing main character) by making the television viewer share her optical point of view, and therefore the viewer is ultimately invited to assume her position as an antithesis to Wormley. While Abby is distanced from Wormley, in 'Garland's War' she is presented in close proximity to Garland, enjoys his hospitality, and is seen in his arms in a romantic embrace, signifying the relationship between Abby's and Garland's positions in the binary patterns of the drama.

*Mise en scène* is also important to communicating the binaries of autocracy/democracy and resignation/militance in the dystopian *Blake's 7* opening episode 'The Way Back'. In the opening scene, the director Michael E. Briant at first chooses a shot that establishes a surveillance camera within the fiction, then cuts to people walking through the city's corridor. These isolated individuals walk in single file, they are self-absorbed and do not speak to each other, suggesting that they may be drugged (see figure 10). Being aware of what is going on, and engaging in communication, are the first steps in rebelling against the Federation system and becoming individuals, but these people are literally and symbolically kept walking around in circles. Soon afterwards, a closer shot of these people is offered as the Federation spy Tarrant walks through the corridor. The other people in the dome wander aimlessly with no concern for their surroundings, with heads drooping and sometimes with their hands in their pockets. Blake is notably different from them and dialogue soon reveals that at the rebel Ravella's request, he has for a long time avoided the drugged food and drink that keeps the population under control. When Blake is first represented, he starts to look around for his meeting point with Ravella. Tarrant, like Blake, moves in a much more purposeful manner to follow Ravella and Blake to the secret meeting outside the dome.

Additionally, the incidental music of this opening scene reinforces these binaries. The music is very subdued and relaxing, at first connoting calm and order. But the music shares the connotations of the

Federation's artificially produced and restrictive control over its citizens' behaviour. To be relaxed entails passive acceptance without question, while to be uncomfortable with the surroundings might eventually lead to active rebellion. The musical score thus takes on an ironic force, as a commentary on the false tranquillity against which Blake will fight. The narrative's move from inside to outside, to a natural landscape with a blowing breeze, represents a relief from this stifling setting.

In 'The Way Back' the use of visual space supports the dystopian binary structures associated with oppression/liberty in the 'Discourse of Politics'. Frames confine characters. The dome constrains Federation citizens inside, and the meeting outside the dome revolves around the desire to find freedom. When Federation guards arrive, Blake is, however, framed behind bars as he hides, a composition connoting his oppression and forthcoming imprisonment (see figure 11). Frames also make characters objects of both the Federation's gaze and the viewer's gaze. Later, in his padded cell, Blake is framed on a surveillance screen being watched by Federation officers. The scene begins with a tilt up from Blake to the surveillance camera on the ceiling of his cell. Then a cut shows Federation agents in conversation in a comfortable lounge watching Blake in his uncomfortable cell on a monitor screen. The screen's high-angle shot of Blake emphasises the Federation agents' power over him. *Blake's 7* dramatises the characters' move from being constrained objects of the gaze, and from literally being imprisoned on a prison ship in 'Space Fall' or on a penal colony in 'Cygnus Alpha', to becoming agents of action.

In 'Duel', as in other Nation scripts, a dystopian planet is left barren and lifeless as a result of war, and this was realised under the control of the director and reinforces the binaries of pacifism in relation to militance, which reflect on *Blake's 7* as a whole. As noted earlier, viewers praised the visual realisation of 'Duel', overseen by director Douglas Camfield. Unlike Nation's first *Doctor Who* story 'The Daleks', 'Duel' was shot in colour, and at the start of the episode effective use is made of this to create the deathly atmosphere of the planet caused by the first of the binary terms, militarism. In television drama, colour contributes to *mise en scène* by being organised into codes specific to particular narratives but also influenced by convention. Colours are usually coded either as warm and comfortable, such as yellow, red and brown, or as cold and uncomfortable, such as blue, green and grey. Pale blue and green are used at the beginning of 'Duel' to code the planet as uninviting and deathly. The lighting is also significant. Lighting can be coded generically where, for instance, soft light often connotes romance, and in this case harsh lighting is appropriate for dystopian science fiction. While the scene at the beginning of the episode, including the shot of the cavern and the graveyard, and those later on involving Sinofar and Giroc on the barren planet, use little light, the colours of green and blue that the lightning casts on the cavern introduce connotations of deathly coldness. Upon their initial appearances, Sinofar and Giroc are associated with this colour. When first seen in long shot, Sinofar's face looks pale blue, while her gown is a mixture of white and pale blue. In close-ups, details of Sinofar's face such as her lips appear bluish, showing the contribution of make-up artist Marianne Ford. Similarly, the skin of Giroc's face and hands appear pale blue because of the scene's lighting design. The effect of this colour coding can be contrasted with an opposing system used in Sinofar's and Giroc's appearances later in the episode where their skin is pink, and Sinofar's gown looks yellow and white, all softer colours than the blue that predominated earlier. Nation's script is therefore repetitive but through *mise en scène* the differences also stand out.

Furthermore, as in the realisation of Nation's script for 'The Daleks', in 'Duel' sound connotes the dystopian barrenness of the planet and the violence that caused this, emphasising the binary of militance/pacifism. The very first use of sound in the episode is of incidental music with a succession of deep, funereal notes whose sombre connotations also appear later. Turbulent human emotions are mapped on to nature through sound effects when in shots of the barren landscape at the beginning of the episode, blue flashes of lightning appear combined with sound, a motif also used in the black and white 'The Daleks'. In 'Duel', both when Blake, Jenna and Gan first teleport down to the planet and explore the area, and later when Blake and Travis have been brought to the planet's surface by Sinofar, the sound of wind can be heard in the background. Also when Sinofar has brought Blake and Travis down to the planet and Giroc informs Blake that they are a dead race, a sudden burst of lightning sounds and flashes over Blake's face. Moments of silence in television are extremely rare and here, rather than use a significant silence, the sound and flash of lightning serve as a pause signifying the horror in Giroc's lines. During this scene, the sound and flashes of lightning are not as pronounced during the dialogue between characters as they are at this point, emphasising this moment.

As we have seen, the connection between the graveyard and the statue, with both representing the horror of war and the need for peace, is established at the outset of the episode and this is conveyed through camera techniques. The third shot of the episode, following the zoom in to the unnamed planet and the similar shot of the cavern on the planet's surface, is a zoom in on the landscape's grave markers (see figure 12).

The audience is offered an omniscient point of view, which surveys the scene and moves closer into what the zoom connotes to be significant details. This is only the third shot of the episode, and follows the convention of establishing location and atmosphere. Following this, there is a cut to a long shot of the inside of the cavern with the statue in the centre, connecting the two images.

As we have explored thematically, the binary of pacifism in relation to militance is represented through the connection between the statue and Sinofar, each in this dystopian fiction offering a critique of war that includes war through the very act of attempting to exclude it, and this idea of doubling is also conveyed through a combination of techniques of *mise en scène*. Posture in the shot, for instance, is significant to creating this visual identification. In one important long shot near the start of the episode, doubling is highlighted when the statue is situated in the centre background while Sinofar occupies the right foreground of the frame (see figure 13). When this long shot first appears, only the statue in the centre is visible, yet a flash of lightning fills the screen and then this disappears to leave Sinofar, bathed in the pale blue lighting, who has magically appeared in the foreground. The use of the long shot conventionally establishes the setting, but the presence of both the statue and Sinofar within the frame in a similar posture creates a visual identification between them. While the opening shots of the episode are zooms in, the long shot of the statue and Sinofar is static in every respect. The motionless statue and motionless Sinofar both have their heads turned upwards with arms outstretched. Subsequent shots offer a close-up of Sinofar's lifted head superimposed over the statue, thus keeping the statue in the background and Sinofar in the foreground far longer than if there were a conventional cut between the first shot and a close-up of Sinofar, so there is a greater chance of this shot registering with the audience. Sinofar is also seen later against the background of the statue when she brings Travis and Blake down to the planet, giving repeated emphasis to this composition and again prompting this association.

This visual identification is further represented through the way images of statues are conventionally referenced. A statue is a cold, lifeless object. The pale blue lighting upon Sinofar making the details of her face bluish gives the impression of her, at first, as cold and lifeless like the statue, in addition to communicating the deathly atmosphere of the planet. Furthermore, statues such as those of figures from Greek mythology, are commonly of naked men and women. In 'Duel' the statue is no exception, being of a naked figure with prominent muscles on its torso. In addition to this muscular torso being, as in the case of other statues such as Donatello's David, a Christian figure from the story of David and Goliath, a sign of strength associated with war, the muscular torso connects the statue visually with Sinofar in the long shot that contains them both. While Sinofar is fully clothed, her white costume is tight, emphasising her breasts, just as the torso of the statue is clearly visible.

The identification between the statue and Sinofar and the binary of pacifism in relation to militance are connected with religious meaning and worship, and both embody a critique of war. The visual and aural identification and doubling of the statue and Sinofar through the type of posture in which they are fixed, through the use of costume, and through incidental music invoke connotations of religiosity. An asymmetrical shot is common in visual media, often signifying the natural and every-day, while a shot that involves symmetry connotes deliberate staging. Sinofar's posture is not everyday, and her appearance suggests a performance for the television audience, which contrasts with the use of naturalism referred to in this chapter. Furthermore, Sinofar's costume is used in a particular way. The white silk hanging from her naked arms connotes ethereal and religious meanings through associations with ceremonial robes and paintings of religious subjects, for example. Also, when Sinofar first appears in shot with the statue, followed by a close-up of her face, the incidental music changes from the more haunting tone associated with the cavern and the graveyard, to more spiritual music.

The binary oppositions of pacifism in relation to militance, which are communicated through the two characters of Sinofar and Giroc, who are doubles where these different values are both distributed and connected, is evident through *mise en scène*. The casting of these roles was important as the story is structured by the notions that Sinofar signifies the attractions of peace, and Giroc conversely embodies the unattractiveness of war (see figure 14). Sinofar resembles a mythological goddess and is played by a younger actress, Isla Blair, while the older actress Patsy Smart is cast as Giroc, supporting the coding of Sinofar as an appealing character once the blue deathly lighting has been removed, and Giroc as a grimmer figure whose age suggests death. As we have seen, physical attractiveness added to the meaning of the *Doctor Who* story 'The Daleks'. Blair has long hair, which, as with her pronounced breasts and the exposure of her skin, marks her as feminine. Indeed, Blair is renowned for appearing in other roles in nude scenes connoting her physical attractiveness to the heterosexual male. Contrastingly, Smart's physique is not emphasised and her hair is covered by a hood.

Costume design also contributes to the expression of this binary opposition, through colouring and texture. Sinofar is further coded as warm, following the coldness of the initial scene where pale blue dominates, through the way in which her white gown, designed by Barbara Lane, contains yellow around the collar, and through her headband with yellow silk stretching down behind her head. Sinofar's costume is made from smooth cotton, which associates her with calm and peace. By contrast, Giroc is coded as cold and unfeminine. Lane's costume for Giroc is dark green, appears rag-like, and provides a sense of roughness connoting the harshness of war with which she is largely associated. The techniques mentioned above add to the myth-like quality of the episode. Casting and use of costume also communicate the idea in Nation's work of the literal birthing process or lack of it standing for the construction or lack of formation of the body politic, since Sinofar is presented as a maiden and Giroc as a hag with the mother figure missing, while in 'Deliverance' Meegat is a virginal figure.

### Gender politics in *Doctor Who*, *Survivors* and *Blake's 7*

Television Studies work on the form and content of representations requires study of textuality (see Muir 2000 for textual readings of *Blake's 7*, for example) and of how representations are understood by audiences. Television is approached as something that is actively made, using particular textual forms to communicate some meanings and not others, with meanings that are not simply delivered to audiences but that are appropriated and used by them in complex ways. The prime binary opposition that structures the world is male/female, and the physical and emotional qualities that conventionally distinguish the sexes are given differential value when they take the cultural forms of masculine and feminine qualities that can be attributed to individuals, texts or genres, for instance. This is a distinction discussed in relation to television representation by David Lusted (1998), for example, who notes that the expression of emotion is a marker of femininity, while masculine values entail the suppression of emotion in favour of efficiency, achievement and stoicism. Science fiction's consistent concern with military conflicts, technology and action drama give the genre a reputation as masculine. The media generally, and television specifically, are filled with gender stereotypes that draw on these binary oppositions. The term 'stereotype' (deriving from the Greek word *stereos* meaning 'solid' and *typos* meaning 'mark') was first proposed by Walter Lippmann in *Public Opinion* (1922), and stereotypes have been examined by T. Perkins (1979), R. S. Lichter *et al.* (1986), Graeme Burton (2000) and B. Casey *et al.* (2002) in relation to television generally, by

Joseph Dominick and Gail Rauch (1972), A. Courtney and T. Whipple
(1980), and Linda J. Busby (1975) in relation to television commercials
where women are frequently associated with the domestic sphere, and
by Joseph Turrow (1974) and M. Fine (1981) in relation to soap opera.
We draw on some of this work in our discussion of the science fiction
programmes Nation worked on.

The stories credited to Nation for *Doctor Who* had to fit into the already
established and rigid parameters of format where the production team
members acted as author(ity) figures. Gender stereotypes were embedded in *Doctor Who*'s format from the start with both format and
stereotypes being relatively rigid components. The Doctor was initially
supported in his masculine physical activity by a younger male
character, creating a composite leading masculinity, and this primary
figure was accompanied by female assistants who played passive
secondary roles. This was the case with every new female companion
who entered the series. Nicholas Abercrombie (1996: 72) cites *Doctor
Who* specifically as an example of 'the traditional "males' tale" ' where
there is a rational active protagonist and an emotional passive heroine.
The female companion indeed differed from the male assistant who
appeared far less frequently, and who existed to assume an action
'running and punching role' when the Doctor was played by the elderly
William Hartnell or when it was not yet clear that Pertwee's replace-
ment would be the physically able Tom Baker, for example (Tulloch and
Alvarado 1983: 229). Nevertheless there were attempts to get away from
this stereotype by making the companion a scientific genius, an
independent journalist (as with Elisabeth Sladen's Sarah Jane Smith
whom Nation was told to make stronger), or a street rogue (as with
Sophie Aldred's Ace in the late 1980s). But in Nation's *Doctor Who*
stories, as we saw in chapter 3, there is continual repetition of the motif
of an unseen figure, who would always turn out to be male, unintentionally frightening the heroine. Indeed, in the first story Nation was
credited with writing for the programme, circumstances are deliberately
engineered so that it has to be the young Susan Foreman who proceeds
through the forest to collect anti-radiation drugs from the TARDIS,
putting her in a threatening situation (as seen in chapter 3). The programme could therefore be read by the audience as reinforcing traditional
gender stereotypes and disempowering women, but it also allows for
readings in which women assist narrative progression. We also saw in
chapter 2 how Nation was instructed by the script editor Terrance Dicks
to make one-off female characters less bland.

Nation's series *Survivors* differs from *Doctor Who* since he conceived
the format and the female Abby Grant as the primary active figure of the

programme. Abby, described in the camera script as 'an attractive and sophisticated woman', displays masculine traits once she ceases being a housewife upon the death of her husband, such as the fact that she is emotionally tough and, unlike the more conventionally feminine Jenny Richards, does not run away at the appearance of the hanged looter in the episode 'Gone Away'. In 'The Fourth Horseman' she cuts her long hair with a masculine rational resolve to start a new life and face challenges. But she also displays conventional feminine qualities, ones that invite sympathetic identification. Abby is driven throughout by her maternal instinct to try to locate her son Peter, which at the level of series plotting ultimately leads her out of the programme at the end of the first season to be replaced as head of the community by Greg Preston. Furthermore, Jenny Richards is consistently represented as a stereotypically helpless female having previously been a typist, an occupation often regarded as women's work. Nation's camera script describes Jenny as 'a good looking modern girl', 'nice' and someone who 'gives the impression of being very vulnerable'. In 'The Fourth Horseman' Jenny struggles to fend off attempted rapists who threaten her physically and emotionally as she makes her way out of London. With no law and order to protect her, the danger of male muscular strength and consequent intimidation asserts itself. Jenny continues in a conventional feminine role later after having found security, when she becomes pregnant with Greg Preston's child in 'A Beginning'. Women's vital but stereotypical contribution to this post-plague society is to keep the community flourishing by bearing children and to re-establish the presence of former familial relationships that have been lost, an idea also developed in the episode 'The Future Hour' where another female visiting character gives birth. Nevertheless, the instance of Jenny Richards becoming pregnant by a man she loves is less extreme than the storyline in 'Corn Dolly' (not written by Nation but by Jack Ronder) of the architect Charles advocating impregnating as many women as possible in order to keep the society flourishing. As Alsop (1987: 13) notes, 'the corn dolly is no longer a throwback to antiquated country superstitions, but a symbol of the future'. The view of Charles, who would later become a regular character, is, however, toned down. But importantly *Survivors* mixes science fiction, apocalyptic drama and domestic drama (not Nation's wish). The latter, as is often the case with soap operas, suggests that the woman's place is still in the home as a maternal figure, playing a different role from the male in the rebuilding of society. For example, the camera script describes Greg Preston as someone who 'can be fairly tough' and his profession was the conventionally masculine one of civil engineer. Therefore, *Survivors* invites the audience to see traditional women's roles challenged in a pleasurable way, but only to find them ultimately reasserted.

Nation returns in the format for *Blake's 7* to presenting the lead primary character as a male (Blake). The series generically mixes science fiction with action adventure and military combat, with four of the original six main 'heroic' characters male and only two female (Jenna and Cally), thereby ultimately reducing the women in Blake's crew to secondary characters. Indeed, in Nation's original plan for the programme where Blake was to be accompanied by the team of seven, Avon, Gan, Vila and Jenna, as well as Tone Selman, Brell Kline and Arco Trent (see Stevens and Moore 2003: 18), the over-weighting of male characters was even more apparent. Heroic virtues were, as in *Doctor Who*, embedded primarily in the lead male, while the two females eventually conformed to common stereotypes about women (as David Hipple 2002 shows). The first of these women introduced in the first episode 'The Way Back' was Jenna Stannis, a notorious criminal with a reputation as an interplanetary smuggler, and Vila commented, 'She's a big name; it's an honour to be locked up with her'. The second of these female characters, Cally, was indeed, as Stevens and Moore (2003: 19) point out, 'a late addition to the team, intended to balance out the gender mix of the regulars'. Cally is first introduced in the fourth episode 'Time Squad' as an aggressive woman in leather clothes who is able to surprise Blake and hold him at gunpoint. Despite Blake's ability to trick her and gain control in that scene, Cally curses him and remains unbowed.

Viewers may read these episodes as empowering women, but in later episodes, both Jenna and Cally become weaker and more conventionally feminine characters, signified not only by their actions but also by their costumes and hairstyles. Sally Knyvette, who played Jenna, reported, 'I met Terry Nation at a convention, and he admitted to me that he couldn't write for women characters' (quoted in Nazzaro, 1992a: 29). In 'Duel', Jenna's role is to be captured and bound by Travis so that Blake will walk into a trap in an effort to save his female companion. She becomes a passive stimulus for the male–male fight in the forest between Blake and Travis. Stevens and Moore (2003: 43) focus on the selection of Jenna to stand for the death of a friend as somehow representing the fact that Blake has subconscious romantic feelings towards her, without noting the way in which the episode is playing upon traditional stereotypical roles for women. The earlier sixth episode 'Seek-Locate-Destroy' followed a similar pattern: it involves the Liberator crew teleporting down to a Federation base in order to steal a deciphering machine, which would enable them to read important Federation messages. The mission goes to plan except for the fact that Cally is stranded and captured by the Federation. This is used to strengthen the male Blake's heroic qualities when he insists on returning to rescue Cally from Travis. Another hero–villain, male–male battle occurs in this episode, revolving around the woman. Again, in 'Deliverance' it is Jenna who must be rescued from 'primitives', and it is Cally, the female, who is taken hostage on board the Liberator by the young Ensor so that the crew will follow his orders. Both Jenna's and Cally's roles aboard the Liberator were reduced to those of housewives (see Hipple 2002), and Graeme Wood and Joanne Hillman (1992: 38–9) report that 'Sally did not enjoy playing the role of Jenna, whom she now regards as a kind of Space-going bimbo without depth or very much interest'. This idea is supported by a comment by Sally Knyvette herself, who stated that her character 'started off as this really exciting, intergalactic space pirate, but then she became a sort of housewife on the Liberator – not quite that, but she did very much become Blake's sidekick, with one-liners and supporting remarks to the lads and making sure she looked as sexy as possible'. 'I did a bit of teleporting', continues Knyvette, but adds, 'I usually had to fight for things like that', and concludes that 'the character wasn't anything like the way she had been conceived in the beginning ... the fact is, we were not given our voices' (quoted in Nazzaro and Wells 1997: 91). In the first *Blake's 7* series there was generally an imbalance where the leads were given a lot to do and the secondary characters little. There were attempts to redress this through the inclusion of largely character-orientated stories devoted to the secondary figures, where the male Gan would have played a central role in Nation's aborted script 'The Invaders' (Stevens and Moore 2003: 48), where Gan does have a central part in 'Breakdown' and where Jenna has a large role in 'Bounty', portraying her as slightly stronger, an episode for which script editor Chris Boucher and director Pennant Roberts had considerable input. But these were rare exceptions and even though there were secondary male characters both of the women in the programme were secondary. Jan Chappell (Cally) is quoted reflecting that 'Sally Knyvette and I did spend a lot of time on the Liberator in the second series, not exactly being "housewives" but it was a bit like that' (Andrews 1994: 8–9).

The specific visual representation of the female characters (and of the others too) is of course the responsibility of the director rather than the screenwriter. Vere Lorrimer directed 12 episodes in the first three seasons, and was the producer of the fourth season. Paul Darrow (Avon) reported an occasion when Lorrimer had to deal with a distraught Jan Chappell (Cally): 'Vere didn't understand why she was crying. She told him her best scenes were gone, to which Vere said, "Don't worry about that, I'll give you a close-up; you'll feel better!"' (quoted in Nazzaro and

Wells, 1997: 46). This attitude was supported by Terry Nation's character sketches for the main characters. Nation describes Jenna as 'a good-looking girl who manages to remain female in a very male world. She can be tough, cynical, and also loyal and honest. Not far beneath her surface is a very "nice" girl' (quoted in Russell 1995: 9), and Nation described Cally as 'strikingly beautiful, tall, slim and athletic'. The physical characteristics of the women predominate over their intellectual accomplishments or physical abilities. For the male characters, it is these physical abilities (like Gan's physical strength) and intellectual attributes that distinguish them from each other. Since the production team had imagined *Blake's 7* as a military adventure in space, it is not surprising that the conventional binary oppositions between characters, and the adoption of present-day assumptions about gender, should appear in the programme. The action adventure genre had already offered Nation opportunities to explore gender representation, especially in his work on *The Avengers*, and recent critical work has returned to these 1960s drama series to debate the significance of gender conventions in them and their potential to disturb and reorient conceptions of femininity and masculinity (see Hermes 2001; O'Day 2001; Osgerby 2001; Chapman 2002).

However, a potentially powerful image of womanhood is offered to the female viewer of *Blake's 7*, in the character of Supreme Commander Servalan (Jacqueline Pearce). The fourth season episode 'Sand' (by Tanith Lee) is an appropriate launching point for considering the character as created by Nation since in this episode Servalan offers a definition of herself as 'unique' stating that there are no other women like her. Servalan refuses to fit within the traditional binary categorisation of women in relation to men and blurs the boundaries between these inherited binaries, mixing the category of femininity with masculinity and power. At a time shortly before the accession of Margaret Thatcher to the role of Britain's first woman Prime Minister in 1979, Servalan's appearance as a woman in a leadership role whose gender challenged conventional representations of female power prefigures television codings of Thatcher (see Bignell 2000b). Servalan also preceded the American prime-time soap opera *Dynasty*'s character of Alexis Carrington-Colby who, as Christine Geraghty (1991) has argued, was a successful businesswoman in a man's world (coincidentally pitted against a character called Blake), and later *Knots Landing*'s Abby Cunningham. Critical work on American prime-time soap operas of the 1980s has consistently debated the significance of strong women characters in this genre and their appeal to women viewers (see Ang 1997, for example) and occasionally the significance of women characters in the police series (D'Acci 1994).

Servalan is the strongest female character in *Blake's 7*, who first appears as a Supreme Commander at Space Headquarters, and is therefore, as her title denotes, a primary figure who appoints and rules over secondary male officers such as Space Commander Travis, in a reversal of the binary of male as primary and female as secondary. She later works her way up the power ladder to the position of Federation President, and after she is deposed she returns under the name of Commissioner Sleer. The character was first introduced halfway through the first season in the episode 'Seek-Locate-Destroy', and was, as noted earlier, originally written as a male character, Shervalan (Stevens and Moore 2003: 18), who would appear only in this episode. However, the Servalan character was changed to a woman who would mix feminine and the originally conceived masculine qualities, described by Nation as 'this tremendously sexual, sensual woman, made of ice' and a 'killer', and Nation's belief was that there is 'something in a woman that is ... colder, icier' than in a man (quoted in Nazzaro 1992a: 29).

Servalan's structural position as Blake's main enemy was represented by her unconventionally masculine behaviour. Positive characters conform to gender conventions, while negative characters distort them. The casting of a female actress in the role of the Federation Commander draws attention to the conventionally passive female role in television fiction and in science fiction in particular, and highlights the Federation's conventionally masculine policies of violence and institutionalised aggression. In the fourth season episode 'Sand', mentioned above, Servalan's back-story is revealed where it transpires that Servalan left the familial setting when her lover died, and replaced human love with love of power. Servalan still used her feminine sexuality but now in a masculine aggressive way to exert power over men. This was developed across the four series of *Blake's 7* in scripts that were not written by Nation but that built on the character he created, such as in the third season episode 'Death-Watch' (by script editor Chris Boucher), for example, where she allows herself to be kissed by Avon while she would happily kill him, and in the fourth season episode 'Traitor' (by Robert Holmes) where, in a passionate embrace, she kills a man by lightly pressing an icicle on his neck, the suggestion being that it has a poison tip. In the fourth season episode 'Orbit' (also by Robert Holmes) there is a suggestion of Egrorian's attraction to Servalan meaning that he will abandon the male Pindar, but when Egrorian fails Servalan in her drive for power, she promptly leaves him. Even the feminine domain of motherhood becomes associated with masculine power for Servalan, as in the third season episode 'Children Of Auron' (by Roger Parkes) where she is involved in cloning, aiming to create children in her own image without a masculine partner, as a God-like figure. The mix of feminine and masculine characteristics in Servalan was visually represented by her increasingly revealing costumes versus her short hair. In the second season episode 'Gambit' (by Robert Holmes), for example, Servalan wears a flamboyant red gown, prefiguring those that would be seen on Alexis in *Dynasty*, with red lipstick connoting both sexual appeal and blood. Servalan became a woman on display both for the viewer and for characters in the world in which she moves. In 'Traitor' a painting of her is placed on display, mainly as a means of characters identifying Servalan who now goes under the name of Sleer, but also as a mark of her masculine power, and is the subject of male characters' voyeuristic gaze, just as the heterosexual male viewer of the programme may be sexually interested in such a dominating and attractive woman (see figure 15).

However, while Servalan offers a potentially empowering representation of womanhood, the female audience may be distanced from the portrayal through the fact that Servalan, despite her masculine traits, does not form a common bond with other female characters but actively works against them. This is an idea also discussed by Geraghty (1991: 182) in relation to prime-time American soaps such as *Dallas*, where the 'refusal to acknowledge a common bond between women is a key characteristic of the film noir women in *Dallas*' such as Kristen Shepherd and Katherine Wentworth. These are 'closed characters, driven by one burning necessity and cut off from the audiences' sympathy by their capacity to manipulate', attacking other women. In *Blake's 7* such negation of a bond between women on the part of Servalan is present in 'Pressure Point' where Servalan uses the conventional familial mother–daughter relationship to her advantage by threatening a rebel mother's life in order to get the daughter to betray the main protagonists, although in Nation's original draft the mother Kasabi was a man named Kasabian, held prisoner, and the daughter did not betray the rebels (see Stevens and Moore 2003: 79). In the opening episode to the third season 'Aftermath', credited to Nation, he introduced the black woman character of Dayna Mellanby (Josette Simon) to the programme, largely because Sally Knyvette had left at the end of the second series. Dayna is at first presented in a familial environment: under the ocean, she lives with her adopted sister with whom she shares a familial bond, and her father Hal Mellanby who turned against the Federation years previously. The relationship between Servalan and Dayna is key to considering issues of gender and how they might be understood by the audience. Servalan at first tells Dayna that they should be 'friends' and condescendingly strokes Dayna's cheek, but Servalan's masculine aggression and duty to the Federation leads her ruthlessly to gun down and kill Dayna's father, realising who he is, destroying the feminine familial environment, and leading Dayna on a personal quest to kill Servalan for the rest of the third and fourth seasons. Dayna joins the Liberator crew (later to become the crew of Scorpio) making this her home. In the fourth season episode 'Assassin' (by Rod Beacham), Servalan tells the hired female assassin Cancer, who turns out not to be a hysterical emotional girl but a cold-hearted killer and has the heroic team in her power, that she is a credit to the female sex, but femininity is only important to Servalan when used against the rebels.

## Conclusion

Our analysis of political signification in work credited as written or devised by Nation has demonstrated a relatively consistent set of concerns, which we have argued goes some way to establishing an authorial signature. But we are not interested in attributing all of the ideological patterns we have discussed to Nation himself, since all of the programmes we have addressed are collective products of the production team and the television institutions that made them. Furthermore, we argue that Nation's authorial intention and that of others is dissimilar in principle to the network of interpretations that audiences in fact create when watching these programmes. Nevertheless, there are consistent interests in the dynamics of power in programmes associated with Nation's name. The seizing, maintenance and exercise of political and institutional power frequently either feature as recurrent storylines in series whose format does not necessarily focus on these issues (as in *Doctor Who* and *Survivors*), or are part of the premise of a whole format (as in *Blake's 7*). While the attention to questions of power is hardly a distinctive or unusual focus for television drama, we argue that the particular ways in which the question is addressed do have some distinctive and recurrent features. We have sought to illuminate these features by adopting a method of analysis focusing mainly on narrative structure, and more specifically on sets of binarily opposed ideas, themes and motifs. This methodology, however, can sometimes reduce the complexity of works to oversimplified networks of ideas (see Bignell 2002a), and thus overlook the tone and dramatic emphases of particular programmes, sequences or scenes. We have aimed to reduce this tendency by looking in some detail at the television techniques used to realise the patterns we identify. This has the added benefit of remarking how personnel other than Nation, such as directors and designers, made important contributions to the coherence and significance of narrative structures.

These programmes are examples of popular television drama aimed at a broad audience, and storylines are structured through binary oppositions that communicate economically and easily. The genre and form of programmes (discussed in the preceding chapters) exercised constraining influences on the stories Nation was involved with, and functioned as boundaries circumscribing the degree of conceptual or formal experimentation that these programmes could contain. As we noted in chapter 2, the production teams of all of the programmes Nation worked on imagined their audience as composed of different constituencies as regards age, gender and social class. The diversity of the audience and the requirement to attract and hold viewers made the expression of alternative or radical ideologies in these programmes institutionally impossible. Instead, consensual ideologies in which liberal humanist and democratic values are espoused were the terrain on which the writing and realisation of particular episodes and storylines were based. Within this constraining context, the science fiction television programmes we have explored in this chapter some-times pushed at the boundaries of these ideologies by adopting a largely dystopian imaginary. Rather than celebrating liberal humanism, as for example *Star Trek* has done, the work associated with Nation poses liberal humanism as a strategy of survival in a science fiction setting that militates powerfully against it. The setting of many of Nation's *Doctor Who* stories in devastated environments and in oppressive regimes pits the Doctor's liberal values against characters and problems that seem overwhelmingly more powerful than he is. In *Survivors* the familiar surroundings of England become a similarly devastated world. There is a desire for collectivity, security and hope, which seem vulnerable and marginal forces doomed to submerge under ruthless and savage forms of individual action and social organisation that respond to immediate needs for food, water and safety. In *Blake's 7* a fascistic and ruthless tyranny is established as a dominant force across an entire galaxy, and again the efforts of Blake and his crew to overthrow this system in favour of a more humane and democratic one can seem like futile and insignificant blows against it. Nevertheless, the values of the British (or more accurately English) middle class that these resistant and hopeful characters possess are attributed with potential to become the lynchpins of progress towards a more enlightened future. While this scenario is undoubtedly somewhat parochial and fantastic, the politics of these programmes represent a consistent attempt to shore up British traditions of decency and tolerance against pervasive fears about both the future and the present. Furthermore, work credited to Nation offers scope for discussion of gender, with a similarly conventional ideological form but with significant play at the edges of these conventions. It is also significant that the ideologies borne in the programmes we have discussed are those of the institutions of British television itself. The heritage of public service broadcasting forms the overarching political and institutional context of Nation's creative career, and its own ideological contradictions between paternalism and liberal tolerance versus acquisitiveness, market individualism and responses to external threats are at least analogous if not parallel to those we have found in the programmes analysed here.

# Conclusion

This book has focused on programmes in the popular genre of science fiction that are credited to Terry Nation as writer or creator, but has challenged the assumption that the authorship of, and the authority over, these programmes rests with Nation himself, who can be more accurately described in Murdoch's (1980) terms as a 'craftsman'. This distinction has been frequently made in the field of Television Studies when analysing popular television. In television forms such as the single play and the prestigious classic serial, the writer for television has been assimilated into an understanding of authorship deriving from literary models. The expectation of a distinctive personal style, and recurrent themes and concerns that may amount to an authorial signature, give writers in these culturally valued television forms the characteristics that the theorist Michel Foucault (1980) attributed to literary authors. However, although some of Nation's television writing, and especially the programmes whose formats he devised, prominently display his name in on-screen credits, and foreground the television screenwriter and creator as author, Nation has received no substantial recognition in these terms. Working in popular generic television, Nation never invited such acclaim, and was content to think of television as a medium of popular entertainment where he could receive recognition from fellow television professionals and audiences, and attain financial security. Television writers working in popular generic television often do not have lofty ambitions, writing to earn a living in a commercial industry and scripting for numerous programmes simultaneously.

One important point confuses the issue of authorship with regard to Nation, however. In the medium of literature, the establishment of laws of copyright ownership in the eighteenth and nineteenth centuries aimed both to secure the status of authors as a special kind of cultural producer, and also to guarantee authors a share of the financial reward for their work (Foucault 1980). In television, copyright ownership over programmes generally rests with the institutions whose personnel collectively produce them, rather than with their writers, and the commercial and industrial organisation of television militates against the prominence of the author. In Nation's case, however, some of the public recognition and financial reward that copyright secures for literary writers was gradually available to him. Nation was one of the first writers working for the BBC to negotiate copyright ownership over his creations. The Daleks are almost always attributed to Nation as their creator, and Nation and his creatures have become almost synonymous in the public imagination. As Nation's range of work and public reputation grew, he was able to secure some measure of control over the early episodes of *Survivors*, and on-screen credit for devising *Blake's 7*. It would seem, therefore, that some of the authorship and authority available to writers of 'quality drama' accrued to him. Nation was able to make his own mark in the industry, and to establish himself as a 'brand name' with significant input into programme-making.

Our biographical sketch set out the range and scope of Nation's work, suggesting a line of development in his career that might support a claim for Nation's personal contribution to British television. But we then adopted an opposite framework for our second chapter on the collaborations at the BBC that facilitated the science fiction television programmes for which Nation is now most remembered. The circumstances in which the production of this genre television in series and serial form was carried out, sometimes working with formats devised by others, militated against his ability to achieve the control over programmes that the concept of authorship has conventionally involved. We aimed to show that there was a complex dialectical relationship in which Nation's individual contribution and the roles of the people and forces surrounding him operated together, where the possibilities available to him in the culture of British television were circumscribed by institutional boundaries. We did not seek to suggest that Nation struggled heroically against these forces, as an individual in conflict with institutional structures or unco-operative personnel. This discourse would place Nation in the collaborative context of television production only in order to argue that he was in some way separate from it. Rather, we emphasised that the specific individual by the name of 'Terry Nation' can only be understood as an individual subject in this way in relation to the television production contexts that permeated his professional life and to which he contributed.

Our work on collaboration at the BBC presented a picture of the television industry as largely a world of its own, cut off to some degree from the 'everyday' world, and where a system of relationships, friendships and power struggles involve a binary opposition between internal and external. The television viewer, who eventually watches completed programmes in the familiarity of his or her home, would seem to have no contact with this 'other' world and little part in the production of programmes, although we saw a degree of importance attached by television production staff to audience response. Those in the television industry would seem to be active author(ity) figures while those at home are passive onlookers, often watching television to relax after a hard day at work or at school. There would therefore appear to be a firm boundary between 'them' and 'us', and in looking at Nation's collaborations at the BBC we attempted to enter 'their' world. This always requires a lot of research by academics and 'fans' of television precisely because this world differs from our own, and our research involved conversation and correspondence with various production team members, as well as archival work on the documents that record the production process of programmes Nation worked on and internal comment on them by BBC personnel.

Our third chapter, meanwhile, located the programmes upon which Nation worked, alongside others, in the generic contexts of science fiction and adventure drama and we saw that, as with all writers, Nation's work was accommodated to existing formats, genres and specific television forms. Genre necessarily entails a process of repetition and difference in which any individual television programme perpetuates ideas that have gone before, and at the same time distinguishes itself. Since Nation's work has often been understood as a series of variations on a set of common narrative structures, we were keen to show both that repetition contributes in part to distinguishing Nation's authorial 'signature' separate from others', and also that repetition offers means for audiences to organise their expectations and understanding of programmes. Genre was not Nation's property and he did not originate significantly new generic forms, but he did mix genres. As we have stressed throughout this book, there is a tension between the individual and the collective, the single programme and the programmes to which it can be related, and between difference and repetition. The writing credited to Nation needs to be seen not as unique and free-standing, but rather as engaged in a dialogue with the programme forms that had evolved and were evolving throughout the decades in which he worked. Nation, and other members of the production teams, sought to engage with an existing tradition in British television, and Nation was not only confined to working within particular genres and forms but these also opened up possibilities for authorship. Programmes, therefore, are not organic wholes existing apart from other works. Rather television programmes fit within the boundaries of a much larger culture, just as signs used in television programmes function through their use in culture at large. The ways in which these genres and forms engage viewers and advertise the attractions of programmes make them worthy of study.

We too, in working on this book, have been viewers of the programmes that Nation contributed to, although our own activity of interpretation has been directed towards our writing, and takes account of the interests and enthusiasms that we hope to engage with in our readers. In our lengthy discussion of the political and social meanings that can be read in the programmes credited to Nation, and our detailed dissection of programmes in terms of these possible meanings, we have not argued that Nation himself or his collaborators intended his work to be read in these ways. Neither have we argued that viewers consciously interpreted the programmes along these lines, since there is insufficient evidence to prove the point. Even so, the programmes identified collectively under Nation's name and realised by other members of the production teams exhibit patterns of political and social representation that link them together. Nation sometimes recognised political themes in his work after the fact (in 'The Daleks', for instance) or when writing (in 'Genesis Of The Daleks'), and it is interesting to see what Nation's contribution was and what was contributed by other production team members. Our discussion demonstrated that Nation's writing, programme ideas and their realisation drew on a rich field of social and political ideologies that were and are in circulation. Some of these ideologies remain as persistent forces today, while others need to be located more specifically in the years when the programmes were originally made and watched. For television is an expression of culture and a medium through which culture is mediated to its audiences (see Williams 1981 and Burton 2000), a reason why television is often taught at universities under the title of Cultural Studies.

In keeping with our consistent concern to both construct and deconstruct the identity of Nation's authorship and authority, we saw that programmes do not 'belong' to Nation or to other production personnel since audiences actualise their meanings by watching and responding to them. Viewers interpret not only structures and storylines, but also components of *mise en scène* like shot composition and music, and we drew attention to the contribution that personnel such as the director and composer made to the meanings we have discussed. As a general principle, we believe that the process of creating television, and the unfolding narratives of television programme texts, seek to supervise the meanings of programmes in different but related ways.

Yet this activity of controlling meaning can never fully succeed, allowing dialogue and debate about programmes among audiences and critics to continue. Indeed, it is the perpetually unfinished and unbordered quality of all texts that allows for the production of new ideas about them (and further publication about them, such as this book). The French theorist Roland Barthes (1977) coined the phrase the 'Death of the Author' in order to argue against the conventional function of the author in literary criticism, which has been to set boundaries around texts that limit interpretation by declaring that only authorial intention can make an interpretation legitimate. Barthes argued that texts are filled with meanings by their readers, and break free from their authors' control once they enter the public domain. Whether an author is literally alive or dead, readers and television viewers construct their own ideas of authorship interpretatively, and our interpretive work on Nation's programmes has therefore enabled us to probe questions of authorship and authority, drawing on Sarah Kozloff's (1992) application to television of a common literary-critical model of authorship. She first identifies the narrator (which in television is often the camera's narrating point of view), the implied author (not a flesh-and-blood person but rather the viewer's sense, constructed from the text, of the organising force behind the programme), and finally the 'real' author (the people who either wrote the script or those who realised it). We have discussed the multiple author(ity) functions of figures such as writer, script editor and director. However, there are also multiple Terry Nations, multiple versions of one script editor, and multiple versions of a particular director, since the flesh-and-blood Terry Nation, for instance, is not identical with the 'Terry Nation' who we construct solely from our analysis of the television programmes. There are permeable boundaries around his identity, and influence and activity moves across these boundaries in both directions.

This approach does not belittle television professionals, whose intentions when producing programmes may sometimes be highly serious. For example, Barry Letts told us that he believed in having writers incorporate political sub-texts into the *Doctor Who* stories he oversaw as producer in the early 1970s. Intention always precedes the text while readings follow it; production planning occurs before while viewing comes after. But what comes last can have authority over what came first, and there will always be more to be discovered in a work than its production team had intended. The notion of 'The Death of the Author' collapses the boundaries set by authors' authority, and reveals that texts can be filled with meanings by their audiences, giving them active authority to negotiate interpretations. Interpretations of television programmes need to be justified by the kinds of detailed argument and discussion we have undertaken in this book, where we have identified authorial 'signatures' uniting television programmes but denied such signatures the intentional authority they might have when placed on legal documents, letters and so forth. So even though Nation had a 50 per cent share of copyright on the Daleks, for instance, he does not necessarily intend or own the stories' meanings. Television viewers engage actively with the meanings of programmes and so out of the symbolic death of the author come new meanings, whether intended by television professionals or not. The boundary separating 'them' and 'us' imposes limits but also blurs or erases them.

### Nation-wide influence: *Doctor Who* and *Blake's 7* in the 1980s, 1990s and 2000s

While this book challenges the notion of Nation as a figure with sole authority over the works he was credited with writing, he maintained a grip over the unfolding of programmes into the 1980s, notably *Doctor Who*, after he had emigrated to Hollywood. To an extent, *Doctor Who* developed in the ways it did because of Nation. For one thing, the BBC had to ask his approval for the use of the Daleks. Second, he insisted that the character of Davros, who he had created for the 1975 story 'Genesis Of The Daleks', must accompany the Daleks in each of their subsequent appearances. So, as Howe *et al.* (1996: 46) note, when producer John Nathan-Turner wished to bring the Daleks back in a story called 'The Return' for the 1983 twentieth anniversary season, in which he planned to pay homage to the programme by featuring an element from the series' past in each story, he had to get Nation's consent. Nation was originally approached to write the story himself, but being too busy he allowed the then script editor Eric Saward to take on the job. Saward borrowed from Nation's earlier work: the warehouse in London's deserted Thames-side recalls 'The Dalek Invasion Of Earth', and the character name Galloway from 'Death To The Daleks' recurs, for instance. Nation recommended changes to make the Daleks less vulnerable, suggested that their first appearance in a warehouse should be more spectacular, that Davros reviving the Daleks should be more generically science-fictional, and that a stronger hint that Davros might escape should be left at the end of the story. Nathan-Turner accepted all of this. A BBC strike meant that this story could not be shot as part of the 1983 season but was transmitted the following year under its new title 'Resurrection Of The Daleks', after a Dalek had made a reappearance in the 1983 twentieth anniversary 90-minute special 'The Five Doctors' in a scene featuring the first Doctor (recast as Richard Hurndall), and Susan (Carole Ann Ford). Again, Nation's approval was needed for the 1985 story 'Revelation Of The Daleks' and the 1988 story 'Remembrance Of The Daleks'. When Nathan-Turner sent Nation a storyline for 'Remembrance Of The Daleks' on 21 December 1987, Nation was not happy with it, especially in the way Davros was used, and Nation insisted upon changes (Howe *et al.* 1996: 116).

Since the cancellation of *Doctor Who* in 1989, Nation's and the Daleks' influence was still felt in relation to the series. For example, a Dalek voice-over occurred in the 1996 *Doctor Who* television film staring Paul McGann (originally the Daleks were to have played a much more central role in the film) and in the BBC's charity telethon *Comic Relief* in 1999 the Daleks appeared in a short spoof adventure, 'The Curse Of The Fatal Death'. The Daleks were also used to advertise *Doctor Who* in Britain in the 1990s, along the lines of our earlier discussion of the Daleks as 'ads'. For the week of 13–19 November 1999, the *Radio Times* featured a cover picture of a Dalek to advertise the *Doctor Who* theme night on Saturday 13 November 1999. The slogan on the left of the Dalek reads, 'Look Who's back on Saturday night'. The word 'Who's', in larger silver lettering than the rest of the slogan, is a pun on *Doctor Who*'s title. The fact that the slogan begins 'Look Who's back' encourages readers to associate the slogan with the large dominating picture of the Dalek in the centre of the page. The pun on *Doctor Who*'s title and the invitation to 'Look' establish the Dalek as a metonym (a sign standing for a larger whole) for *Doctor Who* in general. The mention of 'Saturday night' draws attention to the old familiar Saturday night slot of *Doctor Who*. The cover therefore serves as an advertisement for the *Doctor Who* theme night on the Saturday, and the centrality of the Daleks to the series. The theme night featured the final episode of 'The Daleks', screened as 'the' representative episode of the programme. The Daleks as a metonym for *Doctor Who* would be familiar to many *Radio Times* readers and BBC viewers, but even a child who had not heard of the programme may have been drawn to it by the Dalek's appearance in futuristic silver as a threatening 'science fiction other'.

Even in *Doctor Who* fan circles the influence of Nation and the original designer of the Daleks, Raymond Cusick, whose work on their design contributed so much to their success, was still felt in the 1990s and 2000s. As well as being used in merchandise (such as Talking Daleks and an Inflatable 4-foot Dalek), the Daleks appeared in many comic strips in *Doctor Who Magazine* (including 'Party Animals, 'Emperor Of The Daleks', 'Time And Time Again', 'Up Above The

Gods', 'Fire And Brimstone', 'Happy Deathday' and 'Children Of The Revolution'). The Daleks featured in yearbooks and in *Doctor Who Magazine* specials (such as 'Metamorphosis', 'Bringer Of Darkness' and 'Daleks Versus The Martians'), as indeed they did in the late 1970s and 1980s in *Doctor Who Weekly* and *Doctor Who Monthly* (for example, 'Abslom Daak – Dalek Killer', 'Timeslip', 'Dogs Of Doom' and 'The Star Tigers' in the former and in 'Nemesis Of The Daleks' in the latter). Various strips from the 1960s were also reprinted in *Doctor Who Classic Comics* such as 'Sub Zero', 'The Planet Of The Daleks', 'The Trodus Ambush', 'Doctor Who And The Daleks Movie Adaptation', 'The Doctor Strikes Back', 'The Exterminator' and 'The Threat From Beneath'. *The Dalek Chronicles Special* was a reprint of the entire run of the Daleks strips from the 1960s, and the alien Voord, created by Nation for 'The Keys Of Marinus', appeared in the *Doctor Who Magazine* comic strip 'The World Shapers' (1987). The Daleks were used in John Peel's novels *War Of The Daleks* (1997a) and *Legacy Of The Daleks* (1998), in Telos Publishing's fifteenth and final novella *The Dalek Factor* (2004) by Simon Clark, and in audio-dramas.

Big Finish Productions received a licence from the BBC to produce a series of *Doctor Who* audio-plays, which began towards the end of 1999. Difference and sameness characterise these offerings, which both innovate and extend the boundaries of the original television series, and at the same time conform to its parameters. They not only feature the performers who played the different incarnations of the Doctor and his companions on television, and are given production codes indicating that they are set at intervals in the chronology of the television adventures, but also aim to capture the 'essence' of the programme. In order to produce these audio-dramas readings were made of the original *Doctor Who* programme. Big Finish Productions began releasing its official *Doctor Who* audio-dramas every two months, then monthly. The essence of the original programme not only included its mixture of genres, its 'serious messages', and its structure of mystery, but also its 'monsters'. The Daleks were the first monster to be resurrected in Mike Tucker's May 2000 release 'The Genocide Machine' (which also used a favourite Nation character name in Bev Tarrant) and this return was heralded in the pages of *Doctor Who Magazine* where the audios were partly advertised in relation to the Daleks (Tucker, Russell and Briggs, 2000). In the first four years of production alone, when Big Finish was being established, the Daleks also appeared in 'The Apocalypse Element' (w: Stephen Cole, August 2000), 'The Mutant Phase' (w: Nicholas Briggs, December 2000), 'The Time Of The Daleks' (w: Justin Richards, May 2002), 'Neverland' (w: Alan Barnes, June 2002) and 'Jubilee' (w: Robert

Shearman, January 2003), while their creator Davros surfaced in the audio-drama of that name (September 2003), written by Lance Parkin. Such was the popularity of the Daleks that in its first four years Big Finish Productions also produced spin-off audio-dramas under the title *Dalek Empire*, such as the four stories by Nicholas Briggs in series one, 'Invasion Of The Daleks' (6 May 2001), 'The Human Factor' (6 August 2001), '"Death to The Daleks!"' (29 October 2001), and 'Project Infinity' (17 December 2001). For series two, Briggs wrote 'Dalek War' chapters one through to four (2003), and the six chapters of series three (2004). The Daleks remained so crucial to the *Doctor Who* mythology that they could carry the series alone.

The Daleks have also featured in other merchandising. While Nation was not the sole contributor to the science fiction works he was credited with writing, his influence on popular culture and on the public was felt in the late 1990s and 2000s. For the millennium, a set of four stamps was released depicting cult figures or events from the twentieth century. One of these (44p) used the Dalek photograph by Lord Snowdon, which appeared on the *Radio Times* cover discussed above. This joined the ranks of Live Aid Concerts (19p), the World Cup (26p) and Charlie Chaplin (64p), all evidently regarded as highly significant emblems of the century. The commemorative first day cover 'Towards 2000 Entertainers', also featuring a picture of James Bond as portrayed by Sean Connery, tells us about the Dalek stamp: 'The stamp was inspired by the Scottish invention of television and it's [sic] ability to elevate even fictional characters like the Daleks to "Cult" status'. Nation's legacy was literally being spread nationwide, and merchandisers later seized the opportunity to turn the stamp design into paperweights and drink mats.

In 2002, the Daleks were still current enough in popular culture to be used in Kit Kat television advertisements (with the slogan, 'Take a Break, Have a Kit Kat'). The ads contain various shots of people doing the opposite of what they are known for, like the rock guitarist Lemmy serenading people in a restaurant on the violin. Daleks were seen chasing people in a shopping mall saying, 'We love you. Give us a cuddle', and joining in a Hari Krishna group in the street. The success of this ad relied on the spectator's knowledge of the codes of the original Dalek stories in order to detect their reversal, since the Daleks' coding as threatening was vital to the structure of the ad. In 2003, the Daleks were also used in an advertising campaign for Energizer batteries on billboards across the United Kingdom. The posters depict a Dalek alongside the slogan, 'Are You Power Mad?'. In the film *Looney Tunes: Back in Action* Daleks invade Warner studios and they appear in a laboratory among a menagerie of science fiction monsters.

*Survivors* has not had the same continued interest, although there were two novels based on the series (Nation's *Survivors* (1976) and John Eyers' *Genesis of a Hero* (1977)) and episodes were repeated on the satellite channel UK Gold. But *Blake's 7* also saw developments in the 1990s following Tony Attwood's book *Blake's 7: Afterlife* (1984), dealing with events following the final transmitted episode, a novel with which Nation was 'reportedly unimpressed' (Stevens and Moore 2003: 204), and Paul Darrow's *Avon: A Terrible Aspect* (1989), concerning Avon's half-brother wishing to kill him as revenge for a past treason. Amid attempts to bring *Blake's 7* back (perhaps as a film), which persist at the beginning of the twenty-first century, two audio-plays were written by Barry Letts for BBC Radio 4. Both 'The Sevenfold Crown' (1998) (mentioned by Killick 1997: 20) and 'The Syndeton Experiment' (1999) fit within the boundaries of the original series, set before the programme ended, and supplied fans with the hope of further *Blake's 7* adventures. There have also been *Blake's 7* audio-dramas ('The Mark Of Kane', June 1996; 'The Logic Of Empire', March 1998), as well as Chris Boucher's BBC Books novel *Doctor Who: Corpse Marker* (1999) and audio-dramas such as the 'Kaldor City' series (2001–), which mix the worlds of *Doctor Who* and *Blake's 7* together. In 2003, Andrew Mark Sewell, formerly Creative Director at BBC Worldwide, film producer Simon Moorhead and actor Paul Darrow secured the rights to produce *Blake's 7* as a television film or feature film, though Darrow subsequently withdrew from the project. A four-hour mini-series was being planned, set 25 years after the ending of the original, with a new logo, a new generation of characters to take on the Federation and an appearance by Avon.

While it may be unfortunate that Nation's name was so securely attached to the Daleks, the persistence of their appeal (and indeed that of *Blake's 7*) is a final demonstration of the ways in which the authority of the author can be both perpetuated and refracted. The Daleks and *Blake's 7* are a testimony to Nation's contribution to British television science fiction, yet their persistent presence overshadows the complex significance of authorship that we have aimed to explore in this book.

# Appendix: list of television programmes

The listing shows the television programmes for which Terry Nation wrote (w.), in chronological order of the first episode he scripted, and information is given about the seasons in which episodes were placed. Directors (d.) are indicated, as well as the production company and the television broadcaster that screened the programme and the date of first transmission (tx.) in the United Kingdom for British-made programmes, or in the United States for American programmes. Where possible producers (prod.) and script editors (story ed., story consultant or script ed.) are shown, and for some science fiction programmes, designers (des.) are also indicated because of the significance of their contribution to programmes' *mise en scène*. For the entries on *Doctor Who*, working titles and commissioning dates are provided where possible, and for the entries on *Blake's 7* in a few instances working titles are noted, since these may be of interest to readers. Brief synopses of episodes and storylines are provided, and in some cases have been adapted from reference publications listed in the bibliography or from listings posted on the world wide web. In a few cases the information is incomplete, and the authors would be happy to correct or add to the listing in subsequent editions if readers contact them via the publisher with further information.

### The Idiot Weekly, Price 2d

Five untitled episodes. Authorship was credited to a collective group of writers, including Spike Milligan, Nation, Galton, Simpson, Junkin, Sykes and Speight, represented by the Associated London Scripts agency. (d. Dick Lester), Associated Rediffusion, tx. weekly, 24 February–6 April 1956. Comedic sketches.

### Val Parnell's Startime

Regular contributor of comedy material, ATV, tx. 1958. Variety show featuring guest spots.

### Friday The 13th

(w: John Junkin and Terry Nation ) BBC tx. 13 December 1957.
One-off comedy starring Ted Ray.

### The Jimmy Logan Show

BBC tx. 1957–60.
Untitled episodes.

### The Ted Ray Show

Untitled episodes of seasons five and six (w. John Junkin and Terry
Nation, prod. George Inns, Bill Ward, Ernest Maxin and Barry Lupino),
BBC, tx. 1958–59. A mixture of sketches, variety segments and stand up
acts with comedian Ted Ray.

### No Hiding Place (prod. Ray Dicks)

'Run For The Sea' (w. Terry Nation), Associated Rediffusion, tx. 1959.
Detective Chief Inspector Lockhart and Detective Sergeant Bulter
investigate a series of crimes among a detachment of the armed forces.

### Out Of This World (prod. Leonard White, story ed. Irene Shubik)

'Impostor' (w. Terry Nation from a story by Philip K. Dick, d. Peter
Hammond, des. Robert Fuest), ABC, tx. 21 July 1962.
Earth is at war with the Outspacers. Security officer Major Peters believes
that an Outspace robot bomb is masquerading as top scientist Roger
Carter. Carter is condemned to death, and tries desperately to prove his
innocence.
'Botany Bay' (w. Terry Nation, d. Guy Verney, des. Douglas James), ABC,
tx. 28 July 1962.
Psychiatry student Bill Sheridan discovers that patients at a clinic where
he works are possessed by aliens. When he reveals this he has to kill a
possessed orderly in self-defence. Convicted of murder, Sheridan is
committed to the clinic and tries to persuade his brother Dave and
girlfriend Betty that he is not mad himself.
'Immigrant' (w. Terry Nation from a story by Clifford Simak, d. Jonathan
Alwyn, des. Voytek), ABC, tx. 8 September 1962.

No one has ever returned from Kimon, a mineral-rich planet that only allows the best and brightest to immigrate there. The world government asks the latest immigrant, Seldon Bishop, to solve the mystery.

## *Hancock*

'The Assistant' (w. Terry Nation from a story by Ray Whyberd [Ray Alan], d. Alan Tarrant), MacConkey Productions for ATV, tx. 3 January 1963.
Hancock accepts the challenge to work as a sales assistant in a department store for one week without insulting the customers.
'The Night Out' (w. Terry Nation, d. Alan Tarrant), MacConkey Productions for ATV, tx. 28 February 1963.
After a night of heavy drinking, Hancock awakes with a hangover in a hotel, surrounded by guests he does not recognise.
'The Reporter' (w. Terry Nation, d. Alan Tarrant), MacConkey Productions for ATV, tx. 14 March 1963.
Hancock, working as a junior reporter, is sent to cover a society wedding and upsets the wedding party and their guests.
'The Writer' (w. Terry Nation, d. Alan Tarrant), MacConkey Productions for ATV, tx. 21 March 1963.
Hancock persuades a television comedian to sack his writer and replace him with Hancock, but Hancock cannot think of any jokes.

## *Doctor Who*

Episode titles are given where these exist, though later episodes were designated by numbers. Running time: ca. 25 mins.

### William Hartnell as the Doctor

### Season 1 (prod. Verity Lambert, script ed. David Whitaker)

'The Daleks' (w. Terry Nation, d. Christopher Barry and Richard Martin, des. Raymond Cusick), BBC, tx. weekly, 21 December 1963–1February 1964, comprising seven episodes titled: 'The Dead Planet'; 'The Survivors'; 'The Escape'; 'The Ambush'; 'The Expedition'; 'The Ordeal'; 'The Rescue'.
The TARDIS lands on the planet Skaro after a neutronic war, where the Doctor, Susan, Ian and Barbara side with the blonde humanoid Thals in their continuing conflict with the warlike Daleks, creatures existing inside mechanical shells.
'The Keys of Marinus' (w. Terry Nation, d. John Gorrie, des. Raymond Cusick), BBC, tx. weekly, 11 April–16 May 1964, comprising six episodes titled: 'The Sea Of Death'; 'The Velvet Web'; 'The Screaming Jungle'; 'The

Snows Of Terror'; 'Sentence Of Death'; 'The Keys Of Marinus'.

On the strange planet Marinus, the Doctor and his companions undertake a quest for the lost keys to the Conscience of Marinus to save the planet from domination by the Voord. (This story is one of two *Doctor Who* adventures by Nation not to feature the Daleks.)

## Season 2 (prod. Verity Lambert)

'The Dalek Invasion of Earth' (working titles. 'The Daleks', 'Return Of The Daleks'), commissioned as early as March 1964 (w. Terry Nation, script ed. David Whitaker, d. Richard Martin, des. Spencer Chapman), BBC, tx. weekly, 21 November–26 December 1964, comprising six episodes titled: 'World's End'; 'The Daleks'; 'Day Of Reckoning'; 'The End Of Tomorrow'; 'The Waking Ally'; 'Flashpoint'.

A devastated Earth in the twenty-second century, conquered by the Daleks. The Doctor and his companions land in London and foil the Daleks' plan to extract the Earth's core from a huge mine in Bedfordshire.

'The Chase' (working title 'The Pursuers'), commissioned 25 February 1965 (w. Terry Nation, script ed. Dennis Spooner, d. Richard Martin, des. Raymond Cusick and John Wood), BBC, tx. weekly, 22 May–26 June 1965, comprising six episodes titled: 'The Executioners'; 'The Death Of Time'; 'Flight Through Eternity'; 'Journey Into Terror'; 'The Death Of Doctor Who'; 'The Planet Of Decision'.

During his experiments with an alien space-time visualiser, the Doctor sees the Daleks pursuing the TARDIS. A chase through time and space ends with a battle on the planet of the Mechanoid robots.

## Season 3 (script ed. Donald Tosh)

'Mission To The Unknown', commissioned 25 February 1965 (w. Terry Nation, prod. Verity Lambert, d. Derek Martinus, des. Raymond Cusick and Richard Hunt), BBC, tx. 9 October 1965.

Space Special Security Service agent Marc Cory, on a mission to the planet Kembel, uncovers a Dalek plan to attack the Solar System. He is killed but a tape of his findings remains for another traveller to discover.

'The Daleks' Master Plan', commissioned as six scripts to be written by Nation on 16 July 1965, and eventually co-written with Spooner due to increased length to 12 episodes (w. Terry Nation (episodes 1–5 and 7) and Dennis Spooner, prod. John Wiles, d. Douglas Camfield, des. Raymond Cusick and Barry Newbery), BBC, tx. weekly, 13 November 1965–29 January 1966, comprising 12 episodes titled: 'The Nightmare Begins'; 'Day Of Armageddon'; 'Devil's Planet'; 'The Traitors'; 'Counter Plot'; 'Coronas Of The Sun'; 'The Feast Of Steven'; 'Volcano'; 'Golden Death'; 'Escape Switch'; 'The Abandoned Planet'; 'Destruction Of Time'.

Arriving on the planet Kembel in the year 4000, the Doctor finds Marc

Cory's tape and meets agent Bret Vyon. Mavic Chen, Guardian of the Solar System, has betrayed Earth and enabled the Daleks to produce the Time Destructor, which is to be used against it.

## Jon Pertwee as the Doctor

### Season 10 (prod. Barry Letts, script ed. Terrance Dicks)

'Planet Of The Daleks' (working title: 'Destination: Daleks'), commissioned April 1972 (w. Terry Nation, d. David Maloney, des. John Hurst), BBC, tx. weekly, 7 April–12 May 1973, comprising six untitled episodes.

The Doctor and Jo help a crew of Thal space travellers to prevent a dormant Dalek army on the planet Spiradon from being revived to conquer the galaxy.

### Season 11 (prod. Barry Letts, script ed. Terrance Dicks)

'Death To The Daleks' (originally a very different adventure titled 'Dalek Story' before becoming 'Doctor Who And The Exilons' after the elixir to be found on the planet), commissioned 23 March 1973 (w. Terry Nation, d. Michael E. Briant, des. Colin Green), BBC, tx. weekly, 23 February–16 March 1974, comprising four untitled episodes.

On the plant of the Exxilons (now spelt with two x's so as not to make the connection with 'elixir' too obvious) the Doctor and Sarah Jane Smith join a race against time in which the Daleks and humans seek the antidote to a virulent plague that is sweeping across the galaxy.

## Tom Baker as the Doctor

### Season 12 (prod. Philip Hinchcliffe, script ed. Robert Holmes, but story below commissioned by prod. Barry Letts)

'Genesis Of The Daleks' (working title: 'Daleks – Genesis Of Terror'), commissioned 1974 (w. Terry Nation, d. David Maloney, des. David Spode), BBC, tx weekly, 8 March–12 April 1975, comprising six untitled episodes. Edited together as 85 minute programme for repeat tx. 27 December 1975.

The Time Lords send the Doctor, Sarah Jane Smith and Harry Sullivan to Skaro where the war between the Kaleds and the Thals nears its conclusion. The Doctor must prevent the creation of the Daleks and confront the Kaled scientist Davros who designed them. (The story serves as a prequel to the first adventure 'The Daleks'. It was voted the most popular *Doctor Who* story in a nationwide poll at the time.)

## Season 13 (prod. Philip Hinchcliffe, script ed. Robert Holmes)

'The Android Invasion' (working titles: 'The Enemy Within', 'The Kraals'), commissioned 29 November 1974 as 'The Enemy Within', treatment delivered 13 February 1975, final scripts delivered 27 February 1975 as 'The Kraals' (w. Terry Nation, d. Barry Letts, des. Philip Lindley), BBC, tx. weekly, 22 November–13 December 1975, comprising four untitled episodes.

The Doctor discovers that what seems to be an English village is a training-ground for android replicas of humans on the alien Kraals' home planet. The Doctor foils their plan to conquer Earth using the androids. (This story is the second *Doctor Who* adventure by Nation not to feature the Daleks, written long after Nation had achieved runaway success with the creatures).

## Season 17 (prod. Graham Williams, script ed. Douglas Adams)

'Destiny Of The Daleks', commissioned 20 December 1978 (w. Terry Nation, d. Ken Grieve, des. Ken Ledsham), BBC, tx. weekly, 1 September 1979–22 September 1979, comprising four untitled episodes.

On the planet Skaro, the Doctor and Romana find the Daleks searching for their long-buried but still living creator Davros to assist them in their war against the Movellans.

## *Uncle Selwyn* (w. Terry Nation, d. David Boisseau), Associated Rediffusion, tx. 1964

Uncle Selwyn runs an oil-lamp shop in Wales. When anarchists decide to abandon a plan to attack London, they plot the destruction of the local electricity power station, which will rescue Selwyn's business.

## *Story Parade* (prod. Eric Tayler, story ed. Irene Shubik)

'The Caves Of Steel' (w. Terry Nation from a novel by Isaac Asimov, d. Peter Sasdy, des. Richard Henry, Peter Seddon), BBC2, tx. 5 June 1964.

A Spacer scientist from the Outer Worlds is murdered in a future New York and Detective Elijah Baley has just 48 hours to find the killer before Outer World forces destroy the city in revenge. Baley is assisted by a Spacer agent, the positronic robot R. Daneel Olivaw.

'A Kiss Before Dying' (w. Terry Nation from a novel by Ira Levin), BBC2, tx. 1964.

A former war hero and star student is determined to succeed in business, and vows to dispose of anyone who might reveal the macabre truth about the death of his pregnant girlfriend.

*The Saint*

Season 3 (prod. Robert S. Baker and Monty Berman, script supervisor Harry H. Junkin)

'Lida' (w. Terry Nation from a story by Leslie Charteris, d. Leslie Norman), ATV, New World, Bamore Productions/ITC for ITV, tx. 15 October 1964.
Simon Templar (The Saint) helps a young woman who is being blackmailed.

'Jeannine' (w. Terry Nation from a story by Leslie Charteris, d. John Llewellyn Moxey), ATV, New World, Bamore Productions/ITC for ITV, tx. 22 October 1964.
Templar becomes interested in an oriental diplomat's pearl necklace.

'The Revolution Racket' (w. Terry Nation from a story by Leslie Charteris, d. Pat Jackson), ATV, New World, Bamore Productions/ITC for ITV, tx. 5 November 1964.
In a South American country, Templar must deal with a police captain who is also an arms dealer.

'The Contract' (w. Terry Nation from a story by Leslie Charteris, d. Roger Moore), ATV, New World, Bamore Productions/ITC for ITV, tx. 7 January 1965.
A contract killer is sent to murder Templar by an American airman who has a grudge against him.

'The Inescapable Word' (w. Terry Nation from a story by Leslie Charteris, d. Roy Ward Baker), ATV, New World, Bamore Productions/ITC for ITV, tx. 28 January 1965.
Templar investigates mysterious 'death rays' that seem to be coming from a remote research centre in Scotland.

'The Sign Of The Claw' (w. Terry Nation from a story by Leslie Charteris, d. Leslie Norman), ATV, New World, Bamore Productions/ITC for ITV, tx. 4 February 1965.
In a jungle in South East Asia, Templar confronts a terrorist gang.

'Sibao' (w. Terry Nation from a story by Leslie Charteris, d. Peter Yates), ATV, New World, Bamore Productions/ITC for ITV, tx. 25 February 1965.
Templar encounters a young girl who is involved with voodoo.

'The Crime Of The Century' (w. Terry Nation from a story by Leslie Charteris, d. John Gilling), ATV, New World, Bamore Productions/ITC for ITV, tx. 4 March 1965.
Templar and his long-standing adversary Inspector Teal join forces to stop an audacious crime.

Season 4

'The Man Who Could Not Die' (w. Terry Nation from a story by Leslie Charteris, d. Roger Moore), ATV, New World, Bamore Productions/ITC for ITV, tx. 5 August 1965.

A man is trapped underground with someone who wants to kill him, and is rescued by Templar.

## Season 6

'Invitation To Danger' (w. Terry Nation, d. Roger Moore), ATV, New World, Bamore Productions/ITC for ITV, tx. 6 October 1968.
Templar is taken prisoner by a beautiful blonde woman who picks him up in a casino. She is in fact a secret agent.
'The Desperate Diplomat' (w. Terry Nation, d. Ray Austin), ATV, New World, Bamore Productions/ITC for ITV, tx. 20 October 1968.
Inspector Teal asks Templar to find a diplomat who disappeared with $1 million.
'The Time To Die' (w. Terry Nation, d. Roy Ward Baker), ATV, New World, Bamore Productions/ITC for ITV, tx. 10 November 1968.
Templar pursues an avenging killer who draws him into a game of cat-and-mouse.
'Where The Money Is' (w. Terry Nation, d. Roger Moore), ATV, New World, Bamore Productions/ITC for ITV, tx. 29 December 1968.
Templar investigates the apparent kidnapping of a film producer's wayward daughter.

## *Out Of The Unknown*

### Season 1 (prod. and script ed. Irene Shubik)

'The Fox And The Forest' (w. Terry Nation from a story by Ray Bradbury with additional material by Meade Roberts, d. Robin Midgley), BBC, tx. 22 November 1965.
In the year 2165, David and Sarah Kirsten journey back in time to 1938 as a luxury holiday and decide to stay. But as government workers they are too important to the present and so 'hunters', who blend well into the past, are sent to bring them back.

## *The Baron* (prod. Monty Berman, script ed. Terry Nation)

### Season 1

'Epitaph For A Hero' (w. Terry Nation, d. John Llewellyn Moxey), ITC for ITV, tx. 5 October 1966.
John Mannering (The Baron) attends the funeral of Jim Carey, a former

army colleague. After receiving a message that Carey is still alive, Mannering agrees to go undercover for Templeton-Green. Foiling an elaborate plan to steal a $1 million jewel becomes harder when Cordelia Winfield is used as a hostage to ensure that the Baron co-operates with Carey.

'Something For A Rainy Day' (w. Terry Nation, d. Cyril Frankel), ITC for ITV, tx. 12 October 1966.

Mannering co-operates with a scheming insurance agent to recover a £100,000 Aztec mask from a former criminal. But the gang's leader objects and threatens his former friend's daughter in order to get the mask.

'Red Horse, Red Rider' (w. Terry Nation, d. John Llewellyn Moxey), ITC for ITV, tx. 19 October 1966.

When Mannering gets a message to buy The Four Horsemen, a famous statue, he travels to Khakania, a country gripped by civil war. The sale of the statue is intended to fund the rebels, and the Baron tries to escape with the rebel leader's daughter and the statue but is pursued by the secret police.

'Masquerade (1)' (w. Terry Nation and Dennis Spooner, d. Cyril Frankel), ITC for ITV, tx. 2 November 1966.

Mannering is invited by Sir Frederick Alton to his country home, and when Mannering enters the house he hears a woman crying for help. He is knocked unconscious, and awakes to find that he has a double. Mannering changes places with the double and his captors kill the double instead of him. They reveal their plans to steal the Crown Jewels, but Cordelia arrives at the wrong moment.

'The Killing (2)' (w. Terry Nation and Dennis Spooner, d. Cyril Frankel), ITC for ITV, tx. 9 November 1966.

Mannering must convince Cordelia who he is, but must pretend to be his own double to fool his captors. The gang go to London, but one of them is the double's best friend. After he is discovered, Mannering really has to steal the Crown Jewels.

'And Suddenly You're Dead' (w. Terry Nation and Dennis Spooner, d. Cyril Frankel), ITC for ITV, tx. 23 November 1966.

In Switzerland, Mannering and Cordelia meet Peter Franklin, Cordelia's old friend. Franklin is a CIA agent who has stolen a deadly virus from the laboratory where he worked. When Franklin is killed, Mannering competes with Sorenson, the scientist who developed the virus, and the unscrupulous Holmes, to discover the bacteria first.

'Portrait Of Louisa' (w. Terry Nation, d. Roy Ward Baker), ITC for ITV, tx. 21 December 1966.

Mannering offers to help his old friend Louisa Trenton when she sells some rare family miniatures to get out of trouble. She declines, but later asks for help and the Baron goes to meet her in a London club to find that she has been murdered. He discovers that she was being blackmailed by her young lover. When Mannering tries to find out who is behind the plot, more people are murdered.

'There's Someone Close Behind You' (w. Terry Nation and Dennis Spooner, d. Roy Ward Baker), ITC for ITV, tx. 28 December 1966.

Mannering hears that a robbery is planned at the Lynsted Collection. He and the police lie in wait but one policeman is killed by the gang leader, Greg Wilde. Wilde is arrested but his crooked solicitor tells him that all of the witnesses will be disposed of. Mannering escapes an attempt on his life but Wilde escapes from police custody and pursues him.

'Storm Warning (1)' (w. Terry Nation, d. Gordon Flemyng), ITC for ITV, tx. 4 January 1967.

Mannering and Cordelia are at the Macao docks checking a shipment of antiques. A missing crate leads to Cordelia witnessing a murder on board a cargo ship. When she is held prisoner Mannering has to stow away on the ship. They meet an undercover CIA agent working as one of the crew who tells them about the ship's mysterious cargo and its secret destination. The CIA agent is killed and Mannering is forced out into the open.

'The Island (2)' (w. Terry Nation, d. Gordon Flemyng), ITC for ITV, tx. 11 January 1967.

With the ship arriving at the island to deliver its cargo, Mannering learns of the plot to steal an American space capsule. Using the ship's radio he alerts the US Navy of the plot. He and Cordelia escape and they must think up a plan to stop the robbery and hope that the Navy can get to them in time.

'A Memory Of Evil' (w. Terry Nation and Dennis Spooner, d. Don Chaffey), ITC for ITV, tx. 25 January 1967.

Mannering travels to Austria and discovers a fanatical new Nazi regime which is funding its plans for European domination by selling art treasures.

'The Seven Eyes Of Night' (w. Terry Nation, d. Robert Asher), ITC for ITV, tx. 15 February 1967.

Mannering purchases a necklace for $300,000 but discovers it is a fake and uncovers a love triangle where one member is being set up by the other two to take the blame for the robbery of the real necklace and a murder.

'Night Of The Hunter' (w. Terry Nation, d. Roy Ward Baker), ITC for ITV, tx. 22 February 1967.

Mannering investigates the selling of antiques to fund a ruthless dictator who has overthrown the previous ruler and is now swindling his predecessor's wife.

'So Dark The Night' (w. Terry Nation and Dennis Spooner, d. Robert Tronson), ITC for ITV, tx. 15 March 1967.

Set in a remote country house, Mannering discovers his client, once involved in a $1 million gold bullion robbery, murdered, with the accomplice prepared to do anything to get his share.

'Roundabout' (w. Terry Nation, d. Robert Tronson), ITC for ITV, tx. 29 March 1967.

Mannering's Paris store is being used by a drug trafficking ring, leading him into danger.

'The Man Outside' (w. Terry Nation, d. Roy Ward Baker), ITC for ITV, tx. 5 April 1967.

In Scotland, Mannering stumbles across a plan to flood Britain in £6 million of counterfeit money.


## *The Champions* (prod. Monty Berman, script supervisor Dennis Spooner)

'The Fanatics' (w. Terry Nation, d. John Gilling), ITC for ITV, tx. 11 December 1968.

Richard Barrett infiltrates a gang of assassins and learns that his boss Tremayne is one of their intended victims.

'The Body Snatchers' (w. Terry Nation, d. Paul Dickson), ITC for ITV, tx. 19 February 1969.

The Champions discover that a Pentagon defence advisor is being held in cryogenic suspension in Wales.


## *The Avengers*

### Season 6 (prod. Albert Fennell and Brian Clemens, story ed. Terry Nation)

'Legacy Of Death' (w. Terry Nation, d. Don Chaffey), ABC for ITV, tx. 20 November 1968.

An ornate dagger is bequeathed to Steed. It is the key to a secret treasure and, in a spoof of the film *The Maltese Falcon*, a collection of bizarre bounty hunters try to gain possession of the dagger.

'Noon Doomsday' (w. Terry Nation, d. Peter Sykes), ABC for ITV, tx. 27 November 1968.

Gerald Kafka, head of Murder International, is out of jail and bent on revenge against the man who put him there – John Steed who awaits a noon shootout.

'Invasion Of The Earthmen' (w. Terry Nation, d. Don Sharp), ABC for ITV, tx. 15 January 1969.

The fanatical head of the strange Alpha Academy is training astronauts for missions into space. The death of agent Bernard Grant leads Steed and Tara to the academy to investigate.

'Take Me To Your Leader' (w. Terry Nation, d. Robert Fuest), ABC for ITV, tx. 5 March 1969.

Steed and Tara's boss, known as Mother, is suspected of defecting to the enemy. To clear his name, they have to track the destination of an unusual talking briefcase by following a succession of enemy couriers.

'Thingumajig' (w. Terry Nation, d. Leslie Norman), ABC for ITV, tx. 2
April 1969.

A wartime friend of Steed's, the Reverend Shelley, seeks assistance
when archaeologists beneath his church are murdered in mysterious
circumstances. Steed and Tara do battle with a killer black box that feeds
on electricity and shoots out lethal bolts of energy.

'Take-Over' (w. Terry Nation, d. Robert Fuest), ABC for ITV, tx. 23 April 1969.

On the weekend of Steed's visit to the country home of his friends Bill
and Laura Bassett, criminals invade and take the couple hostage, im-
planting explosives in their throats. The gang intend to train a weapon on
a nearby conference.

## Department S (prod. Monty Berman, story consultant Dennis Spooner)

'A Cellar Full Of Silence' (w. Terry Nation, d. John Gilling), ITC for ITV,
tx. 23 March 1969.

Department S are called in to find out why four men in fancy dress have
been murdered in the cellar of an empty house. They are all criminals,
and a man has been shot by a bullet from a revolver in the possession of
one of them. The police suspect that Martin Kyle may be involved, and
Stewart Sullivan must get him to talk.

'The Man In The Elegant Room' (w. Terry Nation, d. Cyril Frankel), ITC
for ITV, tx. 13 April 1969.

A potential buyer comes to see an empty factory, and he and his estate
agent discover an enormous box standing on the floor. They enter the
box through a heavy door, and find themselves inside a magnificent
corridor that leads to an elegant room. Behind a steel-barred gate, they
find a dead girl, and a distraught young man. When Department S are
called in, they call on the help of crime novelist Jason King.

## The Persuaders! (prod. Robert S. Baker, executive prod. Terry Nation, script ed. Terry Nation).

'Take Seven' (w. Terry Nation, d. Sidney Hayers), ITC for ITV, tx. 1
October 1971.

Jenny Lindley inherited her parents' estate, but her long-lost brother
Mark arrives with legal backing and evicts her. Brett Sinclair and Danny
Wilde investigate Mark's claims and discover the diary of the Lindley's
nurse, which reveals the truth.

'Someone Like Me' (w. Terry Nation from a storyline by Robert S. Baker,
d. Roy Ward Baker), ITC for ITV, tx. 29 October 1971.

Brett is lured into the woods, knocked unconscious, and wakes up in a
fake hospital where he is held for a week then returned to his home.

Someone has been impersonating him. A friend of Brett's, Sam Milford, is coming to see him and there have been several attempts on his life. Brett's double may try to kill him.

'Chain Of Events' (w. Terry Nation, d. Peter Hunt), ITC for ITV, tx. 26 November 1971.

Brett and Danny are on a camping holiday when a dying parachutist handcuffs an attaché case to Danny's wrist. Danny is now a target and cannot remove the case. An intelligence officer Emily Major is sent to recover the case and helps Danny get free.

'A Home Of One's Own' (w. Terry Nation, d. James Hill), ITC for ITV, tx. 31 December 1971.

Danny buys himself a cottage in the country that appears to be haunted. The local squire, Rupert Hathaway, owns the land around the cottage and offers to buy it from him, as he does not want people around who could interfere with his illegal activities. Brett and Danny receive help from a bird watcher who turns out to be working for the fraud squad.

'Five Miles To Midnight' (w. Terry Nation, d. Val Guest), ITC for ITV, tx. 7 January 1972.

An assassin, Frank Rocco, lives in exile to avoid tax evasion charges and kills an Italian underworld boss. He agrees to expose a crime syndicate to US authorities for a reduced sentence, but Danny and Brett must smuggle him out of the country with the help of a female photographer.

'A Death In The Family' (w. Terry Nation, d. Sidney Hayers), ITC for ITV, tx. 4 February 1972.

Someone is killing members of the Sinclair family in bizarrely appropriate ways. Brett's cousin Kate thinks a distant relative is after the ancestral title and land. But one of the victims did not die after all.

'Someone Waiting' (w. Terry Nation, d. Peter Medak), ITC for ITV, tx. 25 February 1972.

Brett decides to enter his new car in a race, but receives threats on his life, is beaten up and almost run over. Drivers are being offered money to throw the race, and an attempt to destroy Brett's car is foiled. Brett and Danny try to find out who is behind the plot.

### Drama Playhouse

*The Incredible Robert Baldick*: 'Never Come Night' (w. Terry Nation, d. Cyril Coke, prod. Anthony Coburn), BBC, tx. 2 October 1972.

Scientist and adventurer Dr Robert Baldick, together with his colleagues Thomas Wigham, a literary scholar, and the burly Caleb Selling, are called on to investigate the mysterious deaths of villagers in a ruined chapel.

## *The Protectors*

### Season 2 (prod. Gerry Anderson and Reg Hill)

'Bagman' (w. Terry Nation, d. Johnny Hough), tx. 28 September 1973.
In Copenhagen, the Protectors chase a young woman's kidnapper and end up confronting him in an old fort.

'Baubles, Bangles And Beads' (w. Terry Nation, d. Jeremy Summers), tx. 19 October 1973.
In Denmark, a double cross in a jewel theft places a man and his daughter on the most wanted lists of the partners they swindled and of the Protectors.

'Route 27' (w. Terry Nation, d. Don Leaver), tx. 1 February 1974.
The Protectors confront drug runners at a harbour brewery in Denmark.

'A Pocketful Of Posies' (w. Terry Nation, d. Cyril Frankel), tx. 22 February 1974.
A popular singer, being unknowingly given hallucinogenic drugs, thinks that she is going mad when ghosts start to terrorise her.

## *Thriller*

### Season 2

'K Is For Killing' (w. Brian Clemens and Terry Nation, d. Peter Moffatt), tx. 2 March 1974. (US title: 'Color Him Dead')
An eccentric husband and wife team of private detectives are hired to investigate the murder of a young playboy's tycoon father.

## *Survivors*
Running time. ca. 50 mins

### Season 1 (prod. Terence Dudley)

'The Fourth Horseman' (w. Terry Nation, d. Pennant Roberts, des. Austin Ruddy), BBC, tx. 16 April 1975.
An epidemic of a virus carried by airline passengers sweeps the world, and communications break down. Insurance broker David Grant struggles home from London to his wife Abby, and in the city a secretary, Jenny Richards, watches her flatmate die before leaving on foot. Abby gets ill, but recovers to find her husband dead. She leaves to find her son Peter who was evacuated from his private school.

'Genesis' (w. Terry Nation, d. Gerald Blake, des. Ray London), BBC, tx. 23 April 1975.

Engineer Greg Preston returns from Holland by helicopter to find his wife dead. He encounters the scheming Anne Tranter and the crippled Vic Thatcher holed up in a quarry. Abby briefly stays with ex-union leader Arthur Wormley and his ruthless henchmen, and Jenny meets Greg.

'Gone Away' (w. Terry Nation, d. Terence Williams, des. Richard Morris), BBC, tx. 30 April 1975.

Abby, Greg and Jenny meet up and collect food, but their refuge is raided by the feckless and duplicitous Tom Price. Price tells Abby he has met a man with a boy who may be her son. Long, Wormley's lieutenant, plans revenge against Abby.

'Garland's War' (w. Terry Nation, d. Terence Williams, des. Richard Morris), BBC, tx. 21 May 1975.

Abby looks for her son at Waterhouse Manor and finds it occupied by Knox's community who are hunting down the rightful owner Jimmy Garland who they think wants to impose his own feudal rule. Abby and Garland team up and restore Garland to his home.

'The Future Hour' (w. Terry Nation, d. Terence Williams, des. Richard Morris), BBC, tx. 25 June 1975.

The scavenger and entrepreneur Bernard Huxley tells his partner Laura that she must abandon the baby she is carrying, and she finds help from Abby's community. Huxley demands that she is returned to him, or he will attack the house.

'Something Of Value' (w. Terry Nation, d. Terence Williams, des. Richard Morris), BBC, tx. 9 July 1975.

On a stormy night, Robert Lawson arrives and leaves the next morning after looking around. With fellow raiders Buckmaster and Thorpe, he attacks the community, demanding the valuable petrol tanker, which Greg is taking to trade for supplies.

'A Beginning' (w. Terry Nation, d. Pennant Roberts, des. Richard Morris), BBC, tx. 16 July 1975.

The ailing Ruth is left at the community, and Abby persuades her group to look after her. Greg and Russell persuade local survivor communities to ally against raiders. Abby visits Jimmy Garland and cements their romantic attachment.

## Blake's 7

Running time. ca. 50 mins

### Season 1 (prod. David Maloney, script ed. Chris Boucher)

'The Way Back' (working title: 'Prelude', originally the first episode was to have been titled 'Cygnus Alpha') (w. Terry Nation, d. Michael E. Briant, des. Martin Collins), BBC, tx. 2 January 1978.

Roj Blake, a former resistance leader whose memory has been erased by the Federation, learns of the Federation's oppression and meets some rebels who are killed. He is falsely convicted of child molestation and sentenced to life on the prison planet Cygnus Alpha, and meets fellow convicts Jenna and Vila.

'Space Fall' (w. Terry Nation, d. Pennant Roberts, des. Roger Murray-Leach), BBC, tx. 9 January 1978.

Aboard the prison ship to Cygnus Alpha, Blake leads a failed mutiny. Blake, Avon and Jenna are sent aboard an unmanned spaceship that drifts into their path. The rebels gain control of the ship and escape.

'Cygnus Alpha' (originally the third episode was to have been titled 'The Way Back') (w. Terry Nation, d. Vere Lorrimer, des. Robert Berk), BBC, tx. 16 January 1978.

Blake, Jenna and Avon plan to free the prisoners on Cygnus Alpha using the alien ship, the Liberator. Blake teleports down but is captured by the planet's ruler, Vargas, who demands the ship in order to spread his false religion.

'Time Squad' (w. Terry Nation, d. Pennant Roberts, des. Roger Murray-Leach), BBC, tx. 23 January 1978.

En route to attack a Federation communications complex, the Liberator takes aboard a mysterious drifting spacecraft. Blake, Avon and Vila carry out the raid helped by Cally, while the alien passengers awake from suspension and try to sabotage the Liberator. (This was originally scheduled as the sixth, and not the fourth, episode.)

'The Web' (w. Terry Nation, d. Michael E. Briant, des. Martin Collins), BBC, tx. 30 January 1978.

Outlawed scientists from Cally's race use their telepathic powers to make her bring the Liberator to a planet where it is trapped in a fibrous web. They plan to use the ship's energy for their macabre experiments.

'Seek-Locate-Destroy' (w. Terry Nation, d. Vere Lorrimer, des. Robert Berk), BBC, tx. 6 February 1978.

Blake plans to steal a message decoder from a top security installation on the planet Centero. In the course of the raid Cally is captured and used to trap Blake by Space Commander Travis, acting on the orders of Supreme Commander Servalan.

'Mission To Destiny' (w. Terry Nation, d. Pennant Roberts, des. Martin Collins), BBC, tx. 13 February 1978.

Blake and his companions become involved in murder and intrigue surrounding a crippled spaceship that was on a mission to save its home planet, Destiny.

'Duel' (w. Terry Nation, d. Douglas Camfield, des. Roger Murray-Leach), BBC, tx. 20 February 1978.

Two god-like beings on an uncharted war-ravaged planet force Blake and Travis to fight a duel to the death.

'Project Avalon' (w. Terry Nation, d. Michael E. Briant, des. Chris Pemsel), BBC, tx. 27 February 1978.

Travis devises a plan to kill Blake's crew and capture the Liberator using a plague-carrying android of Avalon, a captured resistance leader.

'Breakdown' (working title: 'Brain Storm') (w. Terry Nation, d. Vere

Lorrimer, des. Peter Brachacki), BBC, tx. 6 March 1978.

The limiter implant in Gan's brain malfunctions and he becomes aggressive towards the Liberator's crew. They seek help from a research station neurosurgeon, Professor Kayn, but Kayn betrays them to the Federation.

'Bounty' (w. Terry Nation, d. Pennant Roberts, des. Roger Murray-Leach), BBC, tx. 13 March 1978.

While Blake and Cally try to inspire a planet's rejected president to return to help his people, the Liberator is lured into a trap by a false distress call from a group of bounty hunters.

'Deliverance' (w. Terry Nation, d. David Maloney and Michael E. Briant, des. Robert Berk), BBC, tx. 20 March 1978.

On the planet Cephlon, a Liberator search party investigating a crashed spacecraft finds one fatally injured survivor, Ensor. Blake learns that Ensor's father has created the computer Orac.

'Orac' (w. Terry Nation, d. Vere Lorrimer, des. Martin Collins), BBC, tx. 27 March 1978.

Blake's crew win a race against Servalan and Travis to get Orac from the dying Ensor Senior. Aboard the Liberator, Orac predicts the ship's destruction.

## Season 2 (prod. David Maloney, script ed. Chris Boucher)

'Redemption' (w. Terry Nation, d. Vere Lorrimer, des. Sally Hulke), BBC, tx. 9 January 1979.

The aliens who designed the Liberator attack and board it to reclaim the ship. With Orac's help the crew escape, pursued by the Liberator's sister ship, which explodes, confirming Orac's prediction.

'Pressure Point' (working title: 'Storm Mountain') (w. Terry Nation, d. George Spenton-Foster, des. Mike Porter), BBC, tx. 6 February 1979.

Blake plans to return to Earth and attack Control, the computer complex running the Federation. The raid fails, and Gan dies after encountering Travis deep underground. (This was originally intended to be the sixth, and not the fifth, episode of the second season.)

'Countdown' (w. Terry Nation, d. Vere Lorrimer, des. Steve Brownsey and Gerry Scott), BBC, tx. 6 March 1979.

Blake's crew arrive on the newly liberated planet Albian to find the population facing destruction from a radiation device activated by the defeated garrison commander. (This was originally intended to be the tenth, and not the ninth, episode of the second season.)

## Season 3 (prod. David Maloney, script ed. Chris Boucher)

'Aftermath' (w. Terry Nation, d. Vere Lorrimer, des. Gerry Scott and Don Taylor), BBC, tx. 7 January 1980.

The Liberator is badly damaged after a war is won in space. The crew get out in escape pods and Avon lands on a tribal planet where Dayna and her reclusive father rescue him, only to encounter Servalan.

'Powerplay' (w. Terry Nation, d. David Maloney, des. Gerry Scott), BBC, tx. 14 January 1980.

Aboard the Liberator, Avon and Dayna uncover Federation Space Captain Tarrant's real identity. Vila and Cally struggle to survive in a hospital where patients are killed and their organs removed.

'Terminal' (working title: 'Finale') (w. Terry Nation, d. Mary Ridge, des. Jim Clay), BBC, tx. 31 March 1980.

Servalan lures Avon to the artificial planet Terminal by sending secret instructions that seem to be from Blake. The crew are stranded and Servalan leaves on the Liberator, but having earlier passed through a strange particle field it breaks up.

### Ticket To Ride (US title *A Fine Romance*)

'The Tomas Crown Affair' (w. Terry Nation).

The dentist Tomas gives Michael Trent a crown for his tooth, which conceals a smuggled diamond, to be extracted by Tomas's bother in San Francisco. A comedy chase through San Francisco ensues before the plan is foiled.

### MacGyver

#### Season 1

Nation wrote the opening pre-credit scenes for three episodes. These dramatic sequences had their own title, were normally unrelated to the main screenplay and were known as the 'opening gambit'. Nation did not write the screenplay of the main body of these episodes and it is the plots of the 'opening gambits' that are provided here.

'The Golden Triangle' (opening gambit 'Crusher' by Terry Nation, d. Donald Petrie, screenplay by Dennis Foley, d. Paul Stanley), tx. 6 October 1985.

Gambit: In a junkyard, MacGyver uses a magnet to retrieve stolen missile codes, then escapes from a car about to be crushed.

'Thief Of Budapest' (opening gambit 'Pegasus' by Terry Nation and Stephen Downing, d. Lee H. Katzin, screenplay by Joe Viola, d. John Patterson), tx. 13 October 1985.

Gambit: MacGyver retrieves a stolen horse in the desert and is rescued by a helicopter.

'Target MacGyver' (opening gambit 'Kitchen Magic' by Terry Nation, d. Lee H. Katzin, screenplay by Mike Marvin, Stephen Kandel and James Schmerer, d. Ernest Pintoff), tx. 22 December 1985.

Gambit: MacGyver rescues a female military general at a beach house, then captures her kidnappers using the kitchen equipment he finds to hand.

# Bibliography

## Archival sources

The BBC Written Archives Centre (WAC) holds contributor files relating to Nation's employment history and the employment of others he worked with, departmental records and policy documents relating to BBC drama, and programme files on the radio and television programmes Nation worked on. The sources consulted for this book included the following BBC WAC files, whose number and title are shown.

Contributor files: SCR1 RCONT1 Scriptwriter File 1: Terry Nation 1955–62; RCONT1: Terry Nation 1957–62; RCONT20 Terry Nation 1970–74; RCONT21 Terry Nation 1975–79; ART IV Waters, Elsie and Doris 1952–62.

Departmental records: T48/445 TV Script Unit: Terry Nation; T5/2239/5 Drama Memos 1962; T5/2239/6 Drama Memos 1963; T5/2239/7 TV Drama Memos 1964; T5/782/3 Drama Memos July–December 1966; T5/782/4 Drama Memos 1967–68; T5/782/5 Drama Memos 1969–70; T5/649/1 Doctor Who viewers' letters.

Programme files (radio): R19/1582/1 Calling The Stars, Light Programme; R19/1953/1 Variety Playhouse, Home Service 1953–56; R19/1953/2 Variety Playhouse, Home Service.

Programme files (television): T5/647/1 Doctor Who, General A; T5/648/1 Doctor Who General B; T65/85/1 Incredible Robert Baldick, 'Never Come Night'; T5/1241/1 Doctor Who 'The Chase'; T5/1242/1 Doctor Who 'The Chase': 'Flight Through Eternity', 'Journey Into Terror'; T5/1243/1 Doctor Who 'The Chase'; T5/1246/1 Doctor Who 'The Daleks' Master Plan'; T5/1247/1 Doctor Who 'The Daleks' Master Plan'; T5/1248/1 Doctor Who 'The Daleks' Master Plan'; T65/29/1 Doctor Who 'Death To The Daleks'; T5/2569/1 Drama Serials: Doctor Who 'Genesis Of The Daleks' 1–6; T65/10/1 Doctor Who 'Genesis Of The Daleks'; T65/31/1 Doctor Who 'The Android Invasion' file one; T5/2574/1 Doctor Who 'The Android Invasion'; T5/2575/1 Doctor Who 'The Android Invasion' file two; T65/79/1 'Destiny Of The Daleks'; T65/197/1 Doctor Who 'Destiny Of The

Daleks'; R9/7/161 Audience Research Report, *Doctor Who* 'Destiny Of The Daleks'; T65/231/1 *Survivors* series 2, episode one and two; T65/72/1 *Blake's 7* series one, two and three copyright billings; T65/90/1 *Blake's 7* General; T65/91/1 *Blake's 7* 'Space Fall'; T65/89/1 *Blake's 7* 'Duel'; T65/242 *Blake's 7* 'Redemption'; R9/7/158 Audience Research Report on *Blake's 7*, 9 January 1979 to 3 April 1979; T51/369/1 *The Lively Arts*: Whose Doctor Who?; T51/370/1 *The Lively Arts*: Whose Doctor Who?.

## Books and articles

Abercrombie, N. (1996), *Television and Society*, Oxford, Blackwell.

Airey, J. (1991), 'The man who killed *Blake's 7*', *Starlog* 163:42–4, 70.

Allen, R. (ed.) (1992a), *Channels of Discourse, Reassembled: Television and Contemporary Criticism*, London, Routledge.

Allen, R. (1992b), 'Audience-oriented criticism and television', in R. Allen (ed.), *Channels of Discourse, Reassembled: Television and Contemporary Criticism*, London, Routledge, 101–37.

Alsop, N. (1987), '*Survivors*: A horseman riding by', *Time Screen* 10, 9–19.

Amis, K. (1969), *New Maps of Hell* [1961], London, New English Library.

Andrews, H. (1994), '*Blake's 7*', *TV Zone* 58, 8–11.

Ang, I. (1997), 'Melodramatic identifications: television fiction and women's fantasy', in C. Brunsdon, J. D'Acci and L. Spigel (eds), *Feminist Television Criticism: A Reader*, Oxford, Oxford University Press, 155–66.

Ang, I. (1996), *Living Room Wars: Rethinking Audiences for a Postmodern World*, London, Routledge.

Ang, I. (1991), *Desperately Seeking the Audience*, London, Routledge.

Armstrong, K., D. Brunt and A. Pixley (1997), *The Doctor Who Production Guide, Volume 2: Reference Journal*, London, Nine Travellers/Global Productions for the Doctor Who Appreciation Society.

Arnold, M. (1932), *Culture and Anarchy* [1869], Cambridge, Cambridge University Press.

Attwood, T. (1984), *Blake's 7: Afterlife*, London, Target Books.

Attwood, T. (1983), *Blake's 7: The Programme Guide*, London, W. H. Allen/Target.

Bacon-Smith, C. (1992), *Enterprising Women: Television Fandom and the Creation of Popular Myth*, Pennsylvania, University of Pennsylvania Press,.

Bakewell, J. and N. Garnham (1970), *The New Priesthood: British Television Today*, London, Allen Lane.

Ballesteros González, A. (1998), 'Doppleganger', in M. Mulvey-Roberts (ed.), *The Handbook to Gothic Literature*, Basingstoke, Macmillan, 264.

Barnes, A. (1999), 'Tales from the crypt', *Doctor Who Magazine* 282, 8–12.

Barrett, M. and D. Barrett (2001), *Star Trek: The Human Frontier*, Cambridge, Polity.

Barthes, R. (1990), *S/Z*, trans. R. Miller, Oxford, Blackwell.

Barthes, R. (1977), 'The death of the author', in *Image, Music, Text*, trans. S. Heath, London, Fontana, 142–8.

Bazalgette, C. and D. Buckingham (eds) (1995), *In Front of the Children: Screen Entertainment and Young Audiences*, London, BFI.

Bentham, J. (1986), *Doctor Who, The Early Years*, London, W. H. Allen.

Bignell, J. (2004), *An Introduction to Television Studies*, London, Routledge.

Bignell, J. (2002a), *Media Semiotics: An Introduction*, second edition, Manchester, Manchester University Press.

Bignell, J. (2002b), 'Writing the child in media theory', *Yearbook of English Studies* 32, 127–39.

Bignell, J. (2000a), *Postmodern Media Culture*, Edinburgh, Edinburgh University Press.

Bignell, J. (2000b), 'Docudrama as melodrama: representing Princess Diana and Margaret Thatcher', in B. Carson and M. Llewellyn-Jones (eds), *Frames and Fictions on Television: The Politics of Identity within Drama*, Exeter, Intellect, 17–26.

Bignell, J. (1999a), 'Another time, another space: modernity, subjectivity and *The Time Machine*', in D. Cartmell, I. Q. Hunter, H. Kaye and I. Whelehan (eds), *Alien Identities: Exploring Differences in Film and Fiction*, London, Pluto, 87–103.

Bignell, J. (1999b), *Writing and Cinema*, Harlow, Pearson.

Bignell, J. (1999c), 'A Taste of the Gothic: Film and Television Versions of *Dracula*', in E. Sheen and R. Giddings (eds), *The Classic Novel: From Page to Screen*, Manchester, Manchester University Press, 114–30.

Bignell, J. (1994), 'Trevor Griffiths's political theatre: from *Oi For England* to *The Gulf Between Us*', *New Theatre Quarterly* 10:37, 49–56.

Bignell, J., S. Lacey and M. Macmurraugh-Kavanagh (eds) (2000), *British Television Drama: Past, Present and Future*, Basingstoke, Palgrave Macmillan.

Bignell, R. (2001), *Doctor Who – On Location*, Richmond, Reynolds and Hearn.

Born, G. (2000), 'Inside television: television studies and the sociology of culture', *Screen*, 41:4, 404–24.

Botting, F. (1996), *Gothic*, London, Routledge.

Boucher, C. (1999), *Corpse Maker*, London, BBC Books.

Brandt, G. (ed.) (1993), *British Television Drama in the 1980s*, Cambridge, Cambridge University Press.

Brandt G. (ed.) (1981), *British Television Drama*, Cambridge, Cambridge University Press.

Briggs, N. (1993), 'After image: Genesis of the Daleks', *Doctor Who Magazine* 197, 50.

Brown, A. (1993), 'Enough to break the glass', *DWB*, 112.

Brown, M. (1979), 'Seven up', *Radio Times* 6–12 January, 10–11.

Brunsdon, C. (1998), 'What is the television of television studies?', in C. Geraghty and D. Lusted (eds), *The Television Studies Book*, London, Arnold, 95–113.

Brunsdon, C. (1990), 'Problems with "quality"', *Screen* 31:1, 67–90.

Brunt, D. and A. Pixley (2002), *The Doctor Who Chronicles: Season Three*, London, Doctor Who Appreciation Society.

Brunt, D. and A. Pixley (2000), *The Doctor Who Chronicles: Season Four*, London, Doctor Who Appreciation Society.

Brunt, D. and A. Pixley (1999), *The Doctor Who Chronicles: Season Two*, London, Doctor Who Appreciation Society.

Brunt, D. and A. Pixley (1998), *The Doctor Who Chronicles: Season One*, London, Doctor Who Appreciation Society.

Buckingham, D. (1996), *Moving Images: Understanding Children's Emotional Responses to Television*, Manchester, Manchester University Press.

Buckingham, D. (1993a), *Children Talking Television: The Making of Television Literacy*, London, Falmer.

Buckingham, D. (1993b), *Reading Audiences: Young People and the Media*, Manchester, Manchester University Press.

Burton, G. (2000) *Talking Television*, Oxford, Oxford University Press.

Busby, L. J. (1975), 'Sex-role research on the mass media', *Journal of Communication* 25:4, 107–31.

Buxton, D. (1990), *From The Avengers to Miami Vice: Form and Ideology in Television Series*, Manchester, Manchester University Press.

Carson, B. and M. Llewellyn-Jones (eds) (2000), *Frames and Fictions on Television: The Politics of Identity within Drama*, Exeter, Intellect.

Casey, B., N. Casey, B. Calvert, L. French and J. Lewis (2002), *Television Studies: The Key Concepts*, London, Routledge.

Caughie, J. (2000), *Television Drama: Realism, Modernism, and British Culture*, Oxford, Oxford University Press.

Caughie, J. (1984), 'Television criticism: a discourse in search of an object', *Screen* 25:4–5, 109–20.

Chapman, J. (2002), *Saints & Avengers: British Adventure Series of the 1960s*, London, I. B. Tauris.

Clark, S. (2004), *The Dalek Factor*, Tolworth, Telos.

Cook, B. (2002), 'Shoot to thrill!', *Doctor Who Magazine* 314, 8–13.

Cornell, P., M. Day and K. Topping (1996), *The Guinness Book of Classic British TV*, second edition, London, Guinness.

Corner, J. (1999), *Critical Ideas in Television Studies*, Oxford, Clarendon.

Corner, J. (1998), *Studying Media: Problems of Theory and Method*, London, Arnold.

Corner, J. (ed.) (1991), *Popular Television in Britain*, London, BFI.

Courtney, A. and T. Whipple (1980), *Sex Stereotyping in Advertising: An Annotated Bibliography*, Cambridge, MA, Marketing Science.

Creeber, G. (ed.) (2001), *The Television Genre Book*, London, BFI.

Crisell, A. (1997), *An Introductory History of British Broadcasting*, London, Routledge.

D'Acci, J. (1994), *Defining Women: Television and the Case of Cagney and Lacey*, Chapel Hill and London, University of North Carolina Press.

Darrow, P. (1989), *Avon: A Terrible Aspect*, London: Citadel.

Derrida, J. (1980), 'The law of genre', *Glyph* 7, 202–13.

Dickson, L. (1973), 'Who's who among Who's friends', *Radio Times*, 13–20 December, 6–7.

*Doctor Who Poster Magazine* (1994), 1, December.

Dominick, J. and G. Rauch (1972), 'The image of women in network TV commercials', *Journal of Broadcasting* 16:3, 259–65.

Drummond, P. (1976), 'Structural and narrative constraints in *The Sweeney*', *Screen Education* 20, 15–36.

Dunkley, C. (1975), 'Could you survive the end of the world?', *Radio Times* 10–17 April, 6–7.

Dyer, R. (1977), 'Entertainment and utopia', *Movie* 24, 2–13.

Eco, U. (1990), *The Limits of Interpretation*, Bloomington, Indiana University Press.

Ellis, J. (2000a), *Seeing Things: Television in the Age of Uncertainty*, London, I. B. Tauris.

Ellis, J. (2000b), 'Scheduling: the last creative act in television', *Media, Culture & Society* 22:1, 25–38.

Ellis, J. (1982), *Visible Fictions: Cinema, Television, Video*, London, Routledge and Kegan Paul.

Evans, C. (1977), 'Roaming a naughty universe', *Radio Times* 24 December 1977–6 January 1978, 114–17.

Eyres, J. (1977), *Survivors: Genesis of a Hero*, London: Weidenfeld & Nicolson.

Feuer, J. (1992), 'Genre study and television', in R. Allen (ed.), *Channels of Discourse, Reassembled: Television and Contemporary Criticism*, London, Routledge, 138–60.

Fine, M. G. (1981), 'Soap opera conversations: the talk that binds', *Journal of Communication* 31:3, 91–107.

Fiske, J. (1992a), 'The cultural economy of fandom', in L. Lewis (ed.), *The Adoring Audience: Fan Culture and Popular Media*, London, Routledge, 30–49.

Fiske, J. (1992b), 'British cultural studies and television', in R. Allen (ed.), *Channels of Discourse, Reassembled: Television and Contemporary Criticism*, London, Routledge, 284–326.

Fiske, J. (1990), *Introduction to Communication Studies*, London, Routledge.

Fiske, J. (1987), *Television Culture*, London, Routledge.

Fiske, J. (1983), 'Dr Who: ideology and the reading of a popular narrative text', *Australian Journal of Screen Theory* 13/14, 69–100.

Foucault. M. (1980), 'What is an author?', in J. Harari (ed.), *Textual Strategies: Perspectives in Post-Stucturalist Criticism*, London, Methuen, 141–60.

Freeman, N. (1999), 'See Europe with ITC: stock footage and the construction of geographical identity', in D. Cartmell, I. Q. Hunter, H. Kaye and I. Whelehan (eds), *Alien Identities: Exploring Differences in Film and Fiction*, London, Pluto, 49–65.

Freud, S. (1955), 'The uncanny', *The Standard Edition of the Complete Psychological Works*, trans. and ed. J. Strachey, vol. 17, 217–52.

Fulton, R. (2000), *Encyclopedia of TV Science Fiction*, London, Boxtree.

Garnett, T. (2000), 'Contexts', in J. Bignell, S. Lacey and M. Macmurraugh-

Kavanagh (eds), *British Television Drama: Past, Present and Future*, Basingstoke, Palgrave Macmillan, 11–23.

Geraghty, C. (1991), *Women and Soap Opera: A Study of Prime Time Soaps*, Cambridge, Polity.

Geraghty, C. and D. Lusted (eds) (1998), *The Television Studies Book*, London, Arnold.

Gilbert, S. M. and S. Gubar (1979), *The Madwoman in the Attic: The Woman Writer and the Nineteenth-century Literary Imagination*, New Haven, Yale University Press.

Gillatt, G. (1998), *Doctor Who – From A To Z*, London, BBC Books.

Griffiths, N. (1999), 'Who goes there?', *Radio Times* 13–19 November, 28–31.

Griffiths, P. (1998a), 'A run for the money', *Doctor Who Magazine* 270, 46–50.

Griffiths, P. (1998b), 'Speak of the Devil', *Doctor Who Magazine* 263, 46–50.

Gunn, J. (ed.) (1998), *The Road to Science Fiction, Vol. 6: Around the World*, Clarkston, GA, White Wolf.

Haining, P. (1983), *Doctor Who: A Celebration*, London, W. H. Allen.

Hall, S. (1980),'Encoding/decoding', in S. Hall, D. Hobson, A. Lowe and P. Willis (eds), *Culture, Media, Language*, London, Hutchinson, 128–38.

Hancock, F. and D. Nathan (1975), *Hancock, A Personal Biography*, London, Coronet.

Hanson, H. (2000), 'Painted women: framing portraits in film noir and the Gothic woman's film', unpublished PhD thesis, University of Southampton.

Harbord, J. and J. Wright (1992), *Forty Years of British Television*, London, Boxtree.

Harris, M. (1983), *The Doctor Who Technical Manual*, London, Severn House.

Harrison, T., S. Projansky, K. Ono and E. Rae Helford (eds) (1996), *Enterprise Zones: Critical Positions on Star Trek*, Boulder, CO, Westview.

Hartley, J. (1982), *Understanding News*, London, Routledge.

Hearn, M. (1993), 'Directing Who: David Maloney', *Doctor Who Magazine* 202, 13–15.

Hearn, M. (1991), 'Directing Who: Christopher Barry', *Doctor Who Magazine* 180, 10–14.

Hermes, J. (2001), '*The Persuaders!* A girl's best friends', in B. Osgerby and A. Gough-Yates (eds), *Action TV: Tough Guys, Smooth Operators and Foxy Chicks*, London, Routledge, 159–68.

Hills, M. (2002), *Fan Cultures*, London, Routledge.

Hipple, D. (2003), 'From pulp to programming: the Americanisation of science fiction on British TV', unpublished MA dissertation, University of Reading.

Hipple, D. (2002), 'Cosmic housewives: women in *Blake's 7*', unpublished MA essay, University of Reading.

Hopkins, G. (undated a), *Doctor Who: Adventures In Space And Time – The Daleks' Master Plan 1–6*, London, Cybermark.

Hopkins, G. (undated b), *Doctor Who: Adventures In Space And Time – The Daleks' Master Plan 7–12*, London, Cybermark.

Hopkins, G. (undated c), *Doctor Who: Adventures In Space And Time – Mission To The Unknown*, London, Cybermark.

Hopkins, G. (undated d), *Doctor Who: Adventures In Space And Time – The Chase*, London, Cybermark.

Houldsworth, R. (1992), 'Fantasy flashback: *Survivors* The Fourth Horseman', *TV Zone* Special 5, 12–14.

Houldsworth, R. and M. Wyman (1990), 'Redemption', *TV Zone* 13, 25–7.

Howe, D., M. Stammers and S. J. Walker (1996), *Doctor Who – The Eighties*, London, Virgin.

Howe, D., M. Stammers and S. J. Walker (1994), *Doctor Who – The Seventies*, London, Virgin.

Howe, D., M. Stammers and S. J. Walker (1993), *Doctor Who – The Sixties*, London, Virgin.

Jameson, F. (1982), 'Progress versus utopia; or, can we imagine the future', *Science Fiction Studies* 9, 147–58.

Jenkins, H. (1992), *Textual Poachers: Television Fans and Participatory Culture*, London, Routledge.

Johnson, C. (2002), 'Histories of telefantasy: the representation of the fantastic and the aesthetics of television', unpublished PhD thesis, University of Warwick.

Kellner, D. (1999a), '*The X-Files* and the aesthetics and politics of postmodern pop', *Journal of Aesthetics and Art Criticism* 57:2, 161–75.

Kellner, D. (1999b), '*The X-Files*, paranoia, and conspiracy: from the 70s to the 90s', *Framework* 41, 16–36.

Kilgour, M. (1995), *The Rise of the Gothic Novel*, Routledge, London.

Killick, J. (1997), 'The way forward', *Cult Times* Winter Special 4, 18–25.

Kozloff, S. (1992), 'Narrative theory and television', in R. Allen (ed.), *Channels of Discourse, Reassembled: Television and Contemporary Criticism*, London, Routledge, 67–100.

Kristeva, J. (1984), *Revolution in Poetic Language*, trans. M. Waller, New York, Columbia University Press.

Lacey, N. (2000), *Narrative and Genre: Key Concepts in Media Studies*, Basingstoke, Macmillan.

Ledwon, L. (1993), '*Twin Peaks* and the television gothic', *Literature/Film Quarterly* 21:4, 260–70.

Lévi-Strauss, C. (1970), *The Raw and the Cooked: An Introduction to a Science of Mythology*, trans. J. and D. Weightman, London, Jonathan Cape.

Lewis, J. E. and P. Stempel (1999), *The Ultimate TV Guide*, London, Orion.

Lewis, J. E. and P. Stempel (1996), *Cult TV: The Essential Critical Guide*, London, Pavilion.

Lewis, L. (ed.) (1992), *The Adoring Audience: Fan Culture and Popular Media*, London, Routledge.

Lichter, R. S., L. S. Lichter and S. Rothman (1986), 'From Lucy to Lacey: TV's dream girls', *Public Opinion* 9:3, 16–19.

Linford, P. (1994), 'It's the end of the world as we know it', *DWB* 124, 12–13.

Linford, P. (1993), 'The Fourth Horseman/Genesis', *DWB* 113, 24.

Lippmann, W. (1922), *Public Opinion*, London, George Allen & Unwin, Ltd.

Lock, A. and A. Stevens (1991), 'Jacqueline Pearce', *TV Zone* 21, 25–7.

Lusted, D. (1998), 'The popular culture debate and light entertainment on television', in C. Geraghty and D. Lusted (eds), *The Television Studies Book*, London, Arnold, 175–90.

Macdonald, M. (1995), *Representing Women: Myths of Femininity in the Popular Media*, London, Arnold.

MacDonald, P. (1998), 'Morals and monstrosity: Genesis of the Daleks', *Doctor Who Magazine* 265, 26–9.

Marx, K. and F. Engels (2002), *The Communist Manifesto*, trans. and ed. G. Stedman-Jones, London, Penguin.

Meinhof, U. H. and J. Smith (ed.) (2000), *Intertextuality and the Media: From Genre to Everyday Life*, Manchester, Manchester University Press.

Miller, T. (1997), *The Avengers*, London, BFI.

Millington, B. and R. Nelson (1986), *Boys from the Blackstuff: The Making of TV Drama*, London, Comedia.

Mittell. J. (2001), 'A cultural approach to television genre theory', *Cinema Journal* 40:3, 3–24.

More, Sir T. (1965), *Utopia*, London, Penguin.

Morford, M. P. O., and R. J. Lenardon (1991), *Classical Mythology*, fourth edition, New York, Longman.

Morley, D. (1992), *Television, Audiences and Cultural Studies*, London, Routledge.

Moylan, T. (2000), '"Look into the dark": on dystopia and the *novum*', in P. Parrinder (ed.), *Learning from Other Worlds: Estrangement, Cognition and the Politics of Science Fiction and Utopia*, Liverpool, Liverpool University Press, 51–71.

Muir, J. K. (2000), *A History and Critical Analysis of Blake's 7, the 1978–1981 British Television Space Adventure*, Jefferson, McFarland.

Mulkern, P. (1988), 'The Dalek Invasion of Earth', *Doctor Who Magazine* 141, 18–22.

Mulkern, P. (1987), 'Behind the scenes', *Doctor Who Magazine* Autumn Special, 22–9.

Murdoch, G. (1980), 'Authorship and organization', *Screen Education* 35, 19–34.

Nation, T. (1983), 'Introduction', in T. Attwood, *Blake's 7: The Programme Guide*, London, W. H. Allen/Target, 7–8.

Nation, T. (1976a), *Survivors*, London, Weidenfeld & Nicolson/Futura.

Nation, T. (ed.) (1976b), *Doctor Who and the Daleks Omnibus*, London, Artus.

Nation, T. (1975), *Rebecca's World: Journey to the Forbidden Planet*, London, G. Whizzard/Andre Deutsch; Beaver Books 1976.

Nation, T. and J. Peel (1988), *The Official Doctor Who and the Daleks Book*, New York, St. Martin's Press.

Nazzaro, J. (1993), 'Mary Ridge: the final days of Blake's 7', *TV Zone* 45, 30–2.

Nazzaro, J. (1992a), 'Terry Nation's *Blake's 7* part one', *TV Zone* 33, 28–30.

Nazzaro, J. (1992b), 'Terry Nation's *Survivors*', *TV Zone* 31, 28–30.

Nazzaro, J. (1989), 'Terry Nation', *Doctor Who Magazine* 145, 17–21.

Nazzaro, J. and S. Wells (1997), *Blake's 7 – The Inside Story*, London, Virgin.

Neale, S. (2000), *Hollywood and Genre*, London, Routledge.

Neale, S. and G. Turner (2001), 'Introduction: what is genre?', in G. Creeber (ed.), *The Television Genre Book*, London, BFI, 1–7.

Nelson, R. (1997), *TV Drama in Transition: Forms, Values and Cultural Change*, Basingstoke, Macmillan.

Newcombe, H. (1974), *Television: The Most Popular Art*, New York, Anchor.

O'Day, M. (2001), 'Of leather suits and kinky boots: *The Avengers*, style and popular culture', in B. Osgerby and A. Gough-Yates (eds), *Action TV: Tough Guys, Smooth Operators and Foxy Chicks*, London, Routledge, 221–35.

Olson, R. J. M. (1992), *Italian Renaissance Sculpture*, London, Thames and Hudson.

Osgerby, B. (2001), '"So *you're* the famous Simon Templar": *The Saint*, masculinity and consumption in the early 1960s', in B. Osgerby and A. Gough-Yates (eds), *Action TV: Tough Guys, Smooth Operators and Foxy Chicks*, London, Routledge, 32–52.

Osgerby, B. and A. Gough-Yates (eds) (2001), *Action TV: Tough Guys, Smooth Operators and Foxy Chicks*, London, Routledge.

Osgerby, B., A. Gough-Yates and M. Wells (2001), 'The business of action: television history and the development of the action TV series', in B. Osgerby and A. Gough-Yates (eds), *Action TV: Tough Guys, Smooth Operators and Foxy Chicks*, London, Routledge, 13–31.

Peel, J. (1998), *Legacy Of The Daleks*, London, BBC Books.

Peel, J. (1997a), *War Of The Daleks*, London, BBC Books.

Peel, J. (1997b), 'Terry Nation: Dalek man', *Starburst* 19:8, 8–9.

Peel, J. (1992), 'Nation states', *In-Vision* 39, 4–5.

Perkins, T. (1979), 'Rethinking stereotypes', in M. Barrett, P. Corrigan, A. Kuhn and J. Wolff (eds), *Ideology and Cultural Production*, London, Croom Helm, 135–59.

Pixley, A. (2003), 'The *DWM* Archive: The Mutants', *Doctor Who Magazine* 331, 28–41.

Pixley A. (2001a), 'The *DWM* Archive: The Keys of Marinus', *Doctor Who Magazine* 310, 26–32.

Pixley, A. (2001b), 'The *DWM* Archive: Day of the Daleks', *Doctor Who Magazine* 301, 26–33.

Pixley, A. (1999a), 'The *DWM* Archive: Destiny of the Daleks', *Doctor Who Magazine* 283, 12–19.

Pixley, A. (1999b), 'The *DWM* Archive: The Dalek Invasion of Earth', *Doctor Who Magazine* 280, 16–23.

Pixley, A. (1999c), 'The *DWM* Archive: Death to the Daleks', *Doctor Who Magazine* 278, 36–43.

Pixley, A. (1998a), 'The *DWM* Archive: The Daleks' Master Plan', *Doctor Who Magazine* 272, 18–30.

Pixley, A. (1998b), 'The *DWM* Archive: Mission To The Unknown', *Doctor Who Magazine* 271, 22–5.

Pixley, A. (1997a), 'The *DWM* Archive: Genesis of the Daleks', *Doctor Who Magazine* 250, 34–41.

Pixley, A. (1997b), 'Nation's creations: a biographical history of the work of Terry Nation', *Horizon Newsletter* 36, 9–20.

Pixley, A. (1993a), '*Doctor Who* Archive Feature Serial SSS, Planet of the Daleks', *Doctor Who Magazine* 202, 23–30.

Pixley, A. (1993b), '*Doctor Who* Archive Feature, The Chase', *Doctor Who Magazine* Summer Special, 43–50.

Pixley, A. (1992), '*Doctor Who* Archive Feature: Serial 4J, The Android Invasion', *Doctor Who Magazine* 193, 23–30.

Pixley, A. (1987), '*Survivors* season one episode guide', *Time Screen* 10, 18–19.

*Radio Times* (1999), 13–19 November.

*Radio Times* (1983), *Doctor Who 20th Anniversary Special*, 19–26 November.

*Radio Times* (1973), *Doctor Who 10th Anniversary Special*, undated.

*Radio Times* (1972), 30 September–6 October.

*Radio Times* (1964), 28 May–5 June 1964.

Richards, J. and P. Anghelides (1992), *In-Vision: Destiny Of The Daleks*, London, Cybermark.

Richards, J. and P. Anghelides (1988), *In-Vision: Genesis Of The Daleks*, London, Cybermark.

Robins, T. (undated a), *Doctor Who: Adventures in Space and Time – The Dalek Invasion Of Earth*, London, Cybermark.

Robins, T. (undated b), *Doctor Who: Adventures in Space and Time – The Keys Of Marinus*, London, Cybermark.

Robins, T. (undated c), *Doctor Who: Adventures in Space and Time – The Daleks*, London, Cybermark.

Rose, H. J. (1958), *A Handbook of Classical Mythology*, sixth edition, London, Methuen.

Russell, G. (ed.) (1995), *Terry Nation's Blake's 7 Summer Special 1995*, London, Marvel.

Russell Taylor, J. (1964a), 'In the hands of the adaptor', *The Times*, 13 June.

Russell Taylor, J. (1964b), 'Television of the month', *The Listener*, 16 July.

Scannell, P. (1990), 'Public service broadcasting; the history of a concept', in A. Goodwin and G. Whannel (eds), *Understanding Television*, London, Routledge, 11–29.

Scholes, R. (1975), *Structural Fabulation: An Essay on the Fiction of the Future*, Indiana, University of Notre Dame Press.

Scholes, R. and E. Rabkin (1977), *Science Fiction: History, Science, Vision*, New York, Oxford University Press.

Search, G. (1983), 'In the beginning' *Radio Times Doctor Who 20th Anniversary Special*, 19–26 November, 4.

Seiter, E. (1992), 'Semiotics, structuralism, and television', in R. Allen (ed.), *Channels of Discourse, Reassembled: Television and Contemporary Criticism*, London, Routledge, 31–66.

Seiter, E., H. Borchers, G. Kreutzner and E.-M. Warth (eds) (1989), *Remote Control: Television, Audiences and Cultural Power*, London, Routledge.

Shubik, I. (1975), *Play for Today: The Evolution of Television Drama*, London, Davis-Poynter.

Silverstone, R. (1985), *Framing Science: The Making of a BBC Documentary*, London, BFI.

Stevens, A. and F. Moore (2003), *Liberation: The Unofficial and Unauthorized Guide to Blake's 7*, Tolworth, Telos.

Suvin, D. (1979), *The Metamorphoses of Science Fiction: On the Poetics and History of a Literary Genre*, New Haven, Yale University Press.

Tolson, A. (1996), *Mediations: Text and Discourse in Media Studies*, London, Arnold.

Tucker, M., G. Russell and N. Briggs (2000), 'The Emperor's new clothes', *Doctor Who Magazine* 288, 8–15.

Tulloch, J. (2000), *Watching Television Audiences: Cultural Theories and Methods*, London, Arnold.

Tulloch, J. (1990), *Television Drama: Agency, Audience and Myth*, London, Routledge.

Tulloch, J. and M. Alvarado (1983), *Doctor Who: The Unfolding Text*, Basingstoke, Macmillan.

Tulloch, J. and H. Jenkins (1995), *Science Fiction Audiences: Watching Doctor Who and Star Trek*, London, Routledge.

Tunstall, J. (1993), *Television Producers*, London, Routledge.

Turner, G. (2001), 'Genre, format and "live" television', in G. Creeber (ed.), *The Television Genre Book*, London, BFI, 6–7.

Turrow, J. (1974), 'Advising and ordering: daytime, prime time', *Journal of Communication* 24:2, 138–41.

Tymms, R. (1949), *Doubles in Literary Psychology*, Cambridge, Bowes and Bowes.

Vahimagi, T. (1994), *British Television: An Illustrated Guide*, London, BFI.

Walker, S. J. (undated a), *Doctor Who: An Adventure in Space and Time – Death To The Daleks*, London, Cybermark.

Walker, S. J. (undated b), *Doctor Who: An Adventure in Space and Time – Planet Of The Daleks*, London, Cybermark.

Walker, S. J. (undated c), *Doctor Who: An Adventure in Space and Time – The Daleks' Master Plan*, London, Cybermark.

Walker, S. J. (undated d), *Doctor Who: An Adventure in Space and Time – Mission To The Unknown*, London, Cybermark.

Walker, S. J. (undated e), *Doctor Who: An Adventure in Space and Time –The Chase*, London, Cybermark.

Wheatley, H. (2002), 'Gothic television', unpublished PhD thesis, University of Warwick.

Wiggins, M. (1997), 'Terry Nation', *Doctor Who Magazine* 252, 6–11.

Wildermuth, M. (1999), 'The edge of chaos: structural conspiracy and epistemology in *The X-Files*', *Journal of Popular Film and Television* 26:4, 146–57.

Williams, R. (1981), *Culture*, London, Fontana.

Williams, R. (1974), *Television, Technology and Cultural Form*, London, Collins.

Wilmut, R. (1978), *Tony Hancock 'Artiste'*, London, Methuen.

Wolfe, G. K. (1979), *The Known and the Unknown: The Iconography of Science Fiction*, Kent, Ohio State University Press.

Wood, G. and J. Hillman (1992), '*Blake's* 7 Sally Knyvette, disenchanted space rebel', *TV Zone* Special 5, 38–40.

# Index

Notes: Page numbers in *italics* indicate illustrations. Names showing initials only for first names indicate academic references as found in the Bibliography. Full names indicate the names of actors, writers, producers, etc.

ABC network (US) 15, 22
ABC television (UK) 13, 14, 29, 35, 190, 200
Abercrombie, N. 72, 169
*Ace Of Wands* 32
action adventure drama 14–17, 19, 84–6, 91
Adams, Douglas 37, 40, 82, 194
advertisement 73, 88, 89, 103, 104, 107, 127, 185
Airey, J. 22
Alan, Ray (Ray Whyberd) 191
*All My Eye And Kitty Bluett* 10
allegory 123–5
Allen, R. C. 87
Alsop, N. 65, 83, 141, 170
Alvarado, M. *see* Tulloch, J. and Alvarado, M.
Alwyn, Jonathan 190
*Amazing Stories* 116
*And Soon The Darkness* 19
Anderson, Gerry 17, 202
Andrews, H. 172
*Andromeda Strain, The* 73
Ang, I. 173
Anholt, Tony 17
anthology drama 12, 13, 14, 17, 20, 27, 28
*Armchair Theatre* 29–30
Asimov, Isaac 194
Associated British Elstree Studios 15, 107

Associated London Scripts (ALS), 10–11, 12, 36
Associated Rediffusion 12, 14
Attwood, T. 32, 188
ATV 12, 17, 36, 59, 107, 189, 191, 195, 196,
audiences
   as makers of meaning 3, 114, 115–16
   ratings 6–7, 16, 30, 49, 51, 57
   *see also individual programmes*
Austin, Ray 196
authorship 1–3, 6, 7, 9, 17, 23–4, 25–6, 28–9, 67, 69, 83, 84, 101–2, 103, 113–14, 158–68
*Avengers, The* 15–16, 17, 36, 68, 76, 80, 115, 173
   'Invasion Of The Earthmen' 199
   'Legacy Of Death' 199
   'Noon Doomsday' 199
   'Take Me To Your Leader' 199
   'Take-Over' 200
   'Thingumajig' 200
*Avon: A Terrible Aspect* 188

Bacon-Smith, C. 68
Baker, Robert S. 195, 200
Baker, Tom 126, 169, 193
Bakewell, J. and Garnham, N. 107
Bamore Productions 195, 196
*Baron, The* 15, 68, 80
   'And Suddenly You're Dead' 197
   'Epitaph For A Hero' 196

'The Island (2)' 198
'The Killing (2)' 197
'The Man Outside' 199
'Masquerade' 197
'A Memory Of Evil' 198
'Night Of The Hunter' 198
'Portrait Of Louisa' 197
'Red Horse, Red Rider' 197
'Roundabout' 198
'The Seven Eyes Of Night' 198
'So Dark The Night' 198
'Something For A Rainy Day' 197
'Storm Warning' 198
'There's Someone Close Behind
    You' 198
Barrett, M. and Barrett, D. 68
Barry, Christopher 38, 42, 43, 87, 88,
    90, 98, 191
Barthes, R. 76, 183
Baugh, Ann 49
Baverstock, Donald 46, 59
BBC 190, 191, 192, 193, 194, 202, 203,
    204, 205, 206
  role 140
  working practices 6, 25–66
BBC Worldwide 188
Beacham, Rod 176
*Bedouin* 21
Bentham, J. 43, 88, 105, 157
*Beowulf* 146
Berk, Robert 204
Berman, Monty 15, 16, 195, 196, 200
*Beyond Omega* 19
Bible, The 83
Big Finish Productions 186–7
Bignell, J. 8, 71, 72, 90–1, 106, 114, 119,
    173
Bird, Michael. J. 41
Blackman, Honor 16
Blair, Isla 112
*Blake's 7* 1, 21–2, 26, 38, 60, 102, 103,
    105, 108, 119, 120, 122, 123, 130,
    151–2, 180, 188
  advertisement 73, 127
  'Aftermath' 56, 92, 152, 175–6, 205–
    6
  'Assassin' 176
  audiences 57
  audio plays 188
  'The Beginning' 92

binary oppositions 131–2, 141–6,
    149, 150, 159
'Blake' 22, 38
'Bounty' 85, 205
'Brainstorm' *see Blake's 7,*
    'Breakdown'
'Breakdown' 172, 204–5
budgets 48–9, 56
characters 127–9, 132
'Children of Auron' 92, 174–5
'City At The Edge Of The World' 38
cliffhangers 103–4
'Countdown' 90, 92, 125, 159, 205
'Cygnus Alpha' 92, 127, 128, 129,
    132, 145, 164, 204
  *see also Blake's 7,* 'The Way Back'
'Death-Watch' 38, 174
'Deliverance' 37, 92, 96–7, 155, 168,
    172, 205
directors' role 42
'Duel', 37, 49, 57, 85, 92, *110, 112,*
    122, 159, 171, 204
  *mise en scène* 164–8
  and mythology 157–8
  political binary oppositions 143–
    6, 148–9, 152, 153, 154, 155, 164–5
'Finale' *see Blake's 7,* 'Terminal'
flexi-narrative form 91–2, 132–3
format 29, 31–2, 34, 37, 56, 126–9
'Gambit' 175
gender in 57, 171–6
genres in 56, 73–4
  mixed 85–6
intertextuality 73
'The Invaders' 172
'The Liberator' 127
merchandising 65
microcosms 125
'Mission to Destiny' 85, 133, 158,
    204
'Orac' 92, 103, 152, 205
'Orbit' 174
parallel montage 96–7
pitch 21, 32
political activism 132–3
political binary oppositions 131–2,
    141–6, 149, 150, 159
'Powerplay' 42, 92, 158, 206
'Prelude' *see Blake's 7,* 'The Way
    Back'

'Pressure Point' 42, 85, 92, 145, 146,
    152, 175, 205
'Project Avalon' 85, 152, 204
promotion 31, 65
realism, psychological 128–9
'Redemption' 56, 205
repetition in 158–9
'Rescue' 38
'Rumours Of Death' 38, 92
'Sarcophagus' 34
scheduling 56, 57, 106
'Seek-Locate-Destroy' 37, 85, 92,
    102, 128, 150, 171–2, 174, 204
serial form 33
series form 33
'Shadow' 38
'Space Fall' 85, 92, 127, 129, 143,
    164, 204
special effects in 48–9, 57
'Star One' 38, 92
'Storm Mountain' *see Blake's 7*,
    'Pressure Point'
storyline separation 96–7
studio taping 49
'Terminal' 21, 42, 127, 152, 155, 206
'Time Squad' 85, 92, 96, 129, 171,
    204
title sequence 73, *111*, 127
'Traitor' *112*, 174, 175
'Trial' 38, 92
'Voice From The Past' 151
'The Way Back' 92, *112*, 122, 125,
    146, 148, 151–2, 158, 203–4
    music 163–4
    political binary oppositions 141–
    3, 150, 163–4
'Weapon' 38
'The Web' 133, 204
writing process 36–7, 40–1
*Blake's 7: Afterlife* 188
Bochco, Steven 41
'body politic' 146–55
Boisseau, David 194
Botting, F. 146
Boucher, Chris 32, 33, 37, 38, 40, 85, 86,
    103, 104, 122, 129, 141, 172, 174,
    188, 203, 205
Brachacki, Peter 43, 205
Bradbury, Ray 196
*Brave New World* 73–4

Braybon, Ray 71
Briant, Michael E. 42, 163, 193, 203,
    204, 205
Briggs, N. 97, 186, 187
British National Studios 107
Brown, A. 21
Browning, Tod 81
Brownsey, Steve 205
Brunner, John 32
Brunsdon, C. 3
BSB television 22
*Buccaneers, The* 51
*Buck Rogers* 70
Burton, G. 27–8, 72, 105, 168, 182
Busby, L. J. 169

*Calling the Stars* 11
Calvert, B. *see* Casey, B. *et al.*
Camfield, Douglas 42, 164, 192, 204
canons 4
Casey, B. *et al.* 3–4, 123, 168
Casey, N. *see* Casey, B. *et al.*
*Cat And The Canary, The* 19
Caughie, J. 115
Cazenove, Christopher 22
Chaffey, Don 198, 199
*Champions, The* 15, 68
    'The Body Snatchers' 199
    'The Fanatics' 199
Chapman, J. 4, 79, 173
Chapman, Spencer 192
Chappell, Jan 129, 172
characters, realism 122–3
*Charmed* 83
Charteris, Leslie 14, 195
Chaucer, Geoffrey 157
cinema, writing for 13, 19, 22, 24, 63, 91
Clark, Simon 186
classic realism 117–18, 122–3
Clay, Jim 206
Clemens, Brian 17, 19, 21, 199, 202
cliffhangers 30, 32, 87–8, 89–90, 93,
    103–4
*Close Encounters Of The Third Kind* 49
Coburn, Anthony 36, 201
cognition 116
Coke, Cyril 201
Cole, Stephen 186
Collins, Martin 203, 204, 205
colour, use of 160, 162, 164–5

comedy 10–12, 13, 14, 22, 39, 82
*Comedy Playhouse* 12
*Comic Relief* 186
*Communist Manifesto, The* 139
communities 138–41
*Compact* 30
Cook, B. 42, 43, 88
Corner, J. 72, 127
costume 43, 167–8
Courtney, A and Whipple, T. 169
Creasey, John 15
Cribbins, Bernard 20
Crichton, Michael 73
Croucher, Brian 102, 128
cult figures 102
Curse Of The Fatal Death', 'The 185
Curtis, Tony 16
Cusick, Raymond P. 43, 46, 160, 185,
     191, 192

D'Acci, J. 173
*Dalek Chronicles Special, The* 186
*Dalek Empire* 187
*Dalek Factor, The* 186
'Dalek War' 187
Daleks 124–5, 134–5, 160, 184–7, 188
     audio plays 186–7
     comic strips 185–6
     copyright ownership of 1, 9, 18, 44
     cult status 102
     design 43
     first appearances 87–9
     media coverage 18, 23, 52, 60–4, 67
     merchandising 18, 63, 185, 187
     monstrosity of 30, 39, 58
     problems in studio 46
     spin-off texts 18, 37, 61–4
     *see also Doctor Who*
*Dallas* 175
Dare, Daphne 43
Darrow, Paul 22, 32, 93, 128, 172, 188
Davies, Hywel 13
Davros 19, 39, 44, 136–7, 138, 147–8,
     184, 185, 187
Day, Peter 44
de Souza, Edward 107
'Death to The Daleks!' 187
*Department S* 16, 17, 80
     'A Cellar Full Of Silence' 200
     'The Man In The Elegant Room' 200

Derrida, J. 74
designer's role 42–4
Dick, Philip K. 190
Dicks, Ray 190
Dicks, Terrance 18, 37, 39, 54, 169, 193
Dickson, Liz 61
Dickson, Paul 199
director's role 42
*Dirty Dozen, The* 32, 86
*Doctor Finlay's Casebook* 30
*Doctor Who* 1, 9, 13, 14, 17–19, 26, 37–9,
     102, 103, 105, 118, 120, 122, 184–
     7, 188
     advertisement 88, 89, 185
     allegory 124–5
     'The Android Invasion' 19, 39, 47–
        8, 79–80, 194
     audience 30, 50–5
     'Beyond The Sun' *see Doctor Who,*
        'The Daleks'
     'Black Orchid' 37–8
     'The Brain of Morbius' 81
     budgets 45–6, 47–8, 59
     'The Chase' 18, 39, 46–7, 52–4, 78,
        79, 80–1
     'The Death Of Doctor Who' 192
     'The Death Of Time' 192
     'The Executioners' 192
     'Flight Through Eternity' 192
     'Journey Into Terror' 192
     'The Planet Of Decision' 192
     'Colony In Space' 102
     creation 30, 32, 58
     'The Creature From The Pit' 121–2,
        158
     'The Dalek Invasion Of Earth' 18,
        38, 43, 52, 59–60, 61, 62, 71, 76,
        77, 78, 108, 122, 126, 135
     'The Daleks' 192
     'Day Of Reckoning' 90
     'The End Of Tomorrow' 192
     'Flashpoint' 192
     repetition in 158
     'The Waking Ally' 90
     'World's End' 192
     'Dalek Story' *see Doctor Who,* 'Death
        To The Daleks'
     'The Daleks' 18, 32, 67, 71, 76–7, 78,
        79, 87, 97, 98, 108, 110, 111, 119,
        126, 130, 135, 136, 185

'The Ambush' 89–90, 191
audience 50, 51–2, 59
'The Dead Planet' 87–8, 143–4,
191
directors' role 42
'The Escape' 160–1, 191
'The Expedition' 191
*mise en scène* 160–1, 164
and mythology 157
'The Ordeal' 191
parallel montage 96
political binary oppositions 134–
5, 150, 151, 153, 159–60
production 46
repetition in 158
'The Rescue' 191
storyline separation 94
'The Survivors' 154, 191
writing process 13–14, 36, 38, 43
*see also* Doctor Who, 'The Dalek
Invasion Of Earth'
'Daleks: Genesis Of Terror' *see*
Doctor Who, 'Genesis Of The
Daleks'
Daleks' Master Plan', 'The 18, 39,
47, 55, 60, 82, 98–9, 108, 135,
158, 159
'Day Of The Daleks' 18
'Death To The Daleks' 18, 39, 54,
88, 97, 158, 193
designer's role 43–4, 45, 46
'Destination: Daleks' *see Doctor
Who*, 'Planet Of The Daleks'
'Destiny Of The Daleks' 39, 82, 88,
89, 97, 98, 194
'Doctor Who And The Exilons' *see
Doctor Who*, 'Death To The
Daleks'
'Doctor Who And The Mutants' *see
Doctor Who*, 'The Daleks'
educational aspects 30, 50, 52
'The Enemy Within' *see Doctor Who*,
'The Android Invasion'
'The Evil Of The Daleks' 18, 47
'The Five Doctors' 185
format 29, 31, 33–4, 50–1, 70–1, 75–
6, 126
'Four To Doomsday' 37
gender in 39, 169
'Genesis Of The Daleks' 18, 39, 71,

76–7, 81, 82, 88, 90, 111, 119,
122, 124, 125, 157, 184, 193
parallel montage 96
political binary oppositions 135–
8, 147–8, 149–50, 151, 153, 154,
155, 159, 161–2
repetition in 158–9
stalking motif 98, 99–100
storyline separation 94–5
genres in 30, 50, 52–4, 58–9, 71
mixed 75–82
'The Image Of The Fendahl' 38
intertextuality 71
'The Keys Of Marinus' 18, 43, 46,
63, 76, 78, 97, 135, 137, 147, 151,
158, 186
'The Keys of Marinus' 192
'The Screaming Jungle' 191
'The Sea of Death' 191
'Sentence of Death' 192
'The Snows of Terror' 191–2
'The Velvet Web' 191
'The King's Demons' 38
'The Kraals' *see Doctor Who*, 'The
Android Invasion'
microcosm, allegorical 124–5
'Mission To The Unknown' 18, 107,
108
'The Abandoned Planet' 192
'Coronas Of The Sun' 192
'Counter Plot' 192
'Day Of Armageddon' 192
'Destruction Of Time' 192
'Devil's Planet' 192
'Escape Switch' 192
'The Feast of Steven' 82, 192
'Golden Death' 192
'The Nightmare Begins' 192
'The Traitors' 192
'Volcano' 192
moralism 128
music 100–1
parallel montage 96–7
'Planet Of Giants' 107–8
'Planet Of The Daleks' 18, 20, 39,
76, 78–9, 88, 89, 95, 97, 98, 193
parallel montage 95–6
repetition in 158
politics 124–5
'The Power Of The Daleks' 18

promotion 30, 31, 60–4
'The Red Fort' 18
'Remembrance Of The Daleks' 185
'Resurrection Of The Daleks' 184–5
'The Return' 184
'The Return Of The Daleks' see
    Doctor Who, 'The Dalek Invasion
    Of Earth'
'Revelation Of The Daleks' 185
'The Robots of Death' 38
scheduling 50, 51, 54, 106
serial form 28
    episodic 87–8, 90, 93, 103
series structure 108
special effects 44–9, 54, 55, 100–1
storyline separation 93–6
studio taping 44–8
'The Survivors' see Doctor Who, 'The
    Daleks'
'An Unearthly Child' 51
writing process 33, 38
see also Daleks
Doctor Who: Corpse Marker 188
Doctor Who Classic Comics 186
Doctor Who Magazine 68, 97, 135–6,
    185–6
Doctor Who Monthly 186
Doctor Who Then And Now 22
Doctor Who Weekly 186
domestic drama 83
Dominick, J. and Rauch, G. 169
Doomwatch 20–1, 37
doubling, body politic 146–54
Downing, Steven 206
Drama Playhouse
    The Incredible Robert Baldick 19–20,
    201
Drummond, P. 121
Dr Who – Daleks Invasion Earth 2150 AD
    18
Dr Who And The Daleks 18
Dudley, Terence 35, 37, 40, 41, 55–6, 123
Dunkley, C. 31
Dyer, R. 120
Dynasty 173
dystopia 7, 119–21, 126–7

Ellis, J. 28, 73, 127
Engels, F. see Marx, K. and Engels, F.
epic drama 83, 85

episodic serial form 28, 86–90
episodic series 90–3
Evans, C. 86
Exton, Clive 19, 41, 141
Eyers, John 102, 188

Faerie Queene, The 159
Faith, Adam 13
fantasy drama 68
Fenady, Andrew J. 22
Fennell, Albert 199
Fine Goings On 11
Fine, M. 169
Fine Romance, A see Ticket To Ride
Fiske, J. 74, 76, 121–2, 126, 134, 135,
    136–7, 138, 142, 149, 158, 159–
    60
Fixers, The 11
Flash Gordon 70
Fleming, Lucy 64
Flemyng, Gordon 198
flexi-narratives 90–3
Foley, Dennis 206
Ford, Carole Ann 59, 185
Ford, Marianne 165
format 9, 23, 27–9, 31–5, 69, 74
Forrest, Steve 15
Foucault, M. 179–80
Frankel, Cyril 197, 200, 202
Frankie Howerd Show, The 11
Freeman, Dave 11
French, L. see Casey, B. et al.
Freud, S. 81
Frick, Alice 71
Friday The 13th 190
Friedlander, John 44
Fuest, Robert 190, 199, 200

Galton, Alan 11, 13, 189
Garnham, N. see Bakewell, J. and
    Garnham, N.
gender, representations of 7, 160, 168–
    76
Genesis Of A Hero 102, 188
genres 7, 16, 17, 19, 20, 22, 23, 25–30,
    67–8, 69–70
    mixed 74–5
    see also individual programmes
geographical space 150–2
Geraghty, C. 173, 175

Gernsback, Hugo 116
Gilbert, S. and Gubar, S. 146
Gillatt, G. 31, 61, 62, 63, 113
Gilling, John 195, 199, 200
Gonzalez Ballesteros, A. 146
*Good Life, The* 83
*Goon Show, The* 10, 11, 12
Gorry, John 191
Gothic genre 19, 80–1
Gothic parody 147
Gough-Yates A. *see* Osgerby, W. and
    Gough-Yates, A.
Grade, Lew 12, 17, 107
Green, Colin 193
Greif, Stephen 102, 128
Grieve, Ken 194
Gubar, S. *see* Gilbert, S. and Gubar, S.
Guest, Val 201

Hammond, Peter 190
*Hancock* 13
    'The Assistant' 191
    'The Night Out' 191
    'The Reporter' 191
    'The Writer' 191
Hancock, F. and Nathan, D. 13
Hancock, Roger 11, 13
Hancock, Tony 11, 13
*Hancock's Half Hour* 13
Hanson, H. 146–7
Hardy, Robert 20
*Hart To Hart* 121, 160
Hartley, J. 121
Hartnell, William 126, 169, 191
Hayers, Sidney 200, 201
Hearn, M. 42, 161
Henry, Richard 194
Hermes, J. 173
heroic figures 15, 102–3, 118, 123, 129,
    161–2
Hill, Benny 11
Hill, Jacqueline 110
Hill, James 201
Hill, Reg 202
*Hill Street Blues* 41
Hillman, J. *see* Wood, G. and Hillman, J.
Hinchcliffe, Philip 35, 47–8, 79, 81, 194
Hipple, D. 171, 172
*Hitch-Hiker's Guide To The Galaxy, The*
    37, 82

Holmes, Robert 37, 39, 81, 135, 174, 175,
    193, 194
Hope, Bob 22
Hough, Johhny 202
Houldsworth, R. 72–3
*House In Nightmare Park, The* (*The
    House of the Laughing Dead*) 19
Howe, D. J. *et al.* 42, 43, 71, 124, 135,
    160, 161, 184, 185
Howerd, Frankie 10, 11, 19
Hulke, Malcolm 70
Hulke, Sally 205
Human Factor', 'The 187
Hunt, Peter 201
Hunt, Richard 192
Hurndall, Richard 185
Hurst, John 193

*Idiot Weekly, Price 2d, The* 12, 189
*Incredible Robert Baldick, The see* Drama
    Playhouse
Independent Television 12
Inns, George 190
intertextuality 69, 71
'Invasion Of The Daleks' 187
*Italian Job, The* 22
*It's A Fair Cop* 11
ITC television 12, 14–17, 18, 22, 37, 80,
    107, 123, 195, 196, 197, 198, 199,
    200, 201
ITV network 107, 195, 196, 197, 198,
    199, 200, 201

*Jackanory* 20
Jackson, David 129
Jackson, Pat 195
Jacques, Hattie 12
James, Douglas 190
Jameson, F. 119
Jameson, Susan 102
Jenkins, H. 4, 68
*Jimmy Logan Show, The* 190
*Juke Box Jury* 50
Junkin, Harry H. 195
Junkin, John 11, 12, 189, 190

Kandel, Stephen 206
Katzin, Lee H. 206
Keating, Michael 128–9
Kellner, D. 68

Kilgour, M. 147
Killick, J. 188
Kneale, Nigel 70
*Knight's Tale, The* 157
*Knots Landing* 173
Knyvette, Sally 129, 171, 172
Kozloff, S. 183
Kristeva, J. 153

Lacey, N. 28
Lambert, Verity 14, 35, 36, 38, 39, 42,
    45, 51, 52, 54, 55, 59, 64, 80, 108,
    191, 192
Leaver, Don 202
Ledsham, Ken 194
Ledwon, L. 147
Lee, Tanith 34, 173
*Legacy Of The Daleks* 186
Lenardon, R. *see* Morford, M. P. O. and
    Lenardon, R.
Lester, Dick 189
Letts, Barry 18, 35, 39, 79, 102, 158, 183,
    188, 193, 194
Levin, Ira 194
Lévi-Strauss, C. 121, 156
Lewis, J. *see* Casey, B. *et al.*
Lewis, L. 68
Lichter, R. S. *et al.* 168
lighting 164–5
Lindley, Philip 194
Lippman, W. 168
Littler, Prince 12
Llewellyn Moxey, John 195, 196, 197
London, Ray 202
London Films 48
*Looney Tunes: Back in Action* 187
Lorrimer, Vere 22, 35, 42, 172, 204, 205
Lucarotti, John 36
Lucas, George 86
Lupino, Barry 190
Lusted, D. 168

MacConkey Productions 191
MacDonald, P. 97, 135–6
*MacGuyver* 22, 95
    'The Golden Triangle' 206
    'Target MacGyver' 206
    'Thief Of Budapest' 206
Macnee, Patrick 16, 76
Maine, Charles Eric 32

Maloney, David 35, 41, 42, 81, 86, 93,
    99, 161, 193, 203, 205, 206
*Maltese Falcon, The* 199
*Man From U.N.C.L.E., The* 16–17
Marks, Louis 18
Marsh, Ronald 21, 48, 49
Martin, Richard 39, 42, 191, 192
Martinus, Derek 192
Marx, K. and Engels, F. 138
*Masterpiece Of Murder* 22
Maxin, Ernest 190
McCoy, Sylvester 76
Medak, Peter 201
Meinhof, U. H. and Smith, J. 74–5
microcosms 123–5
Midgley, Robin 196
Milland, Ray 19
*Millennium* 83
Miller, T. 15, 68, 115
Milligan, Spike 10, 11, 12, 189
Millington, B. 8
Milne, Alistair 48
*mise en scène* 159–68
Mittell, J. 69–70
Moffat, Peter 202
*Monty Python's Flying Circus* 16
Moore, F. *see* Stevens, A. and Moore, F.
Moore, Roger 14–15, 16, 123, 195, 196
Moorhead, Simon 188
More, Sir Thomas 119
Morecambe, Eric 12
Morford, M. P. O. and Lenardon, R. 156
Morris, Richard 203
Morton, Anthony *see* Creasey, John
Muir, J. K. 168
Murdoch, G. 2, 9, 179
Murray-Leach, Roger 204, 205
music 100–1, 163–4
mythological narratives 156–8

Nance, John J. 73
narrative structures 118, 121–2
Nathan, D. *see* Hancock, F. and Nathan,
    D.
Nathan-Turner, John 184, 185
Nazism 124–5, 137
Nazzaro, J. 10, 41, 88, 130, 171, 174
Nazzaro, J. and Wells, S. 172–3
NBC network 47
Neale, S. 117

Neale, S. and Turner, G. 69, 74
Nelson, R. 8
Newbery, Barry 43, 192
Newley, Anthony 12
Newman, Sydney 29–30, 31, 32, 35, 38,
    42, 45, 46, 47, 50, 51, 52, 58, 59,
    70, 105
New World 195, 196
Nineteen Eighty-Four 73, 127, 142
No Hiding Place 12
    'Run For The Sea' 190
No Place Like Home 20
Norman, Leslie 195

O'Day, A. 115, 173
Official Doctor Who And The Daleks Book
    23
Ortega y Gasset, Jose 133
Orwell, George 73, 127, 142
Osborn, Andrew 19, 20, 41
Osgerby, W. 173
Osgerby, W. and Gough-Yates A. 4, 107
Out Of The Unknown 14, 27, 62, 67
    'The Fox And The Forest' 196
Out Of This World 13, 27, 67
    'Botany Bay' 190
    'Immigrant' 190–1
    'Impostor' 190

Paice, Eric 70
Pal, George 71
Pandora's Clock 73
parallel montage 95–7
Parkes, Roger 151, 174
Parkin, Lance 187
Parnell, Val 12
Patterson, John 206
Pathfinder In Space 51, 70, 71
Pearce, Jacqueline 102, 112, 173
Peel, John 18, 23, 82, 186
Pemsel, Chris 204
Persuaders!, The 16
    'Chain Of Events' 201
    'A Death In The Family' 201
    'Five Miles To Midnight' 201
    'A Home Of One's Own' 201
    'Someone Like Me' 200
    'Someone Waiting' 201
    'Take Seven' 200
Pertwee, Jon 61, 65, 79, 169, 193

Petrie, Donald 206
pilot episodes 141–2
Pinfield, Mervyn 38, 43, 45
Pintoff, Ernest 206
Pixley, A. 10, 11, 12, 13, 14, 18, 20, 38,
    39, 43, 44, 62, 71, 76, 80, 82, 87,
    90, 99, 108, 160, 161
Play For Today 27, 115
plays, television 19, 64
political television drama 114–15, 119
politics 113–76
    binary oppositions 121–2, 130–2,
        134–5, 138–54, 156, 159–68
    popular drama serials 106–7
Porter, Mike 205
Porter, Nyree Dawn 17
post-structuralism 152–4, 161
producer's role 35
production processes 6, 9, 25–6, 44–9
    'Project Infinity' 187
promotion, programmes 6–7, 20, 60–1
Protectors, The 16–17
    'A Pocketful Of Posies' 202
    'Bagman' 202
    'Baubles, Bangles And Beads' 202
    'Route 27' 202

quality 3–4, 7, 113
Quatermass Experiment, The 70, 71

racism 137–8, 149–50, 151
radio, writing for 10–11
Radio Times 185, 187
Rauch, G. see Dominick, J. and Rauch, G.
Ray, Ted 11, 190
realism 117–18, 122–3
Rebecca's World 20
repetition 158–9
Richard, Cliff 12
Richards, Justin 186
Ridge, Mary 206
Rigg, Diana 16
Roberts, Meade 196
Roberts, Pennant 42, 85, 172, 203, 204,
    205
Roddenberry, Gene 41
Romanticism 118, 123, 129
Ronder, Jack 41, 83, 84, 141
Rose, H. J. 156
Ruddy, Austin 202

Russell, G. 173
  *see also* Tucker, M. *et al.*
Russell Taylor, J. 14

*Saint, The* 14–15, 16, 123
  'The Contract' 195
  'The Crime Of The Century' 195
  'The Desparate Diplomat' 196
  'The Inescapable Word' 195
  'Invitation To Danger' 196
  'Jeannine' 195
  'Lida' 195
  'The Man Who Could Not Die' 195–6
  'The Revolution Racket' 195
  'Sibao' 195
  'The Sign Of The Claw' 195
  'The Time To Die' 196
  'Where The Money Is' 196
Sasdy, Peter 194
Saward, Eric 184
scheduling 55, 107–9
  *see also individual programmes*
Schmerer, James 206
Scholes, R. 116, 119, 124
science, representation of 21, 116, 119, 120, 136–7
science fiction 4, 7, 16, 18, 20, 25, 42, 68, 70–109, 123–4
  cinema 30, 49
  fanzines 68
  literature 32
  political origins 115–17
  'soft' 115–16, 119
Scoones, Ian 48–9
Scott, Gerry 205, 206
Scott, Ridley 43
script editor's role 35–6
Seddon, Peter 194
Sellers, Peter 10, 12
serial form 25–8
series form 9, 19, 25–8
Sevenfold Crown', 'The 188
Sewell, Andrew Mark 188
Seymour, Carolyn 64, 65
Sharp, Don 199
Shearman, Robert 186–7
Shubik, Irene 14, 106, 115, 190, 194, 196
Simak, Clifford 190

Simon, Josette 175
Simpson, Dudley 100, 101
Simpson, Ray 11, 13, 189
Sladen, Elisabeth 169
Smart, Patsy 112, 167
Smith, J. *see* Meinhof, U. H. and Smith, J.
Snowdon, Lord 187
*Softly, Softly: Task Force* 48
sound 165
space, geographical/symbolic 150–2
special effects 44–9, 54, 55, 57, 100–1
Speight, Johnny 12, 189
Spenser, Edmund 159
Spenton-Foster, George 205
Spielberg, Steven 22
Spode, David 193
Spooner, Dennis 14, 15, 16, 36, 37, 39, 47, 64, 82, 108, 192, 197, 198, 200
Stafford, Jo 12
stalking motif 19, 97–101
Stammers, M. *see* Howe, D. J. *et al.*
Stanley, Paul 206
*Star Cops* 38
*Star Trek* 41, 57, 74, 126, 143
*Star Wars* 49, 74, 78, 86, 159
*Starburst* 68
*Starlog* 68
Steele, Tommy 12
*Steptoe And Son* 12
Stevens, A. and Moore, F. 21, 33, 34, 36, 37, 40, 42, 85, 92, 93, 97, 102, 104, 125, 127, 128–9, 132, 133, 141, 142, 143, 145, 146, 150, 151, 155, 158, 171, 172, 174, 188
*Story Parade* 14
  'The Caves Of Steel' 194
  'A Kiss Before Dying' 194
storyline separation 93–5
Strutton, Bill 36
sublimation 116
Summers, Jeremy 202
*Survivors* (novel) 102, 188
*Survivors* 1, 20–1, 26, 37–8, 60, 105, 108, 119, 120, 122, 123, 158, 180, 188
  advertising 73
  audience 40, 55–6
  'A Beginning' 21, 111, 170, 203

budgets 48
characters 130–1
contemporary concerns 125
'Corn Dolly' 41, 170
flexi-narrative form 91
format 29, 31, 34, 84, 126
'The Fourth Horseman' 21, 83, 130–1, 170, 202
'The Future Hour' 21, 84, 91, 170, 203
'Garland's War' 21, 40, 84, 139–41, 161, 162, 203
gender in 169–71
'Genesis', 21, 102, *111*, 125, 131, 138, 161–2, 202–3
genres in 72–3
    mixed 82–5
'Gone Away' 21, 84, 151, 170, 203
'Gone To Angels' 41
intertextuality 73
'Law And Order' 41, 91
pitch 19
political binary oppositions 130–1, 138–41, 148, 153, 159, 161–2
'Promised Land' 41
promotion 30–1, 64–5
scheduling 55
serial form 33
series form 33
'Something Of Value' 21, 84–5, 203
storyline separation 96
title sequence 72–3, *110*
writing process 40, 41
suspended enigmas 87–8
*Suspense* 14
Sutton, Shaun 46, 48
Suvin, D. 70, 116, 119, 124
*Sweeney, The* 121
Sykes, Eric 11, 12, 14, 189
Sykes, Peter 199
symbolic space 151–2
Syndeton Experiment', 'The 188
synecdoches 88, 93

Tarrant, Alan 191
Taylor, Don 205
Taylor, Eric 194
*Ted Ray Show, The* 12, 190
telefantasy 68
television 68, 91, 105–7

export of 15, 16, 47, 107
generic 106
    narrative structure 118, 121–2
    and political drama 115
    popular 3–4, 9, 106, 113–14
    quality 3–4, 7
    realism 117–18
    scheduling conventions 107–9
Television Studies 3, 4, 5, 8, 23–4, 25, 179
Telos Publishing 186
Thatcher, Margaret 173
*31 Who* 22–3
Thomas, Gareth 32, *112*
Thomas, Talfryn 64, 65, *111*
Thorson, Linda 16
Thousand And Several Doors', 'The 14
*Thriller* 17
    'K Is For Killing' 202
*Ticket To Ride (A Fine Romance)* 22
    'The Tomas Crown Affair' 206
Time-Life 48
*Time Machine, The* 31, 70, 71, 115–16, 124
title sequences 72–3
*Tomorrow People, The* 32
Tosh, Donald 39, 192
*Town Hall* 30
Tronson, Robert 197
Troughton, Patrick 18
Tucker, M. *et al.* 186
Tucker, Mike 186
Tuckwell, Walter 63
Tulloch, J. and Alvarado, M. 4, 8, 27, 75, 81, 87, 105, 116, 118, 119, 123, 124, 169
Turner, G. 28, 29
Turner, G. *see* Neale, S. and Turner, G.
Turrow, J. 169
*TV Zone* 68
Tymms, R. 146, 147

*Uncle Selwyn* 12–13, 14, 194
utopia 119–20

*Val Parnell's Saturday Spectacular* 12
*Val Parnell's Startime* 12, 189
Valentine, Dicky 11
*Variety Playhouse* 11
Vaughan, Robert 16

Verney, Guy 190
Ventham, Wanda 64
villains 102, 128
Viola, Joe 206
Voytek 190

Walker, S. J. *see* Howe, D. J. *et al.*
'wandering viewpoint' 87
*War Of The Daleks* 186
Ward, Bill 190
Ward Baker, Roy 195, 196, 197, 198,
    199, 200
Waters, Elsie and Doris 11
Webber, Cecil Edwin 31, 50
*Wednesday Play, The* 27
Wells, H. G. 31, 70, 115–16, 124
Wells, S. *see* Nazzaro, J. and Wells, S.
Westerns 72, 84–5, 158
*What A Whoppa!* 13
Wheatley, H. 147
Wheldon, Huw 108
Whipple, T. *see* Courtney, A. and
    Whipple, T.
Whitaker, David 18, 32, 36, 37, 38, 50,
    52, 63, 64, 191, 192

White, Leonard 190
Whitehouse, Mary 81
Whitton, Margaret 22
Whyberd, Ray (Ray Alan) 191
Wiggins, M. 94
Wildermuth, M. 68
Wiles, John 35, 39, 192
Williams, Graham 35, 82, 89, 194
Williams, R. 8, 182
Williams, Terence 203
Wilmut, R. 13.
Wilson, Donald 30, 31, 35, 46, 50, 52, 59
Wise, Ernie 12
*Wish You Were Here!* 14
Wolfe, G. K. 137
Wood, G. and Hillman, J. 172
Wood, John 46, 192
Worth, Harry 10
Worth, Johnny, and the Go-Gos 63
Wyndham, John 32

Yates, Peter 195

*Z Cars* 30